ANOTHER SLICE OF
JOHNNERS

ANOTHER SLICE
OF JOHNNERS

Brian Johnston
Edited by Barry Johnston

TED SMART

For Clare, Andrew, Ian and Joanna

First published in this form in Great Britain in 2001 by
Virgin Books Ltd
Thames Wharf Studios
Rainville Road
London W6 9HA

This edition produced for The Book People Ltd,
Hall Wood Avenue, Haydock, St. Helens WA11 9UL

A catalogue record for the book is available from the
British Library.

ISBN 1-85227-042-X

Phototypeset by Intype London Ltd
Printed and bound in Great Britain by
Mackays of Chatham PLC

Contents

Acknowledgements

A LL TEST AND career records are correct to the end of March 2001 thanks to the excellent player profiles and statistics at www.cricinfo.com. Thanks also to Bill Frindall for his help and advice and for the original records and statistics in *Brian Johnston's Guide to Cricket* and *It's Been a Piece of Cake*.

Introduction

MY FATHER ALWAYS considered himself very lucky to be a cricket commentator. But sometimes he felt a little embarrassed that 'just a game', as he once put it, had played such a large part in his life. 'I often wake up,' he said, 'and think, "Gosh! You've been talking for years about a bit of wood hitting a little bit of leather!"'

Brian first began to take an interest in cricket when he was about six. One day his eldest brother Michael threw him a tennis ball and shouted, 'I'm Jack Hearne, you're Patsy Hendren.' From that moment on Patsy became Brian's hero and he had embarked on a lifelong love of the summer game.

Brian was captain of the Second XI at Eton. He was a good wicket-keeper and an enthusiastic, if slightly unreliable, batsman. At Oxford he kept wicket for New College but was not quite good enough – or, perhaps, serious enough – to win a blue. Contemporaries have said that he would try to put the batsman off by telling jokes and was even known to wear a false nose and moustache.

After Oxford Brian went into the family coffee business in the City but continued to play cricket for the Eton Ramblers whenever possible during the summer. When he was posted to Santos in Brazil for eighteen months, the first thing he did on arrival was to organise a local cricket team.

At the outbreak of war in 1939 he joined the 2nd Battalion Grenadier Guards. But even war could not dampen his enthusiasm for the game. In between training exercises, he played in cricket matches against the other battalions, until going with the Guards Armoured Division to Normandy after D-Day. His first letter from Germany to his mother, after VE Day in 1945, asked her to send him a parcel containing: 'Wicket-keeping gloves, 3 cricket shirts, 3 prs white socks'!

Brian was demobbed in 1945 and really wanted to go into the theatre, but a chance meeting with two 'BBC types' in the Guards Club led to a job in the BBC Outside Broadcasts Department. Then a friend with whom he had played club cricket before the war was put in charge of restarting cricket on BBC

Television. He rang Brian to ask if he would like to 'have a shot' at cricket commentary. Brian could hardly believe his luck.

That telephone call started him on a remarkable career as a cricket commentator, which was to span twenty-four years on television and a further twenty-four years on radio. He officially retired as a member of the BBC staff in 1972, but then went freelance and continued to work for the BBC until his death at the age of eighty-one in 1994.

A Delicious Slice of Johnners was an anthology of Brian's two volumes of autobiography published in the 1970s, along with a collection of his favourite cricket stories. In *Another Slice of Johnners* I have edited together three more of his books from the 1980s and this time the spotlight is firmly on sport and cricket.

Chatterboxes – My Friends the Commentators is an affectionate and humorous account of his former colleagues in the BBC Outside Broadcasts Department. In the original book Brian included several all-round broadcasters such as Richard Dimbleby, Wynford Vaughan-Thomas and Gilbert Harding. But for this anthology I have concentrated on the many radio and television sports commentators with whom he worked, before he retired from the BBC in 1972.

This was a time when the BBC ruled the airwaves in sport. BBC commentators such as John Arlott, David Coleman, Henry Longhurst, Dan Maskell and Peter O'Sullevan were all household names and were the voices of their individual sports. In the book Brian recalls their personalities, their strengths and their weaknesses and, of course, some of their classic gaffes and howlers.

'Commentators are a unique band,' he wrote. 'There are very few of us, and in spite of the travel, long hours, the stresses and the working conditions – often too cramped, too hot or too cold – we should all be extremely thankful for having such a wonderful job.'

The second part of this anthology, *Brian Johnston's Guide to Cricket*, was first published under the title *All About Cricket* in 1972 but was revised and updated by Brian in 1986. The various chapters cover the history, organisation, laws and techniques of the game, as well as a summary of his favourite players and Test matches. I have included what I consider to be the highlight of the book, in which Brian vividly describes the six most exciting Tests he ever saw – and one extra Test which he always *wished* he had seen.

The final part of this trilogy is *It's Been a Piece of Cake – A tribute to my favourite Test cricketers* which was published in 1989 when Brian was seventy-seven. As a result he decided to write about seventy-seven of his favourite Test cricketers. For this anthology I have had to whittle them down to fifty which means I have had to leave out some eminent names such as Les Ames, Bill Edrich, Brian Close and Bob Willis. As a guide to whom Brian himself would have chosen as his 'Top Fifty' I referred back to his original list of forty-two all-time favourite cricketers in the *Guide to Cricket*.

Brian died in 1994 and so more recent cricketing heroes such as Michael Atherton, Brian Lara, Steve Waugh and Courtney Walsh are not included. Many of the original statistics have also been superseded since the books were written, as more Test records continue to be broken, so I have updated them all to the present day.

Brian loved his cricket but above all he enjoyed the camaraderie of the game. 'Far more indelible than memories of games played or watched,' he wrote in *It's Been a Piece of Cake*, 'are the happy recollections of countless friendships resulting entirely from a mutual love of cricket. Beyond my wildest dreams, when I joined the BBC in 1946 and became a commentator, Test and county cricketers gave me their friendship. I shall always treasure this. It has made my time in the commentary box a supremely happy one, and I shall always be grateful to them, and to all my colleagues in the commentary box.'

Here are some of the great voices of British broadcasting and some of the most unforgettable cricketers who ever walked down the pavilion steps at Lord's. I hope they will help you to relive many of the classic moments in cricket history. Simply tune the radio into *Test Match Special*, pop open a bottle of champagne, and help yourself to *Another Slice of Johnners*.

Barry Johnston
March 2001

PART I: CHATTERBOXES

1 The Pre-War Pioneers

ON SATURDAY 27 DECEMBER 1980 I was invited to be the studio guest in BBC Radio 2's *Sport on 2* programme. During the afternoon the presenter, Mike Ingham, suggested that I might like to try out his job, and cue over to the commentator at the various sporting events around the country. I did not do it very well, but I thoroughly enjoyed myself because I found that I knew them all personally.

After the programme it dawned on me that I not only knew, but had probably worked with, all the television and radio sports commentators who had broadcast from the time when I joined the BBC after the war. So I thought it would be fun – at least for me – to recall the characters and techniques of some of my colleagues, not forgetting the slight mishaps or gaffes which may have occurred.

I joined the BBC in January 1946, but of course there had been broadcasting for a quarter of a century before that. This was during my school and university days and, although not a regular listener, I did tune in to the wireless for sport and entertainment. I enjoyed comedians like Tommy Handley, Clapham and Dwyer, and Gillie Potter, and at night listened to the dance bands in their weekly spots from the great London hotels – names like Ambrose, Harry Roy, Carroll Gibbons, Roy Fox, Sidney Lipton and Lew Stone.

So far as sport was concerned I was always fascinated by the 'live' broadcasts of something which was actually happening at the time. The men who described the sports became my unseen heroes. They were the pioneers of commentary and each in his own style left a deep impression on me: R. C. Lyle on racing, Captain H. B. T. Wakelam on rugby and lawn tennis, George Allison on football and Howard Marshall on cricket.

There was then virtually no commentary as we know it today. There had been sporting broadcasts since January 1927, but they were more often than not just eye-witness accounts, reports or summaries at an interval, half-time or close of play. There were exceptions such as the occasional horse race, the Boat Race and snatches of rugby, tennis, soccer and cricket.

What commentary there was, was done by experts in the particular sport, without any training as broadcasters.

The first person to broadcast on cricket was P. F. Warner – 'Plum' – later Sir Pelham. On 14 May 1927 he was at Leyton to 'describe' Essex v New Zealand. He had a very quiet and rather ineffectual, apologetic-sounding voice and was not a great success.

He was followed later in the same year by the Essex player Canon F. H. Gillingham (Gilly). Gilly was a fine preacher with a strong authoritative voice. But, alas, he did not do too well either. He was also at Leyton but unfortunately his first broadcast coincided with a twenty-minute interval. After he had given a ten-minute description of the play so far, he became desperate for something to say. There was no Bill Frindall to talk to about records in those days. So the poor Canon read out the advertisements round the ground. You can imagine the reaction of the BBC in those days. Advertising in any form was strictly forbidden. Even in the 1950s I remember we were doing a broadcast about the motor industry, and we had to say that we were speaking from a well-known car factory at Dagenham. Thank goodness things are far more relaxed today.

Seymour de Lotbinière

My first boss at the BBC was Seymour de Lotbinière, known to everybody as 'Lobby'. He had become Head of Outside Broadcasts ('OBs' as they are called) in 1935 and soon realised that he had to train people to be broadcasters first and foremost. It was no good having an expert who could not communicate with the listener, nor describe what was happening on the field. Of course the mix had to be right. The broadcaster must have knowledge of the sport which he was describing, and should certainly have played it or participated in it. He could then have an international sportsman alongside him as a summariser who would give expert comment as opposed to commentary. Early examples of these were Arthur Gilligan at cricket, Harold Abrahams at athletics and Bernard Darwin at golf.

The first thing Lobby decided to do was to abandon the 'square one' technique which was in existence when he took over. This enabled the listener to follow a game of rugby or soccer by looking at a plan in the *Radio Times* in which the playing area was divided up into numbered squares. The commentator would have a second person in the box with him whose job was to follow the ball and call out the numbered square in which it was. John Snagge was often called on to do this, and as you can imagine his interruptions frequently interfered with the commentary, as there were two voices speaking at once.

Lobby decided that a good commentator must be able to place the ball by his description – 'the ball is on the England 25 line on the far side of the field', or 'the ball has gone out five yards short of Arsenal's right-corner flag'. For a commentator to be able to do this there had to be a definite commentary technique laid down, and so Lobby evolved his now universally accepted Pyramid Method. In this the commentator starts his broadcast at the narrow top of the pyramid by giving straight away the main essentials. Then gradually as the broadcast continues, the commentator broadens outwards by giving less important but still necessary information.

At any game, for instance, a commentator must immediately give the score and say how much time is left or, in the case of limited-over cricket, how many overs are left. At this stage too he should name the goal scorers, or which batsmen are out and how many runs they have each made.

Once this has been done he should set the scene – the weather, the crowd, the condition of the ground or pitch, and where he is sitting in relation to the play. He will then find time to say who won the toss, give the teams and describe briefly any outstanding play by any particular player.

Then can come what is called the 'associative material' – the position of the two sides in the League or Championship Tables, how important this match is for them, likely landmarks for any player, for example his thousand runs for the season or a significant number of goals. When time allows the commentator should always try to weave in a description of the ground, and once again place the position of his commentary box. He is after all the eyes of the listener, who can then imagine that the armchair in which he is sitting is on the balcony of the Lord's pavilion or in some gallery high up in St Paul's Cathedral.

Lobby also added some 'Do's' and 'Don'ts' for commentators:

Do's

1 Always try to build up 'suspense interest', anticipating possible interesting or exciting happenings to come. Enthusiasm for his subject is vital for a commentator but he should never *over* build up a match or event. He soon loses his credibility if he does, especially in radio, since the listener can now often check up on the television.

2 There is also a place for a certain amount of subtle instruction in sport, especially on television. But it must be done casually and not in too schoolmasterly a manner. There is so much that can be explained to the inexpert viewer or listener – the no-ball law, the intricacies of a tie-break at lawn tennis or the reasons for a foul at football.

Don'ts

1 However badly unsighted, try never to say, 'I can't see.' It is natural to think of an excuse if someone gets in your line of vision, or a player runs into a corner of the ground which you cannot see from the commentary box. But it becomes boring for the listener who rightly believes that for his licence fee the BBC should site the box properly, though this is not always possible due to structural difficulties. Similarly some boxes are often cramped, too hot or too cold, and desperately uncomfortable. However, that is not the listeners' fault and they soon become tired of constant moaning.

2 Never take sides. Be completely impartial – something far more easily said than done. The temptation to say 'we' is very strong but inexcusable, even when broadcasting from an overseas tour, when you get the feeling of representing your country. It's so easy to say, 'You'll be glad to hear that Atherton has won the toss,' when of course some listeners will *not* be glad. I know I must have been guilty many times of putting too much obvious delight into my shout of 'He's out!' when 'he' happens to be Australia's best batsman.

The early commentators were having to learn as they went along, with only Lobby to lean on for advice. They could not, as we could, get help from an older commentator – there just weren't any. The conditions under which they worked were appalling by modern standards. They were crammed into a small wooden box either at the back of a grandstand or on top of a van. Sometimes at the Derby they had to broadcast sitting or standing among the crowds on a stand. There is even a photograph of some unfortunate commentator at an outside broadcast at Cambridge perched microphone in hand, up a tree. Mind you, some of our positions are fairly primitive today, but luxurious compared to forty years ago. Their style of dress cannot have helped much either, and in almost every photograph commentators are wearing 'Anthony Eden' Homburg hats – what they did with the headphones goodness only knows.

Then of course they did not have the motorways and Inter-City expresses. A journey which today takes us only three hours could have taken double or even more before the war. And if things went wrong – especially on overseas broadcasts – communications were no way near as good as they are today. Lobby himself found this out when over in Holland for the wedding of Princess Juliana in the late 1930s. The timings for the procession and the service went hopelessly wrong and it became obvious that everything was running at least half-an-hour late.

Today a commentator could dial the number of Broadcasting House in London, and ask them to delay the broadcast. But Lobby could not get through to warn them, so when they came over as advertised he had to waffle for at least half-an-hour before anything happened. Luckily he had practised what he preached and had plenty of associative material about Holland, their Royal Family and so on. But he admitted that in the end he got so desperate that he had to resort to reading out the bulb catalogues!

This became a slightly longer broadcast than the one he did from an aeroplane on the Boat Race. The plane had to cross and recross the winding River Thames and Lobby soon became violently air-sick. When John Snagge cued over to him, he just managed to splutter out, 'Cambridge in the lead by three lengths – back to the launch.' A somewhat expensive eleven words.

R. C. Lyle

R. C. Lyle, the racing correspondent of *The Times*, was the BBC's choice as their first racing commentator. Believe it or not he was said to be colour-blind, so how he picked out the horses I just don't know. Maybe he was so involved in racing and going to every meeting that he knew all the horses – in addition of course to the jockeys – by sight. But anyhow he was a brilliant race-reader and a superb judge of a race. As a result he often decided fairly far out from the winning post which horse was going to win, and used to call it home, hardly mentioning the other horses who were struggling for a place. But of course that is what the listener really wants to know – how *his* horse is doing, however badly.

He was naturally somewhat nervous before his first big broadcast, which was when Felstead, ridden by Harry Wragg, won the Derby in 1928. On his way to the commentary position he happened to run into Edgar Wallace who, besides being a prolific writer of novels and plays, was a keen racehorse owner. He noticed that R. C. Lyle was looking a bit pale around the gills. So not very helpfully he suggested to Lyle that there was only one thing worse than having to give a commentary on such a difficult race as the Derby – and that was to be hung. He made amends, however, by insisting that Lyle drank a bottle of champagne. As a result his broadcast was a great success, though I do not think that such 'medicine' would be included in Lobby's list of what a commentator needs. But from personal experience I can confirm that at least it does not do any harm!

R. C. Lyle (note that some commentators, like E. W. [Jim] Swanton in later years, preferred their initials to be used rather than their Christian names) once shocked many listeners and horrified the Director-General, Sir John Reith. In the Derby when Cameronian beat Orpen he got so excited at the distance (240 yards from the winning post) that he shouted, 'It's the *hell* of a race!' Broadcasting House was inundated with telephone calls of protest. If any of those people who rang up then were alive today, I reckon they would have a pretty hefty phone bill!

In 1938, towards the end of the Northumberland Plate, Lyle suffered a commentator's nightmare. His voice completely dried up and he was unable to broadcast the finish of the race. He was undoubtedly a great expert on racing and knew every horse, trainer, owner and jockey. But were you able to hear him today you would notice the absence of pre-race description, information about the horses, and the subtle build-up of suspense and excitement which you would get from a commentator like Peter Bromley. In fact Lyle really only took over the microphone when the horses were at the start, and another broadcaster – sometimes George Allison – would handle all the preliminaries.

There was one other occasion when Lyle fell foul of Sir John

Reith, who was a teetotaller. During the early stages of the Derby Lyle said, 'The horses are now passing the advertisement hoarding for Booth's Dry Gin,' – this being a conspicuous landmark just after the start. Not only had he broken the BBC rules by advertising, but it was also for drink. Sir John was also not too pleased when a representative of Gordon's Gin rang up not only to protest but also to ask how they too could get in on the act!

George Allison

George Allison was a rotund, cheerful figure. He was too busy with his job as manager of Arsenal FC to give sufficient time to the technique of commentary. But he knew his football and all the players, and in the 1930s he was the voice of soccer. He certainly had the gift of the gab. On one occasion at Loch Lomond when describing an attempt on the speedboat record, he kept going for forty minutes while he waited for Kaye Don to appear in *Miss England III*. In 1936, when Arsenal were in the Cup Final against Sheffield United and he thought it his duty to be with them, he withdrew from the commentary. For the first time *two* commentators – Ivan Sharpe and F. N. S. Creek – did the job which George had previously done on his own.

It is interesting to note that he got little support from his fellow football administrators, who regarded the broadcasting of matches with suspicion and, often, hostility, fearing the effect it would have on their gates. The matches on which George Allison commentated were all connected with the Football Association. The Football League steadfastly refused the BBC permission to broadcast any League matches before the war. At one time the clubs voted not only to bar commentary of the FA Cup Final but also against the players being numbered. What a nightmare that would be for a football commentator! It only emphasises the difficulties of doing commentary in those days. So George Allison was restricted to Cup Ties and international matches and was never a regular commentator every Saturday.

During the war Alan Hardacre, the League Secretary, relented and League matches were broadcast for the Forces. After the war Lobby managed with difficulty to obtain permission to broadcast League matches on a regular basis every Saturday. But there was one stipulation. Until they cued over to the commentator on the ground, the BBC was not allowed to announce where the match was being held. In fact to start with it was made a complete mystery and the studio would cue over to Raymond Glendenning with something along the lines of, 'And now it's time for our soccer commentary on one of today's League matches. Our commentator is Raymond Glendenning so over to him now to find out where he is.' It was not until some years later that the studio was allowed to say which match it was in their cue over to Raymond.

Allison came from Stockton-on-Tees and was a friendly, jolly and popular man. He was a very hard worker and although he could be tough, he always *cared* for his players at Arsenal. It is probably not generally known that he once scooped an interview with Lord Kitchener for the American newspaper magnate Randolph Hearst, and as a result became his press representative in the United Kingdom.

Even in those days before television his voice and face were easily recognised. Once at a railway station a porter approached him and said, 'Excuse me asking you sir, but are you the gentleman what radiates?'

Once when he had remarked that he found it difficult to see over the heads of the crowd, a listener wrote to him suggesting that he gave his commentary from a balloon! There was also the lady who kept a parrot which was normally a very quiet and well-behaved bird. But there was something about George's voice which stirred it to strong language. Whenever George shouted, 'It's a goal, it's a goal,' the parrot would pipe up, 'Damn you – shut up, you old bugger!'

Tommy Woodroffe

Commander Tommy Woodroffe was the only commentator ever to have a West End show named after him – George Black's *The Fleet's Lit Up* at the Hippodrome (later The Talk of the Town). In fact, in spite of the many good things he did, his name will always be connected with that famous broadcast from the Royal Naval Review at Spithead in 1935. It was very bad luck on him because he had to spend all day of the broadcast aboard his old ship, HMS *Nelson*, and among his old shipmates. They were over-hospitable to their old friend, and to make matters worse, they treated the BBC official who was there to look after the Commander in the same way. The result was that by the time dusk fell and it was time for the Fleet to switch on their lights, neither were in a fit state for the broadcast.

I suppose that many people today have never either heard the broadcast, nor the recording. It is certainly one of the classics of broadcasting. Here is an extract from it, and it was delivered, as you can imagine, in a slurred voice, slowly and deliberately:

> ... The Fleet's lit up. When I say 'lit up' I mean lit up by fairy lights. It's lit up by fairy lights ... it isn't a Fleet at all ... the whole Fleet is a Fairyland. If you follow me through ... if you don't mind ... when I say 'the Fleet's lit up' I mean the whole ships ... (extra long pause) ... I was telling someone to shut up. The whole Fleet's lit up ... the ships are lit up ... even the destroyers are lit up. We are going to fire a rocket ... we are going to fire all sorts of things ... you may hear my reaction when I see them ... A huge Fleet here ... a colossal Fleet all lit up with fairy lights ... The whole thing is Fairyland ... it isn't true ... It's gone, it's gone ... it's disappeared ... No magician ever waved his wand with more acumen.
>
> The Fleet's gone ... it's disappeared ... I'm trying to give you Ladies and Gentlemen a description ... the Fleet's gone ... it's disappeared ... the whole thing's gone ... They've disappeared ... We had two hundred warships all round us ... Now they've all gone ... There's nothing between us and heaven ... there's nothing at all ...

The broadcast was then faded out with the announcer saying: 'And that is the end of our relay from Spithead, so now over to the Carlton Hotel for dance music.'

The next morning a tired and rather worse-for-wear Woodroffe reported to Lobby, who had not, unusually for him, heard the broadcast. But Broadcasting House was humming with excitement, and Lobby wisely told Woodroffe to go home and have a good sleep.

Meanwhile Sir John Reith arrived, with his beetling, black eyebrows boding no good for Woodroffe. It was bad luck for the Commander that not only was Sir John strongly against drink on any occasion, let alone at a broadcast, but also that his number two was Admiral Carpendale, a strict disciplinarian in the true naval tradition. So the anti-drink/Royal Navy combination was a formidable force. Sir John's first words to his personal assistant were, 'Has de Lotbinière suspended Woodroffe yet?' Lobby rightly had not done so, since he himself had no first-hand knowledge of what had happened, and refused to take any action until he had investigated.

However, matters were taken out of his hands, and a tribunal was set up to 'try' Woodroffe. Sir John evidently thought that the BBC owed it to the listeners to take strong action. Thanks, largely, I feel sure, to the intervention of Lobby, Woodroffe was only suspended from duty for six months. And so he retired temporarily from the microphone – the best-known broadcaster of all time.

He was in fact extremely versatile and when he returned took part in a variety of OBs, including ceremonials, the 1936 Olympic Games, the 1939 Derby and the 1939 FA Cup Final. He was once hauled over the coals for submitting a large expense sheet for hospitality without naming the lucky recipients. So after the Derby he put in his expenses once again showing a large sum for entertaining. But this time he put: '– to the Clerk of the Course, the Judge, the starter and a gentleman with glasses wearing a pin-stripe suit whose name I didn't quite catch.' And the BBC were happy!

H. B. T. Wakelam and others

There were a number of characters among the pre-war commentators. In lawn tennis there was Colonel Brand, a well-known Wimbledon linesman, who for some reason wore his Homburg hat sideways. After one of his broadcasts in 1929 the *Yorkshire Observer* wrote: 'Tennis-ear-ache! What interest does tennis hold for us? I suppose shortly we shall hear a running commentary on a ping-pong match.' Things have certainly changed fifty years later.

Like R. C. Lyle, Colonel Brand once lost his voice in the middle of a commentary. Nothing came, and he had to be faded out, as he couldn't even manage to say, 'back to the studio.' He once got very excited during a long rally: 'Smash, recovery, smash, recovery, smash, recovery, gosh – it's gone hurtling into the Royal Box at Toque height.' Whether Queen Mary had time to duck is not related.

A Canadian, Bob Bowman, used to do the ice hockey commentaries before Stewart Macpherson. During one particularly vicious and dirty game in Prague, he changed to a boxing commentary in an attempt to describe the fisticuffs out on the rink.

Michael Standing was a member of the BBC staff and before the war did cricket commentary, often in partnership with Howard Marshall. He had a rather slow languid drawl, well suited to the quieter periods of cricket. He was very tall and a useful fast medium bowler, and knew his cricket. Because of his name, John Watt, the then Head of Variety, devised a street-interview spot for him which he called 'Standing on the Corner'.

Michael did commentary other than cricket, including once the Ceremony of the Keys at the Tower of London. He had just said, 'And now silence descends on Tower Hill,' when a roar of half a dozen motorbikes rent the night air. During the war he took over the OB Department from Lobby and afterwards became Head of Light Entertainment.

A highly efficient Jack-of-all-trades was Captain H. B. T. Wakelam, who soon abandoned his initials and was known as 'Teddy'. In giving the first-ever live running commentary, at Twickenham on 15 January 1927, he gained an important place in broadcasting history. At half-time he was heard to say on the air: 'What about a beer?' He deserved it!

After the match the *Spectator* reported: 'That type of broadcasting has come to stay.' How right they were. To prove his versatility Wakelam achieved another 'first' the following Saturday – the first *soccer* commentary on Arsenal v Sheffield United at Highbury. In 1935 he also gave ten-minute comments on the Tests against South Africa during the intervals and close of play. In 1938 he achieved yet another first – in the televising of the Lord's Test between England and Australia, his was the first-ever television commentary on cricket ever given anywhere in the world. He also commentated for television later that year at the Oval and again in 1939 for the West Indies Tests at Lord's and the Oval, assisted by Aidan Crawley and Tommy Woodroffe.

For some reason, however, Wakelam was never enthusiastic about cricket, and thought the game quite unsuitable for lengthy descriptions of play over the air. 'It was too dull,' he said. What sacrilege! But he was not the only one to hold that opinion. After the initial experiment in 1927 of *reporting* from cricket matches the *Daily Telegraph* wrote: 'It is obviously impossible to broadcast anything but short periods of description of a three-day cricket match.' I wonder what the writer would have thought today about our five-day ball-by-ball commentaries on *Test match Special*.

Wakelam also covered lawn tennis with Colonel Brand and there were complaints that with the Colonel, the Captain and the Commander (Woodroffe) the BBC was turning itself into a sort of Cheltenham military establishment. Once on a very hot day at Wimbledon Wakelam caused quite a sensation during his commentary on the Men's Doubles. The commentary box was full of old papers, and while lighting a cigarette he accidentally dropped the match among them. They caught fire and burned his trousers, but he managed to stamp out the blaze without interrupting his commentary. He was one of the main pioneers of commentary and showed remarkable knowledge of all the sports which he covered. He was definitely in the top league of commentators during the last fifty years.

Howard Marshall

The pre-war commentator who made the deepest impression on me was Howard Marshall. I still remember with nostalgia hearing him describe the closing stages of Len Hutton's innings of 364 at the Oval in 1938. I was having a picnic by a river in Yorkshire with some friends, and his slow, deep, burbling voice came through loud and clear. '. . . Bradman with his arms akimbo, the bees are buzzing, and the Oval sparrows are pecking away at the grass by the pavilion gate . . .' It was evocative stuff and paced exactly right for cricket. I think it's fair to say that of all the pre-war commentators he would be the only one totally acceptable today, so good was his technique and his knowledge of cricket. He was a rugby blue at Oxford, but only a good class club cricketer. Unlike most of the others he was a member of the BBC staff, and so had the advantage of accumulating experience as a broadcaster. Besides cricket and rugby he did boxing and ceremonials including the Coronation of

1937. He was thus able to build up time at the microphone which is the best possible way of learning to broadcast.

During the war he was a war correspondent for the BBC and landed in Normandy on D-Day with the invasion forces. I remember hearing his report on the first evening from Broadcasting House in London. He had landed in Normandy early in the morning, and had then been rushed back to Broadcasting House – still in his dirty battledress.

It was some time before he did actual live cricket commentary in the 1930s. Like the Football League, the cricket authorities were frightened of the effect it would have on their gates, so it was not until 1938 that he was allowed into the grounds to describe play as it was happening. Before this he used to sit in the press box and rush out of the ground at intervals and close of play to broadcast from some nearby building where the BBC engineers had set up their equipment.

In 1934 I heard his reports on the Lord's Test match against Australia – Hedley Verity's match when he took 15 wickets for 104 runs. The reports must have been good because I can still recall his description of Patsy Hendren's tumbling catch at silly point, where he caught Tim Wall off Verity, and finished the match.

It was during this Test that Howard had to rush to the basement of a borrowed house in nearby Grove End Road to do his reports. For one of them he arrived breathless to find that the young daughter of the house was having a piano lesson upstairs. The first part of his report had a background of scales, until one of the engineers persuaded the young girl to stop. But her mother was not too pleased, and after a minute or so came down and rapped on the window of the basement, shouting, 'How much longer? My little girl's wasting her music lesson!'

Howard was normally quiet and unexcitable, but on one occasion a listener did write in to complain. She said that when McCabe was bowled by Farnes, Howard let out a fearful shout of 'He's out!' and sounded as if he had swallowed his tonsils. She went on, 'The Prince of Broadcasters had raised his voice!'

As you may have gathered, in the days of Sir John Reith (as he was when Director-General) a commentator had to be very careful what he said on the air. Goodness knows what Sir John would have said about some of our goings-on in the *Test match Special* box today. As an example of what I mean, Howard was once describing the bowling of the Australian, Bill O'Reilly. The

Tiger, as he was called, was bowling magnificently and skittling out the England side. So Howard plucked up courage and actually sang over the air:

> If you're the O'Reilly,
> They speak of so highly,
> Gor' Blimey, O'Reilly,
> You *are* bowling well.

It was the Gor' Blimey which did it, and in addition to an internal reprimand, Howard received a lot of letters of rebuke from the listeners. One anonymous writer wrote:

> My dear Slobber-Chops,
>   Now you've done it. 'Gor' Blimey' indeed. We know you're not the Archbishop of Canterbury but need you descend to blasphemy? I hope they excommunicate you!

2 Links in the Chain

W HEN I JOINED THE BBC after the war, there were several people working on outside broadcasts who had joined the department before and during the war, who therefore formed a link with the early pioneering years. On the administrative side there was Lobby himself, Michael Standing and Charles Max-Muller.

Charlie was never a broadcaster but for years before the war was General Manager of OBs. After war service he returned to the BBC in the overseas service and then became Head of Outside Broadcasts in 1952, when Lobby went to television. His contacts outside the BBC were wide and varied and this was of great value to the department in setting up broadcasts and fixing contracts. He was a superb organiser of such big broadcasting operations as the Coronation, Olympic Games and so on. Certainly under his guidance the OB Department spread its wings and became an even more important part of the BBC.

On the engineering side, R. H. Wood was Engineer in Charge of OBs for just under thirty years, from 1935 to 1964. He was responsible for the vast technical operations involved in all big outside broadcasts, and these included two Coronations, the funerals of King George VI and Sir Winston Churchill, and three Royal Weddings.

He was a special favourite of King George VI and Queen Elizabeth, and did much to help the King over his difficulties with his stammer. He was regularly 'in attendance' each Christmas for the King's Christmas Broadcast which in those days was done 'live', with the King in his study at Sandringham, and his family all listening in another room. The King – and later our present Queen – always expected RH to be there to nurse them through any important broadcast.

He had a quiet confidential way of speaking, almost in a whisper, and unintentionally amused the Royal Family – and all of us – with his famous malapropisms. Here are a few examples: 'He ran out of the room like a house on fire'; 'Now he's buttered his bread he must lie on it'; 'He's as happy as a sandbag'; 'He puts his finger into every tart'.

He had a long reign and ran his department with an apparent remoteness and vagueness about what was going on. But of course he *did* know, and rightly had confidence in, all his OB engineers, who both as men and technicians were the pick of the engineering staff. They are a vital part of any broadcast, not only for their technical skills, but because they are ambassadors for the BBC wherever they go to set up a broadcast. Commentary has always been a team effort and the friendly cooperation and partnership between commentator and engineer has been one of the strengths of the OBs, and has always made this type of broadcast a real pleasure to do.

John Snagge

On the broadcasting side the main link between pre-war and post-war OBs was John Snagge – possibly the most versatile of all broadcasters, certainly one of the best, and definitely the longest standing. He joined the BBC as Assistant Director of BBC Stoke-on-Trent – a lofty title but he actually had to do all the bits and pieces, including announcing. This was in 1924 and until 1981 he was broadcasting from then on.

He became an announcer at Savoy Hill in 1928 in the days when they all had to put on dinner jackets to read the news. They also used to have a pianola in the studio, which the announcer was responsible for playing to fill in occasional interludes. One day John was off duty in the rest room when he heard strangled noises coming from the studio. He rushed in, to find that the tie of one of his colleagues had caught in the pianola roll, and he was gradually being pulled into the pianola and strangled to death.

In John's early days at Stoke he was a conspicuous figure in his Oxford bags, unexpected gear for an old Wykehamist and son of a judge. But when he came to London the standard of dress was higher and if anyone's shoes were down at heel the offender was sent out immediately to get them mended. He will always be famous all over the world for his commentaries on the Oxford and Cambridge Boat Race. He did his first commentary in 1931 and was main commentator on the race for the next fifty years, until he retired in 1980 – and then in 1981 it took *four* commentators to replace him.

He had plenty of memories of those fifty years. He once said of an Australian blue: 'He's the only overseas blue rowing in *both* boats!' And in 1952 he missed the thrilling Oxford victory by a canvas because his launch broke down, and radio had to take the television commentary for the exciting finish.

John told one lovely story about the Boat Race. Every year when the boats reached Duke's Meadows on the Middlesex bank there was a man there who ran up the dark- and light-blue flags on a pole, showing the approximate distances between the crews at that stage. John was normally quite a long way back, so he used to look to see which flag was in the ascendancy. He then based his judgement of the crews' positions by the two flags on the pole. Once at some rowing function John met the man who operated the flags. The man did not recognise John, who asked him how he always worked out the correct distances between the boats so accurately. 'Oh,' replied the man, 'I always listen to John Snagge's commentary!'

There are actually not so many stories about the Boat Race. But a few years ago, on the day before the race, a lady on the towpath was watching the crews in their final practice. She approached Tom Boswell – one of our commentary team – and said: 'I wonder if you can explain something to me. I come to see the Boat Race every year. How does it happen that the same two crews are always in the final?'

Some people thought that the Boat Race would be no more when John retired in 1980 aged seventy-five. For fifty years his voice had told the world about it and he must have been one of the few people alive who had never heard the Boat Race commentary. His great strength was his complete knowledge of all things to do with rowing. He had known all the world's great oarsmen over the period and knew all the inside talk and gossip. Every year he used to dine with both crews in the last week before the race and presented them with a George IV golden sovereign dated 1829 – the first year of the race – for them to toss with. He was remarkably impartial and never let his Oxonian background influence his commentary, either in the many years when Oxford were generally the losers, nor in the last decade when they were on top. Unlike so many of us other commentators he never got overexcited and kept his cool even in the most exciting moments.

The Boat Race, Henley Regatta and Olympic Games, which John covered throughout his career, were actually only a small part of his broadcasting life. He joined OBs in 1933 and covered almost every sport either as commentator, reporter, or as the 'Square One' man. In addition he did a variety of what can be called stunts in a programme called *Let's Go Somewhere*. (This title was 'pinched' by a certain B. Johnston for his live four-minute spot in *In Town Tonight* 1948–52.) He also commentated on a number of events such as the Aldershot Tattoo when, on seeing the royal car arrive escorted by a military policeman on a motorbike, he said, 'Here comes Queen Mary and her motorcycle.'

During the war John moved over to become Presentation Director, and in addition to becoming an announcer once again, was in charge of all the others as well. His rich, deep voice, unlike any other, was so easily recognisable that it was ideal for wartime. It gave a feeling of trust, confidence and credibility, and soon earned him the sobriquet of The Voice of London. Perhaps his most famous wartime broadcast was the announcement of the Normandy landings on D-Day. I remember hearing it in Hove where the Guards Armoured Division was waiting with its tanks. But in addition to D-Day he also announced VE Day, VJ Day and the deaths of King George VI and Queen Mary.

His job as Head of Presentation meant that he had little time for commentary but in 1953 he was the radio commentator in Westminster Abbey, against strong opposition from Richard Dimbleby who covered the Coronation on television.

In 1954 he was told by the Director-General: 'Don't make any announcements without my personal permission. Your voice is so associated with important announcements that as soon as you come on, people will assume that Winston Churchill has died.'

His career came full circle when in the last few years before he finally gave up broadcasting in 1980, he did a series for Radio London called *John Snagge's London*. He recorded over a hundred of these in which he met people, tried out their jobs or visited interesting and historic places. It was *Let's Go Somewhere* all over again and he even went down in a diver's suit, rode on a fire-engine to a fire and travelled on the Post Office underground railway. An apt comment might have been: 'Back to Square One.'

For the record, John was *not* responsible for the following, which was said by an unknown commentator one year at Henley Royal Regatta: 'It's a very close race. Lady Margaret and

Jesus are rowing neck and neck. Perhaps Lady Margaret is just ahead . . . but no, Jesus is now definitely making water on Lady Margaret!'

Harold Abrahams

Another, less obvious, link was Harold Abrahams, the only broadcaster whom I knew who had a film made about him – that splendid British picture *Chariots of Fire*. He was a Cambridge athletics blue and won a gold medal in the one hundred metres in the Olympic Games at Paris in 1924. Before the war he was used mostly as a commentator but from 1945 was more often the expert-comments-man, keeper of records, and unofficial time-keeper, with Rex Alston doing the commentary. That time-keeping was absolutely vital to him. Wherever he went he was armed with at least three stopwatches. I swear that when one was speaking to him he would often time the conversation. Although it was a fetish with him, the reports on lap-times in a race were of tremendous help to the commentators in building up the interest and excitement.

Harold himself occasionally showed bias in his commentary. In the 1936 Olympic Games in Berlin he was commentating on the 1,500 metres. Jack Lovelock, the New Zealander, was a personal friend of Harold, and he could not suppress his pride in the Empire when he saw that Lovelock was going to win: 'Jack, Jack, come on Jack,' he cried. 'He's done it, my God he's done it! Lovelock, Lovelock, Lovelock!'

In those pre-war years he was always formally attired and in 1927 at the Varsity Sports there is a picture of him wearing his black Homburg hat whilst talking into the microphone. He was one of the few experts in the early days who was prepared to find the time to analyse and discuss his broadcasts, in spite of his busy life as a civil servant and athletics administrator. He formed a splendid team with his old friend Rex Alston who had been his number two in the sprints.

Harold had a dry sense of humour and a quick wit. In 1955 he was describing the finish of the Windsor to Chiswick marathon. By mistake he did not notice the leading runner McMinnis enter the stadium, and wrongly gave the winner as Iden, who was actually second. When his mistake was pointed out to him, he quickly apologised, claiming it was a case of mistaken *Iden*tity.

Right up to the end Harold took tremendous trouble with his broadcasts and attended all the meetings before and after a big event. Even though his knowledge of everything to do with athletics was better than anyone else's, he was still willing to learn.

He once showed me a little booklet which he had produced. It was typical of his love of detail and must have involved much journeying to and fro on the Underground. The booklet showed where all the WAY OUT signs were situated on every London Tube Station, and the number of the carriage which always stopped exactly opposite the exit. For instance, if you were travelling from St John's Wood to Oxford Circus you would need to travel in the third coach. But for Charing Cross it would be the first one. I don't know about you but I always seem to get into the wrong end of the train, and would dearly love to have had a copy of Harold's *Guide to the Exits*.

Stewart Macpherson

I personally owe a great deal to Stewart. It was through meeting him both during and immediately after the war that I got the chance to do my test for the BBC at the end of 1945. Although it was not very good, it was sufficient to gain me an interview with Lobby. After much heart searching, I am sure, Lobby took the plunge and offered me a job in the Outside Broadcasts Department. Although he guaranteed neither permanency nor much money, I accepted.

So *I* owed everything to luck. But Stewart owed *his* own job in the BBC to a mixture of cheek and persistence, and, of course, to a large amount of ability. He came over from Canada in 1937 with some sort of introduction to John Snagge – already a broadcasting name well known to listeners overseas. Stewart had done ice hockey commentaries in Canada and had heard that another Canadian ice hockey commentator – Bob Bowman – was switching jobs at the BBC. So Stewart just turned up at Broadcasting House and asked to see John Snagge. John was very busy and sent down a message to reception to say that he was sorry but he could not see Stewart that day. Three hours later he went down in the lift to go to lunch, and saw waiting at reception a short, bespectacled man with a large head. It was Stewart, who somehow recognised John, waylaid him, and persuaded him to ask the BBC to give him a test.

The BBC were looking rather desperately for someone to replace Bowman and they quickly organised a board of high-up officials to try out Stewart in Broadcasting House. They obviously could not produce an ice hockey match, so asked Stewart to sit in a studio and give an imaginary commentary. The board sat in the control room, and gave him the signal to start. For most people it would have been an impossible task to make up the names of players and describe the run of play and the score in a game which was not taking place. But Stewart took it in his stride and went off at a tremendous pace, giving a very exciting commentary packed with action, fouls and goals. After about five minutes he stopped, thinking he had done enough. The panel were visibly impressed. In fact he had made it so realistic that one of the board asked him to continue the commentary, as he wanted to know the final score!

He was, of course, taken on and became the ice hockey commentator. Then when war was declared he did a number of broadcasts for OBs before becoming a distinguished BBC war correspondent.

After the war he was the number one boxing and ice hockey commentator. He was ideally suited for both, with his quick-fire delivery and racy style of description, spiced with a number of transatlantic expressions new to British listeners. He was certainly in the top three of fast talkers, with another Canadian called Gerry Wilmot and Raymond Glendenning as his rivals. He became famous for his close harmony with W. Barrington Dalby, signalling the end of each round with a crisp invitation to 'Come on in, Barry.'

In addition to commentary Stewart also made his name – and good money! – by being chairman of *Twenty Questions* and *Ignorance is Bliss*. In late 1946 and early 1947 he had also tried his hand as the first presenter of *Down Your Way*, which started only in London. There was no preliminary research as there is today. Then, *Down Your Way* just selected a street or a district and with a list of house occupiers knocked haphazardly on doors. On his twelfth programme Stewart did this once too often. After he had knocked on one door, a large man appeared and Stewart, looking down at his list of names, said, 'Good morning, sir. Is Mrs Brown in?' 'Oh,' said the large man, 'you're the chap who's been after my missis, are you?' – and proceeded to slug Stewart a nasty blow. Hasty retreat of the *Down Your Way* party and the last programme which Stewart did. He found the calm and peace of boxing and ice hockey safer!

It was a great loss to British radio when early in the 1950s he decided for family reasons to return to his native Canada. He would have made a big impact too on television and – funnily for such a naturally fast talker – would surely have made a hit on one of the slowest of all sports, golf, which was his favourite hobby.

He was always ready to help with advice and encouragement and I picked up many tips just by watching him at work. One of these can be especially helpful for a commentator at a big state occasion or procession, or even more so at a firework display, which was where I saw Stewart doing it.

He merely had a blank pad of paper in front of him and wrote on it all the adjectives he thought he might need during the display: brilliant – fantastic – magnificent – sparkling – beautiful – colourful – and so on. Then during the broadcast he carefully crossed off each adjective as he used it, and so avoided any repetition. It sounds simple and perhaps unexpected from such a great natural broadcaster. But it is the end result which counts and he certainly nearly always achieved the best.

By the way, we all have to fight against repetition. We often find ourselves plagued by the same adjective coming out of our mouth, time and time again. I wonder if any of you have noticed that my particular *bête noire* is 'marvellous'.

Raymond Glendenning

In the 1930s Teddy Wakelam was the first of the multi-sport commentators with his rugby, soccer, tennis and cricket. The war produced two more, Raymond Glendenning and Rex Alston.

Raymond came to London from the BBC in Northern Ireland in the early 1940s and found the world of sport wide open to his talents. Because of shortage of staff he took on anything and by the end of the war numbered racing, soccer, boxing and tennis as his top sports. Because of Rex he did not do athletics, but was used in the 1948 Olympic Games for the show jumping, and also covered the Greyhound Derby and other races. In fact he was once strictly timed at 176 words in thirty seconds during one race, and over 300 words in a full minute.

So as you can gather he was nothing if not versatile. He had a rich, plummy, mellow voice and had remarkable powers of description. He could describe anything, even our exit from the church when my wife and I were married, and OBs gave us a recording of the ceremony. He had a wonderful memory for facts and figures on any sport but of course he never could devote enough time to any one of them. As a result the boxing public were apt to think that he knew more about racing; or the soccer world thought he should concentrate on boxing. It is in fact an impossible task to be the number one expert on such a diversity of sports.

For instance, to be a racing commentator you must live racing, go to all the meetings and get to know all the racing personalities well. But Raymond could not do this, so had what was called a 'race-reader' who would stand alongside him feeding him with facts, and the position of the horses during the race. This was made possible by the invention of the 'lip-mike', which the commentator held right up to his mouth so that nothing except his voice could be heard by the listener. But you can imagine how difficult it made his job, trying to speak and listen at the same time. The race-readers were full-time racing journalists and one of these was Claude Harrison, followed for a short time by Peter O'Sullevan. The BBC did not try to hide what they were doing, and the race-reader was given his credit over the air.

In boxing Raymond had the help of W. Barrington Dalby – an ex-referee who knew the sport backwards. He summed up for fifty seconds or so between the rounds, but then of course Raymond was left on his own to describe the actual fighting. There was a tremendous furore when Raymond was accused of favouring and shouting home Sugar Ray Robinson in the fight which was in fact won in the end by Randolph Turpin.

Raymond was an easily distinguishable and much carica-tured figure. With his horn-rimmed spectacles, his handlebar moustache and his somewhat ample figure he looked in fact not unlike Billy Bunter with a moustache. He was a gregarious person, a great mixer, and greeted by everyone wherever he went. He enjoyed his drink and would recommend a swig of honey in whisky to maintain stamina and the voice during a broadcast. He could speak at a remarkable speed and his voice at the end of a race, or when a goal was scored, reached an incredible crescendo.

It was lucky that he was a good improviser and a bit of an actor, because on several occasions during the war, he had to commentate on games or races which he could not see. The point was that the BBC was monitored by the Germans, and so no commentator could ever mention anything about the weather. For the same reason no broadcast could ever be cancelled because of fog. When the game or race itself was cancelled because of bad ground conditions, then no commentary took place. There was no explanation to the listener of why not – except perhaps that famous 'technical hitch'.

Certainly on one occasion at Cheltenham Raymond had to invent what was happening while the horses were 'out in the country', only picking them up as they came through the fog in the home straight. Luckily it was not television and he was able to readjust the position of the horses, having been careful to avoid any falls during his fictitious account. There was also fog at Elland Road on Boxing Day 1942, so Raymond could only see one side of the pitch, and had to make up what was happening on the other side to coincide with the reactions of the crowd on that side. Not easy!

Raymond's silver tongue let him down seriously only once when during the Grand National he remarked, '. . . and now coming to the rider jump there's a waterless horse out in front!'

Raymond gradually faded away in the 1960s but for twenty years he had been the BBC's outstanding personality amongst the sports commentators and the big sporting events were never quite the same without that ample figure with the glasses and handlebar moustache.

3 Familiar Voices

Henry Longhurst

I F I HAD TO PICK OUT my favourite commentator on any sport – an invidious task – I think I would pick Henry Longhurst. Like John Arlott in cricket and Dan Maskell at lawn tennis, he indelibly imprinted his personality and individual style on golf. It is significant that all three specialised in one sport on which they were an authority, not only on the skill and laws of the game, but even more perhaps on its history, traditions and personalities.

Commentary on cricket and lawn tennis had been broadcast on television and radio before the war. In golf there were some brilliant reports and comments by that great writer, Bernard Darwin. There were also a few attempts at describing the play, including Henry himself on the British Amateur Championships in 1935. But after the war golf was a virtual newcomer – especially to television, whereas now, thanks to the pioneering work done by Henry, it has become one of the top television sports.

Henry had many achievements during his varied life. He captained the Cambridge University golf team to victory in 1931. During the war for a short time he became a Member of Parliament. He wrote one thousand consecutive pieces for the *Sunday Times* as their golf correspondent for forty-five years. In 1965 he became the first Briton to work regularly for the American networks. He was awarded the CBE and in 1969 was given the Journalist of the Year Special Award. But perhaps the honour he valued most of all was when he was made an Honorary Life Member of the Royal and Ancient in 1977. Although a very sick man at the time he insisted on going up to St Andrews for the presentation.

What was his secret? His style was ideally suited to television. More than any television commentator that I have ever known, he knew by instinct when to talk and when to keep quiet. Someone quite rightly once described 'his brilliant flashes of silence'.

His gruff, confidential voice, his slow delivery, his wit and the ability to produce the apt phrase on the spur of the moment, were just what the viewer wanted. He became the friend of us all and the kind critic and friend of all the competitive golfers. He knew their difficulties and could appreciate all their tensions – especially when putting. He himself gave up golf because he got the 'twitch'. 'Once you've had 'em, you've got 'em,' he once said. With a whispered comment he could make the viewer at home in his armchair feel that *he* was actually about to putt.

Humour was never far away when Henry was about, so I am sure he would not mind my telling the story of when he nearly sued the BBC for slander. Henry was a good liver and liked to 'fortify' himself from time to time – not just in the club-house bar. Remember that he often had to stay at the top of the scaffolding tower which held the BBC commentary box for long periods of the day, in the cold, wet or heat. On one occasion Jim Swanton was commentating on television during a Test match at Headingley. We were sharing air time with the Golf Open Championship, and halfway through the morning our producer told Jim to hand over to Henry at Lytham St Annes. This Jim did, ending with the words: 'So over now to Henry Longhurst.' Jim then turned to our summariser Denis Compton and said, '. . . and I bet he's got his bottle of gin up there with him at the top of the tower.'

Unfortunately Jim spoke before his microphone had been switched off, so that Henry and all the millions of viewers heard his remark. Henry was naturally not too pleased, and had it not been his old friend Jim Swanton with whom he used to share a flat before the war, he might well have taken some sort of action for defamation of character.

It was a tribute to Henry's style that he was as popular in the United States as in Great Britain. The golf commentator's job is not easy. He has to speak against a background of silence, so that his every word is like dropping a pebble on to a still pond. Rugby, racing and soccer commentators can all get away with the slight fluff or not-so-perfect English, against the noise of the crowd. But in golf, lawn tennis, snooker and of course cricket, a mistake seems to be magnified by the backdrop of silence.

Henry was as near perfect as any commentator could be, even towards the end when he was sadly struggling against ill health. He was humble but at the same time a great deflater of pomposity. He died aged sixty-nine and in his last year made a typical comment: 'Three under-fours – not a bad score in the circumstances.' When ill health finally forced him to retire from work, he wrote: 'Now it is time to lay down my pen and alas the microphone too, and to reflect in whatever time may be left how uncommonly lucky I have been.'

What a lovely thing to have been able to write at the end of a successful and happy life. As one of his obituaries remarked about his CBE – he was a Commentator Beyond Excellence.

Kenneth Wolstenholme

Most of the present-day commentators are far too young to have taken part in the war. Of those old enough some of us were in the Services, some were war reporters, and others did equally essential work as, say, teachers or police officers. But one commentator who was a bomber pilot and one of the original Pathfinders, actually won a double medal – DFC and Bar – soccer commentator Kenneth Wolstenholme.

He had been a journalist before the war and afterwards became the pioneer of BBC Television soccer commentary. It is not as easy a job as it may appear to viewers, especially when the game is dull or play below standard. Good identification of players is essential every time the ball is touched by another player. So is expert interpretation of the reasons for the referees awarding free kicks. In Kenneth's time it was also necessary to have a photographic memory of all the incidents which took place, like a goal, an off-side or a penalty. Nowadays action replay makes that part of the job far easier.

In these days of statistics every commentator must be armed with an assortment of facts, either in his head or on notes which are easily to hand. These must include such things as the teams' places in the League and Cup, the careers of individual players, and the historical details of each club and the grounds. Kenneth was very good at this, partly because he concentrated on the one sport. His main strength was the reading of a game and the ability to anticipate what the action would be – or rather perhaps *ought* to be. He demanded a high standard of play and could be a severe critic, which perhaps did not endear him to everyone. But he was honest.

Kenneth will always be remembered for his television commentary when England won the World Cup in 1966 and his immortal words: '. . . some people are on the pitch. They think it's all over – it is now!' He left the BBC in 1972 because they would not guarantee him coverage of the top games. I can quite understand his feelings. Having been so long at the top he wanted to stay there – or else. Since then apart from some regional commentary for ITV his authoritative voice has been sadly lost to soccer.

Dan Maskell

'The Voice of Tennis' began broadcasting on radio in 1949 and then took over from Freddy Grisewood as the main television commentator in 1951. He was one of those who specialised in just one sport which in fact was to be his life's work. He started as a ballboy at Queen's Club in 1923 and later became the professional at the club. He was coach to the All England Club at Wimbledon for twenty-seven years and coached the British Davis Cup team for sixteen years, including during its victorious years in the 1930s, when it won the Cup four years running from 1933 to 1936. He was British Professional Champion when aged only nineteen. Because he was a professional all his life he was never able to play in the Davis Cup nor in the Wimbledon Championships, where professionals were not allowed to compete till 1968. But he did not miss a *single day's* Wimbledon, either as spectator or commentator, from 1929 until his retirement in 1991.

He was a warm, friendly, avuncular figure, and one of the most relaxed of all commentators. He seldom got really worked up, though with his high principles he must have been sorely tempted to 'blow his top' over some of the appalling behaviour on the courts at Wimbledon during his later years. He did, however, protest strongly when a teenager once chased Bjorn Borg across the Centre Court: 'This is sacrilege,' he said, raising his voice ever so slightly. 'She's wearing high heels!'

He took tremendous trouble with his broadcasts and did at least two hours' daily homework before setting off to the day's broadcasting. Each evening too he would watch the repeats and playbacks of play to make sure he was not using the same comment too often. After all it isn't too easy with tennis. What *do* you say? Well played, fine shot, beautiful stroke, and so on. I think he found that on occasions he used certain expressions too often, like: 'Oh I say' and 'Oh, my goodness.' But like Henry Longhurst he was a good timer of *when* to speak, and with his deep knowledge and experience of the game, his comments, when made, were always apt and to the point.

He provided viewers with an impartial commentary of what was happening and why. When he did criticise he was kind and constructive, and his good relationship with all the players enabled him to drop in bits of useful information about what was going on behind the scenes. He was awarded the CBE in 1982 for his services to tennis and broadcasting. When he finally retired in 1991, it felt as though lawn tennis – like cricket without John Arlott and the Boat Race without John Snagge – would never be quite the same again.

Dan was an emotional man who expected a high standard not only from the players, but from himself too. Only once did he let himself down when he was so moved and overjoyed for British Tennis when Virginia Wade won Wimbledon in Jubilee Year. But no one noticed. He was just unable to speak a single word. He appeared on television for forty years, though to my mind not enough in vision. His kind, crinkly, craggy face revealed the true man.

After that I must just tell one little tale 'against' him. He, Peter Alliss, John Snagge and myself once appeared on Bruce Forsyth's *Generation Game*. The competitors had to listen to each of us doing a short, out-of-vision commentary on our particular sport and write down who we were. They hardly got any of us right, though one chap did put down the cricket commentator as Brian Robertson. But the final insult to Dan was when one of the competitors guessed that he was Virginia Wade!

Eddie Waring

There is a good chance that if you mention Rugby League to most people they will automatically think of Eddie Waring. If they live south of the Wash most of them will remember him with affection and be grateful for the many hours of amusement which he provided. For thirty years he was a legend even before the television impressionist Mike Yarwood made him into a larger than life character. The ladies, especially, enjoyed his 'ahaas' and 'eees' and expressions like 'up and under' for the high kick ahead, or 'he's taking an early baath' for a player sent off.

'Ruggerby Leeague' was his life. He played it and managed both Leeds and Dewsbury. In his first seven years with the latter they went from bottom of the table to win almost every honour in the game, including two League Championships. So here was a commentator who definitely knew his game from hard experience.

He worked on a local Dewsbury newspaper and then visited Australia with the first Rugby League Team to tour after the war. He did his first television commentary in 1951 and retired in 1981, and was given the full leaving treatment by the entire media.

This cocky little man with his inevitable trilby hat at a jaunty angle, and those twinkling, mischievous eyes, was a slightly mysterious figure. No one – not even his producers – knew where he lived. All his mail and contracts were sent to the Queen's Hotel in Leeds, where he had an office and held court in the bar. He kept his private life entirely separate.

I said that viewers south of the Wash would remember Eddie with amusement. He certainly broadened the appeal of Rugby League away from its traditional home in the north. But though they could never dislike Eddie as a man, most northern Rugby League supporters thought that he did more harm than good to the game. They felt that his light approach and treatment of the game overshadowed its undoubted skills, thrills and tough play. These all became lost in the flow of chatter and often hilariously apt descriptions of what was going on out on the field: 'They've got to keep their hands warm somehow,' he said of two hefty forwards punching each other. Or of a man temporarily knocked out: 'He'll be all right. I saw his eyelids flutter.' Even better perhaps was this comment about a man lying prostrate after a crushing tackle: 'I don't know if that is the ball or his head. We'll know if it stands up.'

Whatever the feelings of his northern critics Eddie will, I am sure, always be remembered by most people for the laughter he gave them and for his chirpy, cheeky approach to television.

Peter O'Sullevan

Peter O'Sullevan was awarded a knighthood for his services to horse racing and retired in 1997 after fifty years with the BBC.

Peter was born in the last year of the Great War, was educated at Charterhouse and then, because of ill health, at the Alpine College in Switzerland. He first came into prominence as the Press Association's racing correspondent, during which period he occasionally acted as race-reader to Raymond Glendenning. In 1950 he joined the *Daily Express* and he was their racing correspondent until 1986. He formed a perfect double act with Clive Graham (The Scout) and they continued this partnership on television when Peter became the first *regular* television or radio racing commentator to commentate without a race-reader. In contrast to Peter's stimulating commentaries, Clive gave his witty and expert comments from his ringside seat in the paddock.

There have been many fast talkers whom I have already mentioned – Stewart Macpherson and Raymond Glendenning to name but two. But in an exciting finish Peter must surely outpace them all. He undergoes a remarkable change in the tempo and character of his voice. When not commentating Peter is quietly spoken and hardly raises his voice above a confidential whisper. But over the last furlong of a race all this disappears. While the horses are out in the country Peter talks fast but in a contemplative sort of way with his voice staying at a constant level and only the occasional increase in tempo and excitement if there is a faller or a badly taken jump. But as soon as the jockeys reach for their whips and the race to the finish is on, Peter becomes a different person. An incredible succession of horses' names spill from his mouth in an ever increasing crescendo.

Peter has proved the point that to be a racing commentator you must 'live' on the racecourses. There is not time for other sports as in the days of Raymond Glendenning. Peter's racing knowledge is unsurpassed but even so he has to do hours of homework to learn the colours of new owners, or to associate a well-known colour with a new horse. It bears emphasising that a racing commentator may have twenty or so horses bearing down on him at full charge. If he is at a course like Newmarket they are coming headlong at him. He not only has to decide which horses are in the lead but having made his decision conjure up in his mind the name of the horse with that colour, the name of the jockey, trainer and owner. Unless he spent his whole life with the trainers, horses and jockeys his job would be impossible. Even so I still think it is near to a miracle.

Of course in addition to naming the right horses in their correct finishing order Peter has to have a cast-iron background knowledge about the breeding of the horses, and their past successes and failures. The same with the jockeys – he can add to the enjoyment of viewers by talking about their personalities and characters, and their particular style and skill.

Nowadays Peter wears a large pair of horn-rimmed spectacles but this has not hampered his use of the large swivelling binoculars which race commentators use. I am sure that like us all he makes mistakes, but I personally have never seen him call the wrong horse home. Although after one race he announced: 'It's a photo between Gold Prospect and Shareblank, and third is probably just in behind these two.'

He has trained himself to hide his own personal feelings. You can never tell if he has backed a particular horse (which he does from time to time, following no doubt his daily tips in the *Daily Express*). Nor when he had to commentate on his own horse, Attino, did he show a trace of emotion when it won, though I believe he did reveal that Attino had a passion for Polo Mints and loved listening to the radio. Talking of backing horses he once gave a very good tip to punters. Saturday is a bad day to bet, as many horses only run because owners want to see them, and many of them are often not fully fit (the horses, not the owners!).

Peter can top most commentators in two things. He is always immaculately turned out and would, I think, get most people's vote as the best-dressed commentator. I can think of only two possible rivals – Richie Benaud and Peter Jones – both natty dressers. Secondly, except for Raymond Baxter, he is surely the fastest driver – at any rate on the road to Newmarket for which he holds some unlikely record. Sportsmen tend to drive fast, especially jockeys and cricketers who have to travel several times a week over vast distances. In cricket I would back Brian Close and Ian Botham to get to most places quicker than anyone else, although the former would be bound to have had one or two 'close shaves' on the way.

Perhaps the best summing-up of Peter O'Sullevan was given

by the person who said, 'Had he been at the Charge of the Light Brigade, Peter would have given rank, name and number of each rider – plus of course, the name of the horse.'

Harry Carpenter

Harry Carpenter had a style peculiar to himself with his short, staccato, clipped sentences. As a commentator he stuck to boxing and greyhound racing, but was of course more frequently seen on the box as a presenter with an attractive smile, whether it was Wimbledon, the Open Golf or *Sportsnight*.

At Wimbledon he stayed in an underground studio (the bunker) from 11.45 am to 7.30 pm or later. He operated in front of a bank of monitors covering action on all the courts and with his producer 'conducted' the proceedings, switching from court to court, giving results and doing interviews. Not surprisingly he was nicknamed 'The Mole' and over the years he earned the extra 'comfort' of his own studio loo. He did virtually the same thing at the Open Golf but in far pleasanter conditions – above ground.

He also used to present the Boat Race and after Oxford had won in 1977 he told the television audience: 'Ah, isn't that nice, the wife of the Cambridge President is kissing the cox of the Oxford crew.'

He was a naval petty officer in the war and then became boxing correspondent of the *Daily Mail*, also specialising in greyhound racing and speedway. He started life as a journalist on the *Greyhound Express* when aged only sixteen. But his real forte was boxing commentary and although he never boxed himself, his judgement and comments were highly respected in the boxing world. He used his staccato style but never shouted or got overexcited, although at one fight he said: 'He looks up at him through his blood-smeared lips!'

Some points of interest about him – he preferred one-to-one sport to team games, always wore a dark suit and tie in case of blood being spattered, and is probably one of the few commentators to have received police protection – in 1965 after threats and accusations of bias against an Irish boxer. Harry was appreciated by producers because he was unflappable and never panicked. Not even on the occasion when Frank Bough handed over to 'Your carpenter, Harry Commentator.' Harry retired from the BBC in 1991. He was one of television's really professional operators and even earned the praise (since that is what it was) of Muhammad Ali himself, who said in a fore-word to one of Harry's books: 'He's not as dumb as he looks!'

David Coleman

In January 2001 David Coleman left the BBC after forty-six years as 'The Voice of BBC Sport'.

David was the first and foremost of the modern style of commentators who surfaced in the mid-1950s with the swift development of television. He was always supremely confident, slick, smartly dressed and insisted on the highest standards. He was intolerant of inefficiency and this would sometimes lead to differences with producers and cameramen. But his intention was to be the best, and from 1954 when he first joined the BBC he soon became the top television sports presenter, linkman, interviewer and commentator. He also became the highest paid of them all. I think that he would agree that he has mellowed slightly over the years, though not at the expense of his confidence and desire for perfection.

Like so many sporting commentators he started on a news-paper, and was editor of a local Cheshire paper when only twenty-three. He was in the Signals in the war, and then joined the Army paper, *Union Jack*. He joined the BBC in Birmingham in 1954, and through *Grandstand*, *Sportsnight* and *Match of the Day* soon became BBC Television Sport's number one. As a soccer commentator he was strong, fluent and forthright in his opinions. Soccer and athletics have been his commentary sports and he had practical experience of both.

He was a first-class runner and was Cheshire champion for the mile and was also the first non-international to win the Manchester mile. This has been of great help in his athletics commentaries and he is a good reader of the tactics being used by the various runners. He is a fast talker and possibly, like most of us, gets a little bit too excited at times. But he is a good judge of pace and distance and always seems to call the right runners home.

David is renowned for his many gaffes, especially at athletics meetings, such as (of an unknown runner): 'This man could be a black horse'; (of a rather short runner): 'He's even smaller in real life than he is on the track'; and (of a favourite who was not winning the race, as expected): 'He just can't believe what's not happening to him!'

It is very difficult when broadcasting from something like the Olympics not to appear biased in favour of your country. In fact rightly or wrongly I would say that most British viewers want to hear their particular champion encouraged and shouted home. Perhaps he did overdo it when David Hemery won a gold medal: '. . . David Hemery's first, Hennige West Germany second and who cares who's third!' (Actually Mrs Sherwood did because her husband John Sherwood of Great Britain was the third man.)

Perhaps his hardest and almost impossible task is the Olympic one hundred metres. He has to cover as many as twelve heats at five-minute intervals with eight runners in each. Each race takes about ten seconds and there can be names like Papageorgopoulos and Ravelomanantsoa. Try getting your tongue round that lot, and imagine the research needed to learn about the ninety-six competitors taking part in those heats.

But David will always be known for his unintentional howlers and here are a few more Coleman classics: 'Morceli has the four fastest 1500 metre times ever. And all those times are at 1500 metres' . . . 'Nineteen Kenyans started in that race and they finished 1-2-3' . . . and last but not least: 'She's not Ben Johnson – but then who is?'

Bill McLaren

Bill McLaren is a bit of a paradox. I would say that he is the most universally accepted and most popular of all the television commentators. And yet he probably talks more than any, and so breaks the golden rule of 'only talk when you can add to the picture'. But I honestly don't think I have ever heard anyone say they did not like Bill as a television commentator and there can be precious few – if any – of whom that can be said.

He has a melodious baritone voice with a rich Scottish accent but is perfectly easy to understand. His rugby background is impeccable. Born and bred in Hawick, he played rugby for the High School and later for Hawick itself. As a flank forward he played for a Scotland XV v the Army, but his rugby career was cut short by tuberculosis. He was completely cured of this by the 'new' drug streptomycin and got a job as a rugby reporter on the local Hawick paper. His editor, John Hood, recommended Bill to the BBC without his knowing and they wrote a letter offering him an audition. He at first thought this was a joke and threw the letter into the wastepaper basket. But eventually he did a ten-minute test with five others. As a result of this he was given fifty minutes' commentary on a match between Glasgow and Edinburgh. His next break-through was when he was squeezed in for ten minutes between Rex Alston and G. V. Wynne-Jones for a Scotland v Wales match in the early 1950s. He continued to do radio until 1962 when he began on television and has never looked back since.

He is respected by all nationalities because of his great knowledge of the game and his complete impartiality. He admits though that on one occasion his nationality nearly got the better of him. In 1969 in the Scotland v France match the score was 3–3 with only one minute to go. Jim Telfer then scored the winning try for Scotland and Bill's voice reached an unnaturally high pitch!

He owes his knowledge to a great deal of hard work, in addition to his playing experience. He does a tremendous amount of rugby research and, following a tip from Raymond Glendenning, prepares cards for each player and a big double-foolscap sheet containing essential details of the teams, grounds, referee, touch judges and coaches. On the morning before each International he reads the laws of Rugby Football. During a match he is therefore well qualified to name the offence after every whistle, not very easy when a mass of players are lying one on top of another.

The same cannot be said about an Irish Rugby Football commentator, obviously not very experienced, who once reported, 'Now one of the forwards has got the ball – I can't say who he is – wait while I look at the programme – number 8 – oh, well, it doesn't matter anyway, the other side has just scored a try'!

Bill has always been prepared to learn from other commentators. Richard Dimbleby told him: 'Collect as much information as you can. You'll only use about three per cent and you'll feel that much of your work was wasted. But don't you believe it!' So spake the master.

Bill also noticed that when Henry Longhurst commentated he seemed to be playing the game with the players. And so it is with Bill. He is the players' commentator who often knows what they are thinking: 'He'll be sorry about that,' or, 'He'll be cursing himself.' That's about as far as he will go with his criticism. But the viewer does often feel like getting out of his armchair and joining in with the scrum. Bill brings it all alive and has undoubtedly been helped by his experience as the Supervisor of Sport and Physical Recreation in Hawick's five primary schools. Every day he had to 'put it across' to young boys and girls. And not just rugby. Gym, soccer, netball and even dancing were included in his curriculum. No wonder he 'puts it across' so well now to all his BBC pupils.

For all his popularity with viewers, his must be one of the least well-known faces among the top commentators. He is rarely seen in vision. He arrives at an International the day before the match in order to watch the practices. After the game whenever possible he catches the first plane or train back to his beloved Hawick. At least he escapes the mass of autograph hunters. They are not sure who they are looking for!

4 And Now Over To . . .

Peter Dimmock

TELEVISION OBS OWE AS MUCH to Peter Dimmock as Radio OBs did to Lobby. Peter was an RAF pilot and instructor during the war, and when he was demobilised in 1945 became the Press Association racing correspondent before joining BBC Television Outside Broadcasts as a producer and commentator in 1946. Most of his commentary was on racing but it was as an administrator that he really made his name. Up to the mid-50s, however, he must have produced as many television OBs as anyone.

I know that in 1950 he was producing at our first ever televised Test match from Trent Bridge. At that time he was in his late twenties and was brash, supremely confident and never believed in taking 'no' from anybody. In this Test we were due to start televising at 11.30 am, which was the actual start of the day's play. This did not satisfy Peter. He thought – rightly – that there should be at least five minutes before play for the commentator to set the scene, give the result of the toss, and to talk about the weather, teams and the pitch.

Although he had been at Dulwich College he did not appear to know too much about cricket. But at least he knew that the umpires went to the wickets five minutes before play started. So he decided to go and see them and came back in triumph. 'It's all right. I've seen Frank Chester and Harry Elliot and they've agreed to come out at 11.30 instead of 11.25.' I told you he was confident! Imagine a television producer being able to alter the start of a Test match. They can – and do – arrange the times of horse races to suit television. But cricket – no!

Anyhow, I expressed surprise without disillusioning him, and of course at 11.25 exactly, out of the pavilion came the two white-coated umpires. Peter was watching in the control van, and in my headphones I heard him shout: 'By God, there go the umpires – they shouldn't be out till 11.30. Stop them someone – quick.'

But of course Frank and Harry continued their slow walk

out on to the field and the match started at 11.30, just as we started our television broadcast. Peter was quite unabashed, and thought that he had been badly let down.

From 1954 to 1972 he was Head of Television OBs, later on adding the impressive title of General Manager. He was a man of tremendous drive and enthusiasm. Nothing was impossible. No one was inaccessible. He would fight to the last ditch for anything he wanted and he usually won. Peter undoubtedly made the BBC supreme in television sport, and determined to get all the big events in every sport on to the BBC screens. He could be ruthless, tough and overriding, which all sounds rather intimidating. But although a lot of people felt they had been 'done' by him, it was difficult not to laugh and forget after it was all over. This was because Peter himself had a quick wit and a good sense of humour and especially in the later years he was able to take a joke against himself, and laugh.

He was always immaculately dressed in a rather traditional way, and he even had a watch-chain across his waistcoat. He had a military moustache, and often a flower in his buttonhole. He was debonair, dynamic and had a wicked twinkle in his eye, with which he won his way with the ladies. He created a television sports unit for the first time and was responsible for the weekly magazine programme *Sportsview*, which he presented for ten years. On occasions when he was away, I sat in for him, and this was not without its anxious moments.

It was the early days of the teleprompter where the script can be seen in the lens of the camera. In those days to keep the revolving script moving one had to press a button in the floor with one's foot, rather like a dentist, or when you want to flush a lavatory on a train. I was a bit inexperienced in its use, and found that if I pressed too hard the script went too fast and disappeared from sight – and there was no way of getting it back. This happened several times, and I had to 'ad lib' the bit that had disappeared. I also found that in reading the teleprompter I was in the hands of Paul Fox, the producer, who wrote what he wanted me to say. On one occasion there was an item about boxing, of which I know nothing. Paul Fox and the promoter Jack Solomons were not the best of friends, and Paul had written into the script something which Jack thought was libellous. Anyway, at the end of the programme the telephone on the desk rang and it was an infuriated Jack threatening to sue *me* for libel. I managed to pacify him, but decided that I preferred my cricket.

Eamonn Andrews

Most people, I suppose, remember Eamonn as a television presenter of such shows as *This Is Your Life, What's My Line?* or *Crackerjack*. But he started life in broadcasting as a boxing commentator. He was a middleweight boxer and a former All-Ireland Amateur Junior Boxing Champion. He first broadcast for Radio Eireann as a boxing commentator and then came over to England and for a dozen happy years presented Angus Mackay's *Sports Report* on the Light Programme. They were a great combination, with Angus in the studio whispering results and latest sports news into Eamonn's right ear. So quick was Eamonn on the uptake that the words seemed to go into his ear one moment and out of his mouth the next. He soon got into boxing and eventually took over from Stewart Macpherson as the BBC's radio commentator, and in fact was not dissimilar in style and voice to Stewart.

In 1951 he was asked by Peter Dimmock to commentate for television at one of those posh boxing evenings, where everyone wears a dinner jacket, including the commentator. He hired his evening clothes for the occasion and at the end of the big fight was told by Peter to get into the ring and interview the winner. He climbed through the ropes and caught his hired clip-on bow-tie on one of them so that it came off. So for his first big television interview in front of millions he appeared in a dinner jacket without a tie.

It was a pity for the listener that he switched from commentary to television presentation, but of course it made him into possibly the best-known face in the country and certainly one of broadcasting's highest paid performers. But he did not just stick to performing and was by far the most successful businessman of all the television stars, combining Chairmanship of Radio Eireann's Statutory Authority with his own private interests, including night clubs.

Eamonn was a deceptive man. At six foot, he was taller than he looked on television, and still had a boxer's figure. His main feature was his crooked smile and his main strength was his affability, modesty and friendliness in dealing with other people. He sometimes looked slightly embarrassed and believe it or not, after all his years of experience, was still nervous before a show. Although *This Is Your Life* was a recorded programme, it was originally done 'live', and Eamonn always expected something to go wrong. But somehow with him, it never did. A just reward for television's 'nice guy'.

Lionel Marson

I admit that I am fairly emotional and that there have been quite a few occasions on the air when I have found it difficult to speak because of a lump in my throat. But there is only one commentator whom I have actually seen cry with tears running down his cheeks. They were tears of happiness for a great victory by a combination of man and beast. The occasion was the White City in 1951 when Foxhunter – ridden and owned by Harry Llewellyn – won the King George V Cup for the third time.

I had somehow got involved in doing commentary on show jumping. I had few qualifications except that as a rather terrified young boy I used to hunt, and later up at Oxford rode once in a point-to-point or 'grind' as they are called there. I hired a horse called Tip Top who was a half-brother of Tom Walls's Derby winner, April the 5th. The horse did not know it but he could have stopped when he liked. However, his racing instinct prevailed and although left at the start we completed the course and finished fifth. Looking back, it was a crazy thing to have done because I took Tip Top's jumping form on trust and never once went over a jump on him before the race. A famous Oxford tipster called Captain Dean summed up my riding perfectly: 'There are jockeys here today,' he told the crowd, 'who could not ride in a railway carriage unless the door was locked!'

Anyhow, it was considered enough for me to share the commentary on the International Horse Show with a real expert, ex-cavalry officer and BBC announcer, Lionel Marson. There he was in brown bowler hat and gaiters sitting alongside me. As Foxhunter completed the clear round which made him winner for the third time, Lionel rose, shouting into the microphone and quite openly sobbing his heart out. He was actually in good company as everyone in the stand around us seemed to be doing the same thing.

Lionel was one of the old school, had perfect manners, wore all the right cricket ties and was in fact a 'proper gentleman'. He made one famous boob on the air when reading the news about the theft of the Stone of Scone from Westminster Abbey. The script read: '. . . it had been placed in the Abbey by Edward Ist.' For some reason Lionel pronounced this as Edward *Isst*. The duty editor sitting alongside him pointed frantically at the Ist and Lionel, after a second's thought, said, 'I am sorry. I evidently got that wrong. I should of course have said, "Edward *Iced*".'

Incidentally, those few show jumping commentaries were the only ones in any sport other than cricket which I have done, with the exception of the Boat Race. Having played a lot of rugby at Eton and Oxford I would like to have had a shot at that, but Rex Alston was firmly in the saddle and I was never given the opportunity.

Maurice Edelston

Maurice came into broadcasting late in life. He joined Outside Broadcasts in 1969 when aged fifty and shared an office with me in Broadcasting House. He had been a schoolmaster and a writer and also had shares in a sports goods business. He brought great sporting ability to the commentary teams. Best known as an amateur footballer, he was also a good tennis player, and had kept wicket for London University.

As an amateur footballer he played for Fulham, Brentford and Reading and appeared five times for England as an inside forward in wartime internationals. He was stockily built and a fast mover with strong, slightly bowed legs. He was a superb passer and distributor of the ball and made many more goals than he scored himself. He had the reputation of being scrupulously clean and fair, and had only one foul given against him in his whole career – a player fell over his foot! He went on playing charity matches until his sudden death in 1976.

As you would expect, he read a game better than any other commentator and was able to anticipate many moves. He had a quiet voice and never appeared to hurry, yet in both football and tennis he always seemed to keep pace with the game. At lawn tennis he was especially easy to follow, even in a fast double with four complicated names. Maurice was much liked wherever he went, and his chuckle was infectious. He was a delightful companion during the three years in which we shared an office – on the few occasions when we were both there!

Max Robertson

So far as I know there has only been one commentator who has ever been a gold prospector – Max Robertson. He was born in India, and educated at Haileybury and Clare College, Cambridge but left early to join some amateur gold seekers in Papua, New Guinea. I am afraid that they were not very successful, so that Max ended up in Sydney, Australia, where his versatile broadcasting career began. In 1937 he joined the Australian Broadcasting Commission as an announcer and general commentator. Two years later he returned to England and became an announcer on the BBC European Service.

During the war he was commissioned in the Royal Artillery (Territorial Army) and became an Adjutant, which gives a clue to his character. Max always organised himself well, and was punctual, meticulous, hardworking and self-disciplined. After the war he returned to the BBC, and although still with the European Service, broadcast from Wimbledon and the 1948 Olympic Games for OBs, whom he finally joined in 1950.

He will always be associated with his lightning radio commentaries on tennis, but in fact he had a variety of television and radio jobs. For radio there was the Coronation, a royal tour in Canada, a number of Olympic Games and some ceremonials. The latter included the occasion when the Queen of Norway arrived at the Guildhall for lunch with the Lord Mayor. Said Max: 'The Queen of Norway is looking very attractive in an off-the-hat face.'

Max's fast vocal style did not suit television commentary, but as he was possibly the best-looking of all the post-war commentators, he was much in demand as a presenter on television. He even took over *Panorama* for a short period, and his *Going for a Song* was one of television's most popular programmes. He was a natural for this as he was a collector of Chinese and Japanese ceramics.

What was the secret of Max's success? Besides the usual hard work and research, and the ability to produce colourful descriptions of what he saw, he was quite simply the fastest and clearest talker on radio. I have already said how much I admire racing commentators. But difficult as their task is they only have to keep going for a few minutes. Tennis commentators may have to keep going for several hours on end. Modern tennis too has become faster with the development of service and hard hitting. The real difficulty comes during a long rally in a doubles match. The commentator not only has to describe the shot but pronounce clearly the name of the player who made it. Just imagine having to commentate on a long rally in which these four ladies' names were involved: Navratilova and Mandlikova v Kiyomura and Sawamatsu.

But somehow Max managed to keep up with the play, with words pouring from his mouth at an unbelievable pace, revealing a remarkable co-ordination between eye and tongue. There has never been anyone else quite like him and I doubt if there ever will be.

Robert Hudson

Of all the leading commentators since the war the most unsung and least known to the public must surely have been Robert Hudson. This was largely due to his quiet, unobtrusive and retiring personality. He was, in fact, one of the very few commentators who was not an extrovert. At the same time he was probably the most conscientious, and put most of us to shame with his meticulous preparation and research before any programme in which he was taking part. He was essentially the broadcasters' commentator. We knew all the difficulties he had to overcome and so appreciated his great skill. To the listeners, however, he made it all sound too easy.

After leaving the army as a Major in the Royal Artillery he did his first cricket broadcast in 1947 for television, and for radio in 1948. His career was spent mostly with radio and he mainly commentated on cricket, rugby and ceremonials. He had two spells as an administrator, first up in North Region, as it was then, and later when he succeeded Charles Max-Muller as Head of OBs in London.

His commentaries on cricket and rugby were hard to fault for accuracy of description, and he made sure that his knowledge of the laws and details of the players' careers was complete. In cricket, for instance, whereas most of us rely on the brains of Bill Frindall in the box, Robert always had his own little black book full of the records of all the players in the match. Most of us stroll casually into the box half an hour or so before the start of a game. But Robert liked to take his place about an hour before, and sit there concentrating on the job ahead.

I always had the feeling that it was quite a strain for him until the first ball was bowled. After that he was a different person and sounded confident and efficient, giving a completely accurate account of what was happening. Although in private life he had a good sense of humour, it did not often come through in his broadcasts, so he lacked some of the colour of someone like John Arlott.

Before I joined *Test match Special*, in 1970, Robert had become Head of OBs and given up regular commentary. It was in fact entirely due to him that I was invited to join the *Test match Special* team when I was dropped by television. Since he had left the commentary box I did not work a lot with him, which is perhaps just as well. I doubt whether he would have wholly approved of all the fun and games which we enjoy in the box today.

In spite of his great concentration Robert did make one amusing gaffe, during the England v New Zealand Test at Lord's in 1969. The two teams were as usual being presented to the Queen in front of the pavilion during the tea interval. 'It's obviously a great occasion for all the players,' Robert said. 'It's a moment they will always forget.'

One rather unusual feature about Robert was that at the end of a day he tended to fade away, and due to his shyness seldom mixed or talked with the players. In one way this is not a bad thing, as it is easier to criticise someone you don't know personally. But it also meant that the players hardly knew Robert and often used to ask, 'Who was that giving that excellent commentary?'

I have dealt with Robert as a cricket commentator but he was equally admired and respected by rugby enthusiasts. He was, however, best known as radio's number one ceremonial commentator. He covered all the big royal occasions and until he decided to give up in 1981 had broadcast twenty-five Trooping the Colour parades. The drill is always the same each year, but somehow, by diligently talking to as many as possible of those taking part, Robert managed to make his commentary sound different. As for the royal occasions his research and meticulous timing put him into the Richard Dimbleby class.

Robert has officially retired but I would not be at all surprised if he was resurrected to take part in some future national occasion. He was always cool, calm and confident, and whoever succeeds him cannot be any better.

Raymond Baxter

When the Outside Broadcast Department moved into the new part of Broadcasting House in the early 1950s, I shared an office with Raymond Baxter. He had come into the BBC via the RAF where he was a fighter pilot in Spitfires serving in North Africa, Malta, Sicily, Italy and with the Tactical Air Force in Europe after D-Day. So he was a well-travelled man, and when he left the RAF started his broadcasting career with Forces Broadcasting first in Cairo, and ending as Deputy Station Director of BFN Hamburg.

He and I were fairly different in character. I try to be five minutes early for everything, he was always late and gave many producers heart attacks waiting for him to turn up for a show. He was extremely knowledgeable in all things mechanical and scientific. I am quite hopeless at both. But we both had a sense of the ridiculous and whenever we did manage to meet in the office, we usually had a good laugh. As a commentator he was a natural for all things to do with cars, rallies, motor shows and Grand Prix racing. Similarly, for any air show or display he was completely in his element. He used to drive as a serious competitor and commentate at the same time in the Monte Carlo Rally, a difficult feat which he did extremely well. His motor racing commentaries for both radio and television were high class and I have never understood why the BBC did not use him more.

Raymond was very likeable and gregarious and this enabled him to know all the racing and rally drivers and have many of them as close friends. Once again I must stress how this affinity with those taking part in a sport is of great help to a commentator. It enables him to add the odd personal titbits which put that extra something into a commentary. Raymond had a very distinct style. He was very precise in his pronunciation and enunciated every syllable deliberately and clearly.

It was this, coupled with his knowledge, that made him such a good presenter of *Tomorrow's World* on BBC Television. He had the ability to explain the most complicated piece of gadgetry or machinery in simple terms which even I could understand. To my mind he was a great loss to the programme when he decided to leave it because of a disagreement with a new producer. He had always been a 'non-knocker' and – rather like in *Down Your Way* – liked to look for the good things. The programme's attitude to Concorde, which it criticised, showed the way things were going. The new producer not only wanted Raymond to cease being the sole presenter and share the programme with two others, but in-depth investigation was going to be the policy. Raymond was in favour of facts, not opinions. So regretfully he did not sign a new contract for another series.

Although he was the king of television technology, the modern whizz-kids tended to think him old-fashioned. 'Dinosaurs were left high and dry when the world evolved away from them,' said the new producer unkindly in explaining his reason for changing Raymond's role as chief presenter. If old-fashioned meant being courteous, fair and good mannered in his handling of people whom he interviewed on the programme then Raymond certainly *was* old-fashioned – and rightly proud of it.

Bryon Butler

Among BBC commentators there seems to be a close affinity with the *Daily Telegraph* – Howard Marshall, Jim Swanton, Rex Alston and Bryon Butler all worked for both. Except for Rex Alston they were all journalists before they became commentators.

Bryon Butler was born in Taunton, Somerset in 1934; he was educated at Taunton School and did his national service with the Somerset Light Infantry. His newspaper apprenticeship took him from Taunton to Exeter, Nottingham and Leicester. His first job in Fleet Street was with the *News Chronicle* which promptly closed after he had been with it for sixty days. He claimed that he was in no way responsible for its demise! He then freelanced for a while, sub-editing for *The Times*, reporting on rugby for the *Guardian* and writing features for the *Daily Express*. In 1960 he did his first freelance job for the BBC's Sports Department under Angus Mackay. He spent six years with the *Daily Telegraph*, writing on cricket and soccer, before joining the BBC staff in 1968, when he took over from Brian Moore as the Association Football correspondent.

So before joining the BBC he had had no commentary experience and was thrown in at the deep end, learning as he went along, as so many of us have done. He became, of course, one of radio's top commentators, with a crisp, staccato style. His varied journalistic experiences made his reports on matches, or soccer's news stories, punchy and full of telling phrases. More than any other commentator, perhaps, he seemed to speak in 'headlines' over the air, without resorting to clichés.

In 1969 he was brought near to tears at the end of a match on which he had been commentating. Leeds United had only to draw with Liverpool at Anfield to win the League Championship; but if they had lost, Liverpool would have been the champions. The score was a draw and Bryon was apprehensive of the reaction of the naturally disappointed Kop. Would they boo, fight, or try to invade the pitch? He need not have worried. After a pause the Kop began to sway, the scarves were held high and the Kop chorus sang out: 'Leeds are the champions, Leeds are the champions.' A pleasant soccer story, for a change.

Bryon came out with his fair share of non sequiturs, including:

'Wilkins pushes the ball to the left – a perfect pass – to no one in particular,' and 'Keegan was there like a surgeon's knife – bang!' In one interview he asked Peter Shreeve: 'Did you have any doubts about yourself when you left Tottenham?' To which Shreeve replied: 'I don't think so'!

Bryon retired as the BBC Radio football correspondent in 1991. Soccer took him all over the world to about sixty countries, but I have a feeling that Bryon's first love was always cricket. He played it whenever he could and once said that his greatest sacrifice was when he was reporting on cricket six days a week throughout the summer for the *Daily Telegraph*. The seventh day was the only free time he had to play cricket, but he gave it up for those six years to spend Sundays with his family. And despite his successful professional career, his finest hour was still the moment when, with the last ball of the last over, he scored the vital two runs needed for a victory over

Taunton's arch-rivals, Blundell's, and was carried shoulder-high off the pitch by cheering Taunton supporters.

Peter Bromley

After commentating on more than two hundred Classics, Peter Bromley announced his retirement from broadcasting in June 2001. His last commentary was at the 2001 Epsom Derby.

If ever someone was suited to his job it is Peter Bromley. From Cheltenham and the Royal Military College at Sandhurst, he served for three years (1948–51) in the famous cavalry regiment, the 14/20 Hussars. They were then of course mechanised but still maintained many of the old cavalry and horsey traditions. When he finished his service he rode for a time as an amateur until an accident forced him to give it up. He also acted as an assistant trainer before doing five years as a racecourse commentator.

In 1959 he joined the BBC under contract as their first-ever accredited sports correspondent. Cricket (myself and Christopher Martin-Jenkins), soccer (Brian Moore and Bryon Butler), lawn tennis (Gerald Williams) followed in the 1960s and early 70s with *their* correspondents, but Peter was the first of all. He added to his qualifications by becoming an owner, and then a consultant on horse-breeding. So, gifted with phenomenal eyesight, with a clear voice and a sense of pace, Peter has been one of the BBC's outstanding commentators, mostly on radio, but with occasional television appearances.

You may have noticed that I mentioned 'a sense of pace'. This is so important in racing, especially over the longer races. It is no good getting excited too early and Peter will calmly go through the horses giving their placings, and mentioning as many of the runners as possible. But as the race develops he will gradually increase his pace and begin to concentrate on the leaders, or those whom he thinks still have a chance. And then in the last two furlongs or so when the race is really on, Peter will speed up his tempo and allow himself to express the excitement which everyone feels when watching a close finish.

I have never heard him get the winner wrong. Even if the judge asks for a photo-finish Peter is not afraid to say, '. . . and in my opinion so-and-so just made it.' Often too – as at Kempton – his commentary box is at an angle to the finish, and yet he seems to outjudge the judge. He also reels off the second and third, and most of the other runners too. As you know, I feel that the racing commentator has the hardest job of all, having to learn and recognise all the colours and then apply to them the name of the horse, jockey, trainer and owner. It can only be done by living on the racecourses and mixing with the racing fraternity, and, of course, by the usual essential for a commentator – hard work. Peter, like most of the other racing commentators, will paint all the colours for a race on a board and then learn them like a saying lesson at school. Of course the big owners and trainers are easy, but nowadays there are more and more syndicates in racing, each with their new set of colours.

Whatever our particular jobs may be in the BBC, people always seem to think it is all glamour, good living and being present at events which they would give their eyes to be at. But for someone like Peter it is never the bright lights and luxury hotels at the end of a day's racing. For a one-day meeting he motors home straight away after his last commentary. But for a three-day meeting he will stay quietly away from the social life and do his homework each night. It is the same with Peter O'Sullevan. He is usually the last to leave the press box, sometimes as late as 8 pm, because he prepares for the next day's racing before leaving the racecourse. How the racing commentators do it, I don't know, especially as I am colour-blind. They must have fantastic memories to register in their minds the details of horses – sometimes twenty runners in one race – for all the races which they are broadcasting.

One interesting thing about Peter. He always has an assistant – more often than not John Fenton – who before the race will give the latest betting odds as they change. But even more important when working with Peter is to write down the names of the winner, second, third and fourth as Peter calls them out. He has been concentrating so hard that he often forgets which horse he has said was second or third, and his assistant has to thrust his piece of paper into Peter's hand as soon as the horses have passed the post.

Like myself, Peter enjoys his life and his job, because apart from his delightful family and the odd shoot or game of squash, racing *is* his life.

5 More Commentary From . . .

Peter Alliss

PETER ALLISS HAS BEEN A worthy successor to Henry Longhurst but in a very different way. He is the epitome of what people expect the modern commentator to be. He is cheerful, witty, gregarious and good-looking. He exudes confidence and not only looks prosperous but is! He writes about golf, he coaches and does interviews and is a course architect. But with it all he has a human and friendly touch. This came over well in his television series *Around with Alliss* which included a good 'mix' of partners such as Lord Scanlon, Michael Parkinson, Sir Douglas Bader and Bill McLaren.

As a player he won twenty-two major tournaments and played for Great Britain in the Ryder Cup. He was a stylish player and always looked better than his results. Even more than Henry he can sympathise with the tensions of the man on the green. For he too got the twitch, or 'yips' as I think he calls it, and once took four from the edge of the eighteenth at Wentworth which contributed to Great Britain's defeat in the 1953 Ryder Cup.

Since starting on television under Henry's wing in 1965, Peter has become the master at telling the average golf viewer exactly what is happening and why. He knows the players so well that he almost seems to read their minds. With experience he has learned the art of being informative, descriptive and colourful in an utterly unpompous manner. He can build suspense without overdoing it, and realises that the personalities and characters of players are the strings which a commentator plucks to bring the game alive. 'Bernhard Langer is considered a good putter from this range,' he observed once, 'irrespective of his reputation!' During another golf tournament he surprised viewers when he confided: 'I like a bit of rough – who doesn't?'

But Peter is never at a loss and as someone once said, 'His putter is not too good, but his patter . . .!'

Dorian Williams

Some commentators seem especially suited by character, appearance and lifestyle to the sport on which they commentate. Even though he retired after Olympia in 1980, I suspect that most people still think of Dorian Williams whenever show jumping is mentioned. I think it is fair to say that BBC Television made show jumping the amazingly popular sport which it is today. And Dorian was not only the voice of the BBC for that sport from 1953 to 1980, but his was the hand which steered the producers to the stage of perfection which we see on our screens today.

In appearance he looked distinguished and was always well and soberly dressed in clothes cut in that special horsey style – jackets longer than most with slanting pockets, narrow trousers and well-polished shoes. Except for the first year he was Master of Foxhounds of the Whaddon Chase for all the time he was broadcasting. His knowledge of the horses, riding and jumping was unsurpassed and founded on his own experience. In fact he wrote more than two dozen books (three of them novels) about horses and the art of training, treating and riding them. He aptly described himself as an 'equestrian commentator' and for all those twenty-eight years covered all the big events for BBC Television, including the Olympic Games, International Horse Show, Horse of the Year Show and Olympia.

In addition to his expertise and close relationships with all the show jumping world, his greatest asset as a commentator was his enthusiasm. His favourite phrase was 'Jolly good' and his 'Oohs' and 'Aahs' and '*Come* on David', 'Go *on* Marion' not only raised the excitement and tension, but often made the armchair viewer feel he was actually in the saddle himself. Dorian was unashamedly partisan, and admitted it, which is rare in a commentator. He was also intensely patriotic, so our successes or failures in international events raised him to peaks of enthusiasm or depths of depression.

He seldom made a mistake though he did once announce Lady Rose Williams as George Hobbs – in spite of the difference in their figures! He was always impeccable in his description and treatment of the Royal Family, whether they were watching or competing. But he did once fall into the trap we have all fallen into in our time – thinking his microphone had been switched off when it hadn't. He once said, as a member of the royal family walked forward to present a cup at the end of a show: 'My God! What a hat!' – much to the delight of millions of viewers, who probably agreed with him.

There was another interesting side to Dorian. After he left Harrow he attended the Guildhall School of Music and Drama, was a schoolmaster from 1936 to 1945 and then in that year founded the Penley Centre of Adult Education at Tring, of which he continued to be a director. And to show his versatility and that horses were not the only things in his life, every August he produced an open-air production of a Shakespeare play in the garden at Tring.

Once again I find myself saying it about a sport broadcast on BBC: horse jumping will never be quite the same again without Dorian.

Alan Weeks

In 1996 Alan Weeks had to retire from broadcasting because of illness and he died three months later at the age of seventy-two.

The man for all seasons, and all sports. Whenever a minor or comparatively unknown sport is televised you can be pretty certain that Alan will be the commentator. He is always reliable and knowledgeable and has commentated on ice hockey, skating, soccer, volleyball, basketball, gymnastics, water-skiing, snooker and swimming. And I bet I have missed something out! I enjoy him best when he is doing dancing or figure-skating on ice. The technical terms for all the varied and intricate movements, such as double axels, camel spins and flying jump sit spins, just roll off his tongue.

It is not really surprising that he seems so much at home by an ice-rink. After leaving the Royal Navy in 1946 at the age of twenty-two, he became secretary of the Brighton Tigers ice hockey team, and general administrator of the Brighton Ice-Rink. In 1951 Peter Dimmock heard him on the public address system and gave him a test, which he passed with flying colours.

He wears rather large glasses and once after a football commentary he was called to the telephone. It was Buckingham Palace: 'We have just seen your spectacles on television; where can we buy a similar pair? They would be good for golf!' I wonder who of the royal family played golf?

Alan is so expert at all the sports which he covers that he is not often caught out. However, in the 1978 World Gymnastics he was commentating on Ronda Schwaudt carrying out some amazing movements on the beam: 'Whichever way you look at it,' he said, 'the improvement by the Americans is really quite – Aaagh!' While he was talking Ronda had mistimed a somersault and landed painfully astride the beam.

He was also responsible for a little gem when swimmer David Wilkie was winning his gold medal in the Olympic Games: 'If Wilkie goes on like this he'll be home and dry!'

John Motson

One of the best of the modern commentators is John Motson, better known for his soccer commentaries, but who has also covered lawn tennis. He went to a rugby-playing secondary school, but learned his soccer from his father – a Methodist minister – who used to take him to watch games all over London. He talks fast in a rather sad-sounding voice and is full of facts and figures which he has accumulated by poring over all the soccer records. He is accurate and objective and because he is a fair critic is popular with managers and players.

He made his name on radio, joining their Sports Department in 1968 after reporting for the *Sheffield Telegraph* and commentating on local radio. Ten years later – as so often happens these days – he was grabbed by BBC Television for their *Match of the Day*. Radio is indeed the nursery for television.

John has been through the usual commentator's nightmares. In the 1978 World Cup the numbers of the Argentinian players were indecipherable against their striped shirts, and John had to commentate for twenty minutes or so without really knowing who was who. He has also made his fair share of gaffes. Once he was describing Tottenham's black forward Garth Crooks who was making space for his colleague Archibald: 'There's Crooks,' he said, 'doing all the *spade*work for Archibald.'

At another match he commented: 'He has those telescopic legs that can turn a Leeds ball into an Arsenal one.' And during a World Cup match he announced: 'Nearly all the Brazilian supporters are wearing yellow shirts – it's a fabulous kaleido-scope of colour!'

Soccer commentary is not easy – unless the commentator knows his game and facts thoroughly, it can become just a recitation of names. There is also intense rivalry for the top position on BBC Television, and the feeling of a rival breathing down your neck makes the job that much more tense and difficult. But John seems to cope admirably and, as he once remarked, 'The unexpected is always likely to happen!'

Nigel Starmer-Smith

Old rugby internationals seem to make excellent commen-tators, far more than old players from any other game. I can think of Peter Cranmer, Cliff Morgan, Ian Robertson, Chris Reay and Rex Alston (who although not an international, captained both Bedfordshire and the East Midlands).

And then of course there is Nigel Starmer-Smith who came to Radio OBs shortly before I left, and now does such admirable commentaries for BBC Television. He gained seven caps for England as scrum half or as Jimmy Hill once said: '. . . he had seven craps as scum half for England.'

Nigel is very much the players' commentator. He seems to know what they are thinking and can of course appreciate from personal experience all the conditions and difficulties under which they are playing. He has a pleasant, cheerful voice and brings the game very much alive. In one memorable commen-tary he said: 'Wales now really are operating inside a telephone kiosk'!

At the age of thirty-four he came on as substitute for Dusty Hare for the Barbarians against the East Midlands. He showed that he had lost little of his skill and, for a commentator, was still remarkably fit, when he made two spectacular tackles.

He has spread his wings and has done some hockey, tennis and soccer commentary, and he once informed his listeners: 'That's the equaliser. Germany go ahead 2–1!'

Ron Pickering

Another commentator whose profession made him a 'natural' as an athletics commentator was Ron Pickering. He was the Amateur Athletics Association coach for Wales and South West England and helped Lynn Davies win his Olympic gold medal for the long jump. Later Ron joined the Greater London Council as the recreational manager of the Lee Valley Scheme. He was born into a cockney family and his father was a boxer. Ron himself was a good athlete at school but abandoned his own hopes of winning a gold medal when his girlfriend beat him in the school long jump. It was not such a disgrace as it sounds because his victor was Jean Desforges who in 1952 captained England's women's team, and in 1954 was European long jump champion.

Ron was always a fighter for good causes – sports facilities for young people, anti-drugs, the Olympics in Moscow and starting the Harringay Athletics Club to encourage good race relations. Ron had quite a large physique, a rather 'with it' hair style and a sense of fun. The goodness of the man came out in his sympathetic commentaries which, added to his vast knowledge of athletics and the athletic world, made him an ideal partner for David Coleman in BBC Television's excellent coverage of the sport in the 1970s and 1980s.

Ron's last television commentary was at the 1990 European Championshops in Split and sadly he died of a heart attack in 1991. Viewers respected him and had confidence in him, because in the complicated variety of athletics he quite obviously knew what he was talking about.

He is credited – or debited! – with several athletics gaffes: 'Watch the time – it gives you a good indication of how fast they're running' . . . 'One thing I must say about this packed meeting. It is absolutely packed!' . . . and the all-time favourite: 'Here comes Juantorena now – every time the big Cuban opens his legs he shows his class!'

Alun Williams

A few years ago OB commentators could have put on quite a good variety show. Tony Lewis on violin; Don Mosey singing anything from Gilbert and Sullivan to *Ilkley Moor*; Christopher

Martin-Jenkins with impersonations; Freddie Trueman as stand-up comic; myself – perhaps as a story-telling compère; and very definitely Alun Williams with songs at the piano.

On many tours overseas he entertained rugby teams and, on every sort of get-together where there was a piano, he was the life and soul of the party. He also travelled round Wales in a professional capacity supporting such artistes as Max Boyce. He was fluent in Welsh and could tell stories and commentate equally well in either language. Perhaps because he had been a permanent member of the staff in BBC Wales ever since the war, until he went freelance in 1982, he was possibly the most versatile of all modern commentators.

There was really nothing that he had not had to cover, not just in Wales, but nationally for the BBC on big occasions. You could bet that you would find him somewhere on the route of the procession, whether it was a coronation, wedding, jubilee or even funeral. He had the Welsh gift of language and rhetoric and also had the *joie de vivre* to bring lightness and laughter into his description of events. He also seemed to attract around him every Welshman who happened to be in the crowd.

In sport in Wales he covered everything, including cricket and soccer. But he was of course best known all over the world – and in the Commonwealth especially – for his rugby and swimming commentaries. It would not be right to say that he did not sound pleased when Wales scored a try. In truth, for a few seconds he was often hysterical. But one easily forgave him for his enthusiasm, because of the skill and knowledge with which he had described the play leading up to *that* try. In swimming his famous '. . . he (she) touches NOW' rang out round the Olympic pools all over the world.

He was in the Royal Navy before joining the BBC and as you will have gathered was a man of terrific energy, travelling many miles on his job ('Four or five times round the world'), and taking on far more than any one man should. He was a delightful companion to be with and a great storyteller and behind the glasses was the wickedest twinkle you will find in anyone's eyes.

He had his awkward and embarrassing moments like all of us. I don't know of any real gaffes in English, but there were probably some in Welsh which we don't know about. His fellow commentators remember with delight the Commonwealth Games in Jamaica in 1966. Lord Swansea won a gold medal for rifle-shooting and Alun with pride in his voice was describing the scene as Lord Swansea stood on the centre dais to receive his medal. Alun's voice broke into a near sob as the medal was hung round Lord Swansea's neck. But then to Alun's horror the local band started to play *Land of Hope and Glory*. Forgetting his BBC job, he rushed out of the commentary box and pointed out the mistake to the conductor. The band then tried to retrieve the position by playing *God Save the Queen*. And then – after further entreaties by Alun – they *did* strike up *Land of My Fathers*, giving Alun time to rush back to the commentary box to restart his commentary when the tune finished.

He also had some of those dreaded long moments to fill when delays in a ceremony mean that the commentator has nothing to describe. This happened to Alun at the return from the round-the-world voyage of Francis Chichester, when he was due to land at a certain time at the steps by Plymouth Hoe. But Mrs Chichester – as she was then – went out in a boat to meet her husband before he landed, and there was a delay of an hour with nothing happening. Somehow Alun coped.

He was, however, struck dumb for some seconds on one occasion early in his BBC career. He had been commentating at the St Helen's Ground at Swansea on a county cricket match between Glamorgan and Lancashire. At the end of the game he had to rush back to the studio to give a close-of-play summary in a sports programme. Because he was then inexperienced he thought he would make sure to get off to a good start by writing down his opening sentence, and after that he felt he would feel more confident and he could then continue his summary unscripted. So he scribbled out something like: 'I've just got back from the St Helen's Ground where in front of a large crowd there was an exciting day's cricket, Glamorgan bowling Lancashire out for 127, and then making 210 for 2 in reply.'

Alun had only time to rush straight back into the studio without talking to his producer first. Still, he knew that he had three minutes to do, and he had his opening sentence all written out, and the score-card of the day in front of him for the details of play. He had hardly sat down in front of the microphone when the presenter of the programme got a signal in his headphones, gave Alun a nod and said: 'Well here in the studio is Alun Williams, who has just got back from the St Helen's Ground, where in front of a large crowd there was an exciting day's cricket, Glamorgan bowling Lancashire out for

127, and then making 210 for 2 in reply. Alun.' As I said, he was struck dumb for a few seconds – who wouldn't be? – but he got out of it somehow and completed his three minutes. But he learned the danger of writing down anything in advance when about to do a *live* broadcast.

By the way, he was a bit touchy about one thing. Alun – as you probably know – should be pronounced 'Alin'. Woe betide you if you cued over to him as 'Alun'. He would not start his piece of commentary until he had pointedly said: 'Yes, it's *Alin* Williams here.' Like myself, he retired as a member of the BBC staff and then continued to do exactly the same jobs as a free-lance – and he got better paid too!

Peter Jones

Welsh broadcasters are so versatile! Alun Williams, Wynford Vaughan-Thomas and Peter Jones put a microphone in their hands and they would talk and commentate about anything. It was not just the gift of the gab. They seemed to have a natural exuberance and enthusiasm, and words streamed out of their mouths like a waterfall. Long, beautiful words too. I honestly don't know where they found them. If anyone could claim to be, then Peter Jones was the *Roget's Thesaurus* of broadcasting. Although he did get a bit carried away once when he said: 'They're floating up on a sea of euphoria, and hoping to drag themselves clear of the quicksand at the bottom'!

Peter had a pleasant, lilting voice to go with it too, which he often dropped on the last word of a sentence. Sadly, he col-lapsed in the BBC launch whilst he was doing the radio commentary on the 1990 Boat Race. He died soon afterwards while still in the prime of his broadcasting career.

He had come into broadcasting late in life and like a few of us had that necessary little bit of luck which was to change his way of living. He got a blue for soccer at Cambridge in 1951 and 1952, and his captain was Peter May, who surprisingly captained Cambridge at soccer but not at cricket. Peter (Jones) also played as an amateur for Swansea under the captaincy of the legendary John Charles. After Cambridge he went to Brad-field where he was master in charge of soccer. Living nearby and playing for Reading at the time was Maurice Edelston, and Peter arranged for him to go and coach the boys at Bradfield.

They became great friends and one day when Maurice was doing a soccer commentary for BBC Radio at Southampton, he took Peter along with him.

After the match they had a drink in a pub with Tony Smith, the BBC producer from Bristol who was in charge of the broadcast. During the conversation Peter mentioned that he would love to have a shot at commentary one day. Tony promptly replied that he wanted a report from a match at Aldershot the following Saturday, and would Peter like to do it. Peter leaped at the chance and did a satisfactory job with his report. So much so that Angus Mackay, then in charge of Radio Sports News, heard it and offered Peter a job in the Sports Department. So Peter left Bradfield after thirteen years as a schoolmaster and became a broadcaster. Like myself, he happened to meet someone at the right time and took advantage of his luck. He was soon to make his mark, because Angus chose him to succeed Eamonn Andrews as the introducer of *Sports Report*, and Peter did this for five years, learning his trade as a soccer commentator at the same time.

He soon found that soccer commentary is not as easy as the commentators make it sound. The ball is constantly changing direction, up field, down field, and across from touch line to touch line. On its way it is passed from player to player. I remember that Raymond Glendenning told me that on average he could only mention one pass in three, unless his commentary was to become a list of players' names. And of course in those days there were the great players such as Matthews, James, Finney, Shackleton and Logie, who tried to beat their man by controlled dribbling. Nowadays the players – because no doubt they are fitter – run all over the place and get rid of the ball to someone else as soon as they receive it. How seldom does one see a player trying to pass his opponent with a dribble or a dummy. This means that there are far *more* passes in modern football and it is quite impossible for the commentator to cover them all.

So Peter evolved what I call a 'thinking aloud' commentary. When play was in midfield and there was little likelihood of a goal, he would speak his thoughts instead of describing the game. 'Poor Graham Shaw,' he said once. 'It was there for the asking and he didn't give the answer!' He might muse over what tactics the team was trying, what was going on in a certain player's mind, how the game would affect the teams' positions in the table, how the manager was feeling, and so on. He would do this for a few moments and then pick up the play again as one of the goals was threatened. Other commentators now do the same, and the soccer commentary is far less descriptive of actual play than it was. Were individual skills to be revived to the standards of say twenty or thirty years ago, then there would be something other than just passes to describe.

And that's quite enough about soccer commentary from me. But I did watch the Arsenal in the golden age of the 1930s, so I *am* biased in thinking that soccer playing standards have deteriorated. Whilst talking about the Arsenal I must digress to tell you the only funny soccer story that I know – or possibly that exists, for that matter, because it is a fact that cricket and golf provide so many stories, leaving the other sports nowhere.

Anyway, in the 1930s Arsenal had a half-back called Copping who for those days was considered an aggressive hard-tackling player. They went to Italy to play a match against a well-known club and after about five minutes Copping whipped away the legs of an opponent with a sliding tackle. The small Italian referee ran up to him wagging a finger and said in broken English, 'No more of that please. We want a clean game.'

Copping nodded but five minutes later did another vicious tackle. Again the referee ran up to him: 'I have already warned you once – next time I send you off – pronto.'

The game went on but Copping continued to play his natural game and soon had another Italian writhing in pain on the ground. Up came the little referee, notebook in hand, and as he approached, Copping muttered under his breath: 'Oh, bugger off.' 'Ah,' said the referee, 'that is good. You apologise, so I do not send you off.'

And now back to Peter in his many other roles, other than soccer commentator. He became radio's number one for the big occasion, be it a jubilee procession, a wedding or a London Marathon. He was, I would say, happier outside than covering a service or ceremony indoors. He had one favourite expression which you could bet he would use at least once in any big radio broadcast. He loved to describe a person or people as 'walking tall'. This he physically did himself. He was tall, good-looking, with wavy hair and bags of charm. He was always debonair and smartly dressed and was in the international class as a chatter-up of the opposite sex! In addition to presenting sporting programmes such as *Sport on 2* and *Sports Report*, he was chairman of innumerable quiz shows like *Sporting Chance, Treble Chance* or *Brain of Sport*.

He also commentated on other sports including rowing and, of course, swimming where he shone at many Olympic or Commonwealth Games, one of them producing the following classic phrase: 'Welcome to the Olympic pool where an enthusiastic crowd are cheering the exciting races which are taking place. I've never seen such excitement. It's the pool that sets them alight!'

Brian Moore

Brian Moore retired as a football commentator after leading the ITV commentary team at the 1998 World Cup Final in France.

BBC's first Association Football Correspondent in 1963, who went across to the other side, was Brian Moore. He went reluctantly at the time and tried hard to get a satisfactory contract with BBC Television, but failed. Not that he should worry now. He is ITV's number one commentator and presenter and is judged by many experts to be the best of the lot – either on BBC or ITV. His skill at both commentary and presentation is perhaps best illustrated by ITV's choosing him – their best commentator – to be their home-based presenter and conductor of their panel of experts throughout the 1982 World Cup.

Brian is different from most commentators who, as I have said, are on the whole extrovert and outwardly, at least, supremely confident. Brian is exactly the opposite. He is modest, diffident and retiring and claims to be afraid of meeting people. Not for him the sporting scene of receptions and dinners – if he can gracefully avoid it. He says that he had an inferiority complex when he won a scholarship to Cranbrook School, because his father was a farm worker. But in spite of it, he didn't do too badly. He became captain of the school, cricket and hockey, and then got a commission in the RAF during his national service. So beneath that friendly, rather sad smile must be a lot of guts and steely determination to succeed in whatever he tries to do.

Why then, without the usual trappings of the successful commentator, has Brian become one of the top commentators in the country? Mainly because he has the vital factor of *knowing* his soccer and in a calm way commentates on the game with fairness and impartiality, and without too much of the frequently overdone excitement and shouting. When conducting a panel of experts he defers humbly to them and doesn't impose his own opinion too strongly, while remaining firmly in control.

So Brian is an extremely rare bird among commentators. What's more he is a very nice person. But thank goodness like all of us he is human and does make mistakes, as when he told the television viewers: 'It's just a sea of voices here at the moment.' During another game he said: 'This is going to be a very long 30 minutes with 26 minutes left.' And finally: 'The referee is now looking at his whistle, and will blow his watch at any moment!'

Gerald Williams

If I were asked to nominate the commentator with the sexiest voice I think that I would choose Gerald Williams. He is a Welshman, but in his long absence from Wales he has lost most of his Welsh accent, though the lilt is still there. But his voice is sympathetic and has a beguiling and cajoling air which in his interviews draws out confidences – and sometimes indiscretions – from the stars of the tennis world.

He started life as a journalist when he left west Wales to come to London. He wrote for a number of newspapers not just on tennis but also on football. He finally became the lawn tennis correspondent of the *Daily Mail*. When he left the *Mail* he did commentaries for ITV on both soccer and tennis, until he joined BBC Radio in the early 1970s and became their first ever lawn tennis correspondent. At first he did interviews and reports but has gradually become one of the BBC's top commentators. He developed his skills during his many assignments abroad where he has covered all the major overseas championships and tournaments. He has not got the speed of a Max Robertson but scores heavily with his great knowledge of the game and its administration, and even more important from his obviously close relationship with so many of the players.

As I write he is probably most admired for his interviewing, when, as I've said, he seems able to draw more out of his 'victims' than the other interviewers. In commentary he has learned the art of slipping in remarks between rallies which build up the tennis scene beyond just the game on the court.

It can be a comment on the character of one of the players, picking out the wife or boyfriend watching, or just a throw-away remark about the weather or the strawberries and cream. It all helps to build up the Wimbledon atmosphere.

And yes, he *has* made a gaffe or two, such as: 'There are two Jonas Strenssons on the tour, but this is the one whose name we will get most used to hearing.' I heard another one myself during the 1982 Wimbledon. He was commentating on a ladies' doubles in which Pam Shriver was playing. She was suddenly stung by a wasp. It had obviously got inside her dress and Pam was peeping down her cleavage to try to find it. As she was looking down, Gerald – to fill in time – innocently remarked to Christine Truman apropos of Pam and her partner: 'They are a fine pair, aren't they?'

6 Voices of Cricket

FTER I HAD BEEN AT the BBC for twelve years, I discovered that I was entitled to something called 'grace leave', which meant I could be given three months off with pay. So in 1958 it occurred to me it was about time I saw some first-class cricket abroad. I applied for leave and bought myself a return air ticket to Australia. I was also prepared to pay all my own expenses out there. But when the BBC heard what I was doing, they decided to use me as a commentator and interviewer and to pay me for each job which I did for them. Luckily I was acceptable to the Australian Broadcasting Commission and they kindly invited me to be a member of their own commentary team for the last four Tests.

People talk a lot about jet lag but I arrived in Melbourne on the afternoon of 30 December and was doing my first ever commentary in Australia on the morning of the 31st. I was soon to notice the difference between the techniques of the Australian commentators and the BBC. As I explained earlier, Lobby's instructions to commentators at cricket were to give the essentials first: the score, the weather, pitch, toss and so on. And of course to continue to give the score every time a run was scored, or if there was a maiden bowled, at least at the end of that over. After that we have always been encouraged to add 'colour' to our broadcasts. By this I mean descriptions of the ground, the crowd, and of course the players or the field. We think it adds to a broadcast to talk about the players' personalities and characteristics. There are also so many stories about cricket which can be subtly woven into the commentary, to say nothing of the many individual and team records.

In Australia it is exactly the opposite. They regard their main purpose as keeping the listener informed of the score and the state of play – to the exclusion of almost everything else. For example, over here we describe the man running up and add a few remarks about him – his style, his long hair, his recent performances or whatever. We then describe the stroke, where it has gone, and say something about the fielder. And then give the score. In Australia, in between giving the score comment is often restricted to '. . . and he bowls and it goes through to the keeper,' or, 'he bowls, and that's a single down to X at third man, and the score is now . . .' In other words the Australian style is terse and accurate. Our style is more flowing and descriptive of *everything*, without, we hope, any loss of accuracy.

There is also the different way of giving the score, which at first took a bit of getting used to. When four wickets are down for twenty runs *they* say 4 for 20, *we* say 20 for 4. By way of compromise, what I used to do in Australia was to use their method when I was broadcasting with their commentary team to Australia only. But when the BBC joined us I would go back to our method. The Australian commentator Alan McGilvray did the same when he was in this country. The other minor differences are that they call extras 'sundries', and close of play 'stumps', but no one really worries which is used.

A newcomer to Australia, as I was then, also discovers that Down Under some words have different meanings from ours. I was once sharing a commentary box in Tasmania with a commentator called Peter Mears. During a pause in the play he asked me how I had spent my day off on Sunday.

'Oh,' I replied, 'I had a lovely day. I had my first bathe for two years.'

I noticed that he looked slightly surprised and edged further into his corner of the commentary box. It wasn't till several days later that I discovered that what I had said, to the Australian ear, was that I had had my first *bath* for two years!

Rex Alston

The majority of sports commentators have played or participated at some level or other in the sport on which they commentate. Some, like Harold Abrahams, Richie Benaud, Jim Laker and Nigel Starmer-Smith, have been of international class. I must emphasise here, by the way, that I am talking about *commentators*, not summarisers.

One non-international but who qualified better than most was Rex Alston. He won an athletics blue at Cambridge and ran in the sprints as second string to Harold Abrahams. From 1924 to 1941 he was a master at Bedford School, and while there captained Bedford at rugby football and also played for

Rosslyn Park and the East Midlands. In cricket he captained Bedfordshire in the Minor Counties Championship. Not surprisingly, his three main sports were cricket, rugby and athletics, to which he added lawn tennis.

Already you will have a clue to his character – a schoolmaster for seventeen years with obvious powers of leadership. He joined the BBC in 1942 and became a freelance when he reached retiring age in 1961. Whilst on the staff he was the office organiser and commentary box leader in all four sports. He was precise, meticulous, fair, unbiased and demanding of a high standard of behaviour on the field, the track, the court and in the commentary box itself. He could at times sound like a schoolmaster, gently reproving any lapse in standards of play or behaviour. But he was a friendly, gregarious person and the commentary box was always a happy place when he was in command.

In my opinion, of the four sports, he was best at athletics, closely followed by rugby. At cricket he was – as we all were – slightly overshadowed by John Arlott. He was prone to slight mishaps and had more difficulties than most with the commentator's five-letter nightmare – 'balls'. At Canterbury once he described the scene during the tea interval: '. . . the band playing, the tents with their club flags, the famous lime tree, people picnicking round the ground, whilst on the field hundreds of small boys are playing with their balls.'

Like all of us he made quite a few general gaffes. One for which he cannot be blamed was in Australia, when he said: 'Lindwall has now finished his over, goes to the umpire, takes his sweater and strides off.' What Rex did not know was that in colloquial Australian, 'strides' are trousers.

E. W. Swanton

Jim Swanton was a big man in both senses of the word. He had a strong personality, held high principles and liked to get his own way – which he usually did. Some people who didn't know him thought he was pompous. So, I suppose, did his many friends, which is why we enjoyed pulling his leg. On tours Jim had a habit of staying with governor-generals or dining with prime ministers and high commissioners. I expect that he himself would have admitted that he was a wee bit of a snob.

Anyhow, the thought prompted a now famous remark about him: 'Jim is such a snob that he won't travel in the same car as his chauffeur!'

Cricket was his life and in addition to broadcasting he wrote or edited more than two dozen books and was the cricket correspondent of the *Evening Standard* in the 1930s, and of the *Daily Telegraph* from 1946 to 1975. So far as I am concerned he wrote and said all the right things about cricket, and he made sure that he was given plenty of space to air his views. He also ensured that none of his copy could be sub-edited without reference to him. How his press colleagues envied him this unique journalistic licence. He was forthright in all he wrote and his often unfavourable comparison of modern cricket with that of the past did not always endear him to modern cricketers.

He began his radio broadcasting with some reports in 1934, followed by commentary on the 1938 and 1939 Tests in England. But his big chance came in the winter of 1938–9. He became the first commentator to be specifically booked by the BBC for an overseas tour – South Africa v England in South Africa. He started off with a commentator's dream when he was able to describe a hat trick by Tom Goddard in the first Test at Johannesburg. During the war he was captured by the Japanese at Singapore and was a prisoner of war in Siam from 1942 to 1945. But in 1946 he took up where he had left off as a member of the radio commentary team with Rex Alston and John Arlott.

Jim had played cricket for Middlesex against the Universities before the war, so with his deep, rich, authoritative voice, was well qualified for the job. He was also a cricket historian with a thorough knowledge of all the developments of the game and its players. Between us we evolved a form of television commentary, trying hard not to speak more than necessary. Our styles were very different. Jim, factual, serious, analytical and critical, myself almost certainly too jokey, and too uncritical. I was also always eager to find extra ingredients to the actual play. To me a cricket match does not consist solely of what is taking place out in the middle. There is so much else which is part and parcel of the game – a member fast asleep – a bored blonde reading a book or some small boys playing a game of their own, oblivious of the cricket they are supposed to be watching. This meant close co-operation with our producers, Peter Dimmock and Barrie Edgar in the early days, and then Antony Craxton, Ray Lakeland, Phil Lewis and Nick Hunter. With a good producer the camera can capture so much of the 'atmosphere' of a game, and I still believe that it gives better entertainment to the viewer than just sticking to bat and ball.

In addition to commentary, Jim used to do close-of-play summaries and both on television and radio these were better than anyone else's, so good was his analysis and reading of a day's play. On television he would sometimes stop and snap his fingers and ask someone moving behind the camera to keep still. It takes a bit of guts to do this, and also breaks the train of thought. But he always seemed to be able to pick up where he had left off.

As I've said he was an ideal subject for leg-pulls. In 1964 for some reason Jim had a chauffeur to drive him around. He was doing the television commentary with us at Trent Bridge, which was packed. At about twelve noon Denis Compton went to the man on the public address system and asked him to read out a note which we had written up in the box. Between overs the crowd heard: 'If Mr E. W. Swanton is listening will he please go to the back of the pavilion, where his chauffeur has left the engine of his car running.' Quite untrue of course, but I've never heard such a roar of laughter from a cricket crowd.

We had many happy days in the television commentary box, and in spite of our irreverence, I know that Jim too enjoyed his time in the box with us. Let me tell one final story at his expense – as related by Colin Ingleby-Mackenzie at the Eton Rambler dinner in 1982. Not having been present at the occasion he referred to, I am unable to vouch for its veracity!

Apparently, on the first night of their honeymoon, as Jim and his wife were getting into bed, Ann's foot touched Jim's.

'God,' she said, 'your feet are cold.'

'It's all right, darling,' he replied. 'In bed you may call me Jim.'

Peter West

My other regular colleague of those days, Peter West, was a complete contrast to Jim. Peter retired surprisingly early in 1986 and lives a quiet country life tending his garden in Gloucestershire. I should think that he could justifiably claim to have commentated more hours on television since the war than any other commentator. He was certainly a Jack-of-all-sports, partly because the producers knew he would never let them down. He quickly learned all the intricacies of television commentary and presentation and was the complete television professional. Of the major sports on television he covered cricket, rugby, tennis, hockey, rowing and field events in six Olympics. In addition he was chairman and presenter of at least twenty games or quizzes on television and radio, including fifteen years of presenting *Come Dancing*. As if this were not enough he wrote and edited books and magazines about cricket and till 1983 was the rugby correspondent of *The Times*, and did rugby commentary for radio. He also found time to be an active chairman of a public relations firm with strong sporting contacts.

All this is proof of his versatility and capacity for hard work – something we seem to find in most commentators. But, as with Raymond Glendenning, versatility had certain disadvantages. Because he did cricket, tennis and *Come Dancing*, rugby supporters were apt to think he could not know much about their game. And so it was with other games. Most of them questioned his ability to be an expert in so many sports. Peter's answer to this would be that the producers had faith in him or they would not have continued to employ him. And, throughout his broadcasting life, working always as a freelance, he was always in full employment as a commentator – which certainly has not been the case with every freelance. He could of course add that he has always been on very good terms with his bank manager!

Peter is a very friendly person with a good sense of humour and much of our happiness in the box was due to him. He came into cricket by pure chance. He once telephoned some copy for C. B. Fry who took a liking to him and admired his efficiency, and recommended him to the BBC. He went to the Royal Military College at Sandhurst and served in the war with the Duke of Wellington's Regiment. He was a good games player, especially at cricket. But a bad back prevented him from playing seriously, except in our many charity matches. As a commentator at cricket he combined his knowledge of the game with quick assessment, and was not afraid to give his opinion with some force. But because he knew all the players so well, he was always a kind critic and enjoyed and engineered quite a few of our pranks in the box.

Peter did not escape the occasional unlucky choice of words. Once, when commentating at tennis, he remarked, 'Miss Stove seems to be going off the boil.' There was one occasion when he made a mess of a proposed joke. Neil Durden-Smith's wife Judith (Chalmers) had just had a baby girl which they were going to call Emma. The same week Neil was a commentator for *Come Dancing* at one of the outside broadcasts. I suggested to Peter that he should congratulate Neil during the television broadcast with the words: 'By the way, Neil, congratulations on the birth of your daughter Emma.' To this I told Neil to reply (here comes the joke!), 'Emma-so-many-thanks.'

Not very funny, I admit, but it went for a complete Burton when on the broadcast Peter said, 'Congratulations on the birth of your daughter,' leaving out 'Emma'. In spite of this Neil replied, 'Emma-so-many thanks,' as arranged. The poor viewers, not knowing her name, must have been very puzzled over Neil's pronunciation of 'ever'. A warning perhaps, when indulging in cross-talk, to listen carefully to your partner's cue.

Jim Laker

In the 1970s and early 80s, BBC Television's other main commentator on cricket, alongside Richie Benaud, was Jim Laker – two experts not just on reading a game, but on summing up the strengths and weaknesses of batsmen and bowlers. After 1956 Jim walked through life with a halo round his head shining '19 for 90'. How can you argue with a man who has performed such a feat? It must have given him the confidence and self-assurance which he undoubtedly possessed. He *was* a fine judge of cricket, knew it and stuck to his opinion.

He had a completely different commentating style from anyone else I have ever heard. His voice was flat and unexciting. His 'battin' and bowlin'', spoken in his Yorkshire accent, would not have been tolerable from anyone else. Who ever heard of a commentator dropping his g's? But he did, and got away with it. He was laconic, with a shy wit and unlike most commentators avoided any frenetic excitement, no matter how sensational the happening. He was as leisurely as he was when, as a bowler, he trod slowly back to his mark, walking on his heels, looking up at the sky, before wheeling round and starting his short run up to the wicket. His commentary style was in fact ideally suited to television cricket, and with his knowledge and authority the viewers could not technically have been in better hands.

His whole temperament matched the pace of his walk – placid. I remember how, after he had achieved that unbeliev-able 19 wickets for 90 runs in the fourth Test against Australia at Old Trafford, I went over to the pavilion to collect Jim for a television interview. There was a hubbub of excitement in the dressing-rooms, everyone laughing and talking at the tops of their voices. But Jim? He was the calmest person there, gra-ciously accepting the many congratulations with modesty and a broad smile. I remember telling someone that instead of having created a Test record which must surely stand for all time, he looked as if he had just taken a couple of wickets in a parents' match.

Jim was only sixty-four when he died in 1986. He was undoubtedly the greatest of all off-spinners. Trevor Bailey once said that facing Jim was like being a rabbit caught in the head-lights: petrified, stationary and instinctively knowing one was about to be slaughtered. My own personal experience of his skill was in one of those Sunday charity matches in which I was keeping wicket. Immediately Jim came on, I noticed the difference between him and the other bowlers. He was extremely difficult to take because he managed to make the ball bounce. He had such a perfect action – his high right arm brushing his right ear, the swivel as he delivered the ball, the flight, the prodigious off-spin, the accuracy, direction and the away floater beautifully disguised. To me it was impossible to spot which one was not going to turn from the off.

I was keeping pretty badly, when the batsman went a long way down the pitch. 'Ah,' I said to myself, 'a chance to redeem myself with a leg-side stumping.' So I positioned myself outside the leg-stump and waited for the off-break to curve round the batsman's body into my waiting hands. Alas, it was the away floater and there I was stranded down the leg-side. Imagine my horror – and Jim's delight – when the ball beat the batsman and went for four byes *outside* the off-stump, leaving me looking a complete clot in missing a stumping by being in the wrong place.

Alan Gibson

One of the earliest commentators on *Test match Special* was Alan Gibson who did his first radio commentary for the BBC in 1948. Although for many years he was associated with the West Country, he was in fact born in Sheffield. He captained Queen's College, Oxford, at cricket and was also president of the Union. He was possibly the most intellectual, articulate and wittiest of all commentators. He had an extensive vocabulary and a strong, confident voice with a 'twinkle' in it. He held strong opinions and was perhaps too honest to please all the producers. If he thought a match boring or pointless he would say so. A commentator should not be required to oversell an event or game. But nor should he undersell it.

He left the commentary box in the early 1970s and subsequently entertained readers of *The Times* with his hilarious accounts of cricket or rugby matches. He travelled everywhere by train, and his adventures in getting to or from a match often filled most of his column. But he had an eye for a cricketer and an appropriate phrase for every happening on the cricket field. He was a very high-class broadcaster and his early departure was a severe loss to radio.

Tony Lewis

Tony Lewis retired as the anchorman of BBC Television's cricket coverage after the 1998 NatWest final at Lord's. He served as President of MCC in 1998-9.

A popular newcomer to the *TMS* team in 1979 was Tony Lewis, known to us all as ARL, to the annoyance of his wife. I'm afraid that I am to blame once again. I was coming to the end of my commentary stint and glanced at the rota for the commentators, pinned up in front of me. Our producer Peter Baxter always puts just our initials, and there, sure enough, I saw that the next man in to follow me was A. R. L., and – I'm sorry, Mrs Lewis – I simply said, 'And now after a few words from Trevor Bailey, ARL will take over the commentary.' And so it stuck.

He brought an air of great distinction to the box. Here we had an ex-Captain of England, and of Cambridge. A double blue for cricket and rugby and to his credit the fine feat of making

95 as a freshman in the Varsity match at Lord's, and then two years later in 1962 making 103 not out when captain. Added to all this were a hundred for England and the winning of the County Championship by Glamorgan when he was captain in 1969.

So we were very proud of our new recruit, who was no stranger to television or radio. In Wales he had hosted both an arts and weekly sports programme on television, while on Radio 4 his *Sport on 4* on Saturday morning had become a high-class sports magazine presented in a friendly and highly personalised style. Later he was to be one of the presenters of the television show *Saturday Night at the Mill*. In fact it was during one of these programmes which always went out 'live' that the string of his violin went flat due to the heat of the studio lights, when he was slap in the middle of the Handel Violin Sonata. Yes, believe it or not, he is also a skilled musician and was a member of the Glamorgan Youth Orchestra. Indeed on one occasion he had to choose between playing for the Welsh National Youth Orchestra, or for Glamorgan v Leicestershire, and he chose the latter.

There was never any doubt in anyone's mind that he would be a success at commentating. Not just because of his cricketing knowledge and experience. But to a man who could cope in a live television interview – as he did one *Saturday Night at the Mill* – with Oliver Reed, who proceeded to take off his trousers in the middle of the interview – being a mere commentator would be a 'piece of cake'. (And he would get plenty of that in the box.)

He started off doing the summaries and reports and gradually eased into the commentary seat. In fact he did not find it too easy at first, partly because he had been doing some television commentary. He found it difficult to keep a flow of talk going, and there were one or two long pauses, which of course would be completely acceptable on television. He had one other difficulty. He got so absorbed in the cricket – as you would expect from an ex-England captain – that he often forgot to give the score and was inclined to ignore Bill Frindall's feed of records then being or about to be broken. He has a soft, lilting Welsh voice with a friendly chuckle, and as if he hadn't got enough already, he is by far and away the best-looking commentator on either radio or television – not that there is too much competition!

His other considerable skill is his writing, and as the *Sunday Telegraph* cricket correspondent he put forward his point of view and opinions in an entertaining and forthright manner. This job also enabled him to tour abroad in the winter and he has broadcast for the BBC from Pakistan, the West Indies, India and Australia. ARL left *TMS* in 1986 and succeeded Peter West as BBC Television's main cricket presenter.

Norman Cuddeford

'Cudders' did not rely on broadcasting for his living. He looked on it as a hobby which took him to big events and faraway places. It was a relaxation from his insurance business, though you would not have realised it from his professional approach. He had a clear, young-sounding voice, and had the ability to speak fast but to be completely intelligible. He had done quite a bit of cricket round the counties but his strong sports were athletics and lawn tennis. In a fast race he could keep up with the best and there was a sense of zest and enjoyment in everything he did.

I suppose he will always be remembered best in broadcasting circles for his appearance on the *Today* programme. He was there to read out the sports bulletins which were normally at about 7.27 am and 8.27 am. All the contributors to *Today* used to sit around a large round table with microphones positioned like the numbers on a clock. When there was an item being broadcast which had previously been recorded, there was momentary relaxation in the studio while the tape was being played. Sometimes the presenters practised their next introduction out aloud to make sure it sounded all right.

On this occasion, at about 8.24 am Cudders was sitting with his script in front of him, waiting for his turn. He was concentrating and checking up on his script when he thought he heard John Timpson *rehearsing* his cue out aloud. He heard John say, 'Norman Cuddeford has been keeping an eye on the sporting scene for us. So Norman can you please bring us up to date with the score in the Test match between Australia and England at Sydney.'

Cudders thought he would join in this 'rehearsal' and to be funny said with a laugh, 'No. As a matter of fact I can't!' The result was the complete collapse of everyone in the studio, with John desperately signalling to Cudders that it was a genuine cue. Cudders, very red in the face, then had to apologise and read out his script to the listeners. That's a moment he will never forget!

Peter Cranmer

One of the most popular commentators on the Test and county circuit in the 1950s and 60s was Peter Cranmer – inevitably known as 'Cranners'. He was a magnificent athlete, a rugger blue at Oxford with sixteen caps for England as a strong-running centre three-quarter. He just missed a cricket blue at Oxford but played first-class cricket for Warwickshire and was their captain in 1938–9 and 1946–7. He was a fine fielder, a hard hitter and a tearaway bowler. As a commentator he was completely natural – almost conversational. He combined his considerable knowledge of cricket with a cheerful exuberance which made him easy on the ear, and a delightful companion to work with.

He sometimes found difficulty in the more basic skills of broadcasting, like time-keeping and cueing over. When we were doing three commentary matches every Saturday afternoon, plus racing, tennis and athletics it *could* become complicated. Remember that in those days we used to work to a pre-arranged timetable on a cue-sheet. We would then cue over to each other at the appropriate time, no matter what was happening in the various matches.

Nowadays the presenter in the studio is completely in charge. He cues over to the commentators, who wear headphones. He then tells them when to stop, saying something like: 'Brian, go to the end of the over, and then give the score.' On hearing the score at the end of the over, the presenter picks up in the studio and cues over to someone else. This is of course a far better method as it is completely flexible, and means that the programme can spend longer on an exciting match with only brief coverage of dull ones.

I remember that one Saturday afternoon Cranners was at Edgbaston and I was at Leyton. As I said, he was not too good on his time-keeping, and cued over to me at least five minutes later than he should have done. I couldn't resist saying, 'Thank you, Cranners. Better Leyton than never!'

Neil Durden-Smith

One of the most versatile of commentators, who came to the BBC after retiring from the Royal Navy and after a spell as aide-de-camp to that very popular Governor-General of New Zealand, Lord Cobham, 'Durders' joined the BBC originally to help organise the broadcasting of the World Cup, a complicated job with such tremendous worldwide coverage. But it wasn't long before his love and knowledge of cricket gained him a seat in the commentary box.

He had played for the Combined Services and at one time was very near to taking over the captaincy of Worcester. He is still a first-class batsman and plays most of his cricket for the Lord's Taverners, of whom he was chairman for two years. He is quietly spoken and almost gentle in his delivery. He did broadcast Tests, but never gained a regular place in the team. I am afraid that first with John Arlott, and then me, broadcasting well over the retirement age, opportunities for the new commentators were scarce. He knew his cricket inside out, and as a result possibly interjected his own opinion rather than consulting our two experts.

His main occupation was his public relations business. He worked for television, both BBC and ITV, and covered hockey, at which he was a class player, show jumping and polo – not the easiest game on which to commentate. For radio he took over from Robert Hudson and brought a touch of the Navy to that most Military of occasions – Trooping the Colour. If you can get away with a commentary on that without incurring the wrath of a dozen or so retired colonels, then you can scale any height.

He will always be known in OBs as the broadcaster with the best excuse when he missed his cue during a broadcast. He was at Leicester during one of the Saturday afternoon round-ups and the presenter cued over to him according to his cue-sheet just after the tea interval should have finished. But there was dead silence except for the distant applause from the crowd. So the presenter went over to the other commentary points for the next ten minutes or so. He then decided to try Durders again: '. . . Are you there now, Neil? We tried ten minutes ago and couldn't raise you.' There was a slight pause, then a very out-of-breath Durders managed to blurt out, 'I am sorry. I can hardly speak. I've just run up the stairs to the box. I'm late because I've been having tea with the Bishop of Leicester.' This was of course greeted with roars of mirth by his colleagues in their commentary boxes all round the country. It was the best – and most unlikely – excuse ever heard on the air. When Durders cued over to Alan Gibson at Worcester Alan said in a sombre voice, 'I regret that there are no episcopal celebrations here.'

7 Overseas Visitors

Richie Benaud

*I*N 1999, AFTER BBC TELEVISION *lost the rights to broadcast Test match cricket, Richie Benaud joined the new cricket commentary team on Channel 4.*

For my first two years of television cricket commentary my fellow commentators included W. B. Franklin (captain and wicket-keeper of Buckinghamshire), Aidan Crawley (Oxford University, Kent and twelfth man for England against South Africa in 1929), R. C. Robertson-Glasgow (wit, raconteur and brilliant cricket writer, of Oxford University and Somerset) and Percy Fender (England and astute, big-hitting captain of Surrey). I was then joined by Robert Hudson for a short period and later by Jim Swanton who with Peter West and myself formed the regular television commentary team throughout the 1950s and 60s.

In 1958 Denis Compton retired from first-class cricket and became an expert summariser, and in 1960 – rather surprisingly, as he was still captain of Australia – Richie Benaud began his long stint as a commentator, which happily still continues. He joined the *Test match Special* team on radio in 1960 and then, when he retired from Test cricket, came to us in television.

He was always a good communicator and appreciated the importance of good public relations. When captain of Australia he started something which had never been done before and, so far as I know, has not been done since. After each day's play in a Test match he would give a press conference for the English and Australian cricket writers. Nowadays this only happens at the end of a match. He gave good value too as he was completely candid and never evasive in his answers. He would talk about the day's play and clear up any misunderstandings about incidents or doubtful umpires' decisions. He was fair in his judgement and assessment of players on both sides. It was ideal for the press as he more or less wrote their articles for them. It was also good for Richie and Australia, because no matter how fair he would try to be, both the English and Australian press were being given an Australian point of view.

When he was over here in 1956 and 1961 he took a great interest in our television commentaries. In fact at the end of the tour he managed to arrange a crash television course for himself at the BBC. He was a quick learner and soon learned all about the use of cameras and the tricks of the trade in commentary. Although during one match he explained to the viewers: 'The slow-motion replay doesn't show how fast the ball really was'!

A good example of Richie's coolness under pressure occurred during the summer of 1969. We had invited Colin Milburn to join our television commentary team of Richie, Denis Compton, Peter West and myself. Ollie, as we called him, was large, jolly, and fat, with a big frame and a tremendous appetite. We always had fun in the box, but with Ollie there it became even better.

It was during a Test match at the Oval, where in those days we had a small wooden hut on the roof of the pavilion. Somehow we had all managed to squeeze in, even with Ollie, but he had to stand leaning against the door. It was a terribly windy day and when someone opened the door from the outside, the gale caught the door and blew it wide open, taking Ollie with it. He landed safely with a plump on the roof, and of course we all got hysterics. We were saved by the professionalism of Richie, who, although the summariser, took over the commentary while we recovered.

He is possibly the best organised commentator that I know. His whole year is carefully mapped out by his wife Daphne and there is not, I suspect, a single *idle* day in his diary. If he is not working you can be sure he will be playing golf. In our winter he is at home in Australia running his sports consultancy business and since 1977 he has commentated for Channel Nine television on any Tests there are out there. His schedule is killing. He is up every day at dawn, dictating, writing or telexing, and after a busy day there are usually dinner parties at night. If you go to his flat for dinner the hospitality is superb, but in the background there is still the ticking of telex and tape machines.

I have always considered Richie the best of all the post-war captains, better even than Bradman or Brearley, and he makes an ideal television commentator. From his experience as captain he reads a game with great skill, and can usually guess which tactics will be employed or suggest which ones should be. He has confidence in his own judgement and is never afraid to give his opinion about anything – even if it differs from that of his colleagues. He has a dry sense of humour and it is a pity that television tends to discourage this.

I remember that he, Peter West and myself used to have a pact that as soon as the batsman had hit the ball we would say, 'That will be one run,' or, 'two', as the case might be, and if we could immediately say, 'That's four all the way,' it was considered a minor triumph. Richie was by far the best at this and seldom got it wrong. I used to be very bold and shout 'Four', but frequently had to make an excuse when the ball was brilliantly fielded or stopped just short of the boundary. We had a lot of laughs – usually at my expense. I was never much of a judge of a run when I played, and often, I'm afraid, ran people out.

One last example of Richie's great energy. After a full day's commentary, which in his off-duty moments includes a close study of the racecourse runners and starting prices, he will appear in front of the camera after close of play, and give a slick and accurate summary. He does it all out of his head without notes and also has to cue in various film inserts to illustrate what has happened. It is not easy to do but he does it supremely well. And one other thing you have probably noticed – even at the end of a long hot day he is immaculately dressed and must certainly qualify as the cricket commentators' nattiest dresser.

Alan McGilvray

One or two older readers may remember someone called Jack Smith, the whispering baritone. He used to sing songs like *Baby Face* and *Miss Annabelle Lee* very softly at the piano during the 1920s and 30s. For more than fifty years the Australian Alan McGilvray – from now on 'McGillers' – was the whispering *commentator*. His style was utterly unique. He spoke right up against the microphone so confidentially and so quietly that even if you were sitting next to him, you could not hear what he was saying. It was a very effective method as it gave the air of intimacy which made the listener at home think that he was the one person to whom Alan was talking. His commentary

flowed freely at about the same level, his voice rarely generating excitement. His description of play was completely factual
and he was always wary of following the English style of
'colourful' commentary.

I would say he was the most unbiased commentator I have
ever heard. He liked to enjoy good cricket, no matter who was
winning, and had very high principles as to the conduct of
players and the spirit in which the game was played. He was
a fine reader of the tactics and cricketing skills and was well
qualified to give his judgement. In addition to the experience
gained during his fifty years of commentary, he also captained
New South Wales in the Sheffield Shield in 1934–6. He succeeded Don Bradman as captain and had people like Bill
O'Reilly and Jack Fingleton under his command, he himself
being a useful fast medium bowler.

One other unusual feature of his commentary was that he
often looked through his binoculars while commentating, the
field glasses resting on the top of the microphone, his elbows
on the desk in front of him. I find this a very difficult thing to
do, and BBC commentators rarely do it and then only for the
odd ball or two. The trouble is that although you get a fine close-
up of the batsman and the stumps, if the ball is hit anywhere, it
goes out of your vision. It is then very difficult to take down
the binoculars, and pick up where the ball has gone.

McGillers did his first cricket commentary in 1934, and so
was by far and away the longest serving and most experienced
commentator. He broadcast his two-hundredth Test at Melbourne in 1980, and received a tremendous ovation from the
crowd when this fact was recorded on the giant scoreboard.
He first came here to represent the Australian Broadcasting
Commission in 1948, but his first Test broadcasts were done
from an Australian studio when they were covering the 1934
and 1938 Test series in England with 'synthetic' commentary.

McGillers and others would sit in front of a studio microphone and be fed with cables sent direct from England
describing *each* ball, where it had gone, how many runs scored
or how a wicket had fallen. There were certain code signs so
that they were able to say, as the cable describing the second
ball of an over was thrust in front of them, 'Bradman has cut
that one down to third man – Leyland fields and returns over
the top of the stumps to Les Ames, while they trot through for
an easy single.' After some experience they could pick that up

easily enough from the cable. But the difficult part was when the next cable was delayed for some reason, and to fill in they had to make up 'drinks coming out', 'a dog running across the pitch', and so on. It was all backed up by sound effects of applause, cheers or gasps for a missed catch or near thing.

I gather it all sounded very realistic and they were even still prepared to use the method in 1948, if the actual commentary being relayed from the grounds became too difficult to follow due to atmospheric interference. (In those days there was no Commonwealth cable laid to take the broadcasts.) It must, though, have been a tremendous strain on the commentators, having to improvise off the cuff, using only their knowledge of the game and their imagination. The first time this unusual system was used was in 1932 during Douglas Jardine's Bodyline tour of Australia. A French radio station in Paris used Alan Fairfax who had played for Australia in England in 1930. He gave a ball-by-ball commentary from cables sent from Australia. He must have been exhausted at the end of the day, as there is no evidence that he had any other assistant.

It must have all been good training for McGillers, who stood head and shoulders above any other Australian radio commentator. With the Sheffield Shield competition, and a regular visit each year from one of the cricketing countries, he got plenty of practice. He did a little television but basically he stuck faithfully to radio. I always remember a conversation that he and I had with Sir Robert Menzies, the former Australian Prime Minister, who was a great cricket enthusiast. I have said that McGillers' commentary flowed along more or less non-stop. So, I suppose, does mine. Anyway, Sir Robert told us that he enjoyed our commentaries but that he preferred so-and-so up in Brisbane, 'because he knows the value of the pause'. McGillers and I understood what he was getting at, but I'm afraid it did not have much effect on our style. Sir Robert was quite right. The commentator in question would say something like: 'He bowls.' Pause. 'Outside the off-stump.' Pause. 'The batsman plays and misses.' Pause. 'It goes through to the keeper.' He would then not say anything until the next ball was bowled, leaving a long gap as the bowler walked back to his mark. Imagine me keeping silent that long!

I had got to know McGillers well on his visits to Great Britain, but as I did television exclusively until the mid-1960s, I had never worked with him until I went to Australia in 1958 for my three months' 'grace leave' with ABC. He was kindness itself in the box and a great help to me in my first attempts to give the score in the Australian way. We went on to enjoy more than twenty-five years of friendship in the commentary boxes of Australia, South Africa and England.

He became used to our somewhat more light-hearted approach, with the jokes and the leg-pulls, and was remarkably tolerant even when he was a victim. I caught him beautifully one year at Lord's. Someone had kindly sent me a large and deliciously gooey chocolate cake for my birthday. I had cut it up into slices and was busy commentating when I heard McGillers enter the box behind me. I pointed at the cake, signalling that he should help himself to a slice. His eyes gleamed and I saw him take a large piece and pop it into his mouth.

As soon as the next ball had been bowled I immediately said, 'And now I'll ask Alan McGilvray what he thought of that last delivery.' There was a spluttering noise and an avalanche of crumbs as he desperately tried to speak with his mouth full. After that he never accepted even a biscuit or sweet in the box.

McGillers retired at the age of seventy-five in 1985. He will certainly be remembered as the longest serving cricket commentator, universally respected by his colleagues as the real professional and with a large number of appreciative friends both in Australia and England. And I am sure that listeners everywhere would universally award him the supreme accolade of 'The man who *always* gave the score' – something I think we could all learn from him.

Charles Fortune

Someone entirely different in style from Alan McGilvray was Charles Fortune, the South African commentator. Charles had no nickname on the air except for the occasional 'Charlie'. The natural one for him was 'Outrageous' but somehow it did not stick, possibly because it was *too* outrageous. After Alan he was the second longest serving commentator and when broadcasting in his mid-seventies he was certainly the oldest. He was born in Corsham in Wiltshire in 1906 but later became a schoolmaster in South Africa and combined it with broadcasting on cricket, tennis and rugby football. His first cricket broadcast for SABC was in 1945. He was a natural broadcaster and was capable of describing and talking about absolutely anything.

You could not mistake Charles. He usually wore a soft trilby hat, smoked cigarettes through a holder and never tied his tie in a knot, but folded it over rather like a stock or cravat. Somewhere, I suspect, there was a monocle hidden away in a pocket. Actually, it is not *quite* true that he never tied his tie. He did make *one* exception. When we asked him to be a member of the Test match Broadcasters Club, we presented him with its tie but only on the strict condition that when he wore it, he would tie it properly. This he always did, and on the first day of any Test match, when we all have to wear it, he appeared with it beautifully tied. I have never really discovered why he did not tie his ties, though I believe he had not done it for nearly fifty years, and that it was in protest against something or other.

I always enjoyed working with him. At Newlands – the beautiful Test cricket ground at Capetown – a goods train used to pass the ground regularly at 11.50 every morning. Whenever I was on I always mentioned it, and the driver must have kept a radio in his cab, because he always gave us a hoot as we called out 'Good morning' to him over the air.

Without wishing to belittle the other cricket commentators, I would say that Charles was near the top of the league for 'best educated commentator'. He was well read, had a fund of general knowledge and a good choice of words and language. If it were possible, he was the nearest thing to John Arlott in style and content. He spoke slowly and clearly and obviously relished a bon mot or choice of phrase. He was always close to the players and brought his knowledge of their personalities and lifestyle into his commentaries. Like me he looked for all those little extra somethings at a cricket match and rolled his tongue round colourful descriptions of the scene in front of him. He knew his cricket well but he was often accused of concentrating on everything except for the play going on and the score. There is a marvellous story told about him, purely apocryphal I know, but near enough to the truth to portray his style of commentary.

South Africa was batting in a Test match against Australia at Adelaide. Charles is reported to have said, 'At the start of this over from Lindwall, South Africa are 63 for no wicket, and from my commentary position I can see the beautiful spire of St

Peter's Cathedral silhouetted against the azure blue sky. Away to the north are the towering Lofty Mountains – magnificent in their grandeur, and making a worthy backdrop to this most lovely of grounds. In a far corner I can see a group of small boys playing their own game of cricket, using a lemonade bottle as a bat. Just below me a flock of seagulls are settled in front of the sightscreen having their afternoon tea, whilst in the George Giffen Stand the ladies make a superb picture in their gaily coloured dresses. And that brings us to the end of that over by Lindwall. South Africa are now 63 for 3 – and my scorer tells me that hat trick by Lindwall was the first of his career.' I told this story in a *This Is Your Life* type of programme about Charles on South African Television in 1981 and he took it very well!

He is also the only cricket commentator I know who has commentated in his pants. It was very hot in our box at Johannesburg one day and when I had finished my stint at the microphone I handed over to Charles who was sitting beside me. I noticed for the first time that his trousers were hung up on a hook and there he was in his pants. I didn't give him away on the air but alas for him the Director-General of SABC was showing a VIP round the various commentary positions. We had just returned listeners to the studio when the Director-General came in and said to the VIP, 'And now I'd like you to meet our senior cricket commentator – Charles Fortune.' Poor Charles stood up rather sheepishly in his pants and shook hands.

Vic Richardson

Vic Richardson was best known for his inter-over comments and his famous cross-talk act with Arthur Gilligan. But in Australia he also did some commentary and at Adelaide in 1966 for the fourth Test against England, he was a member of the ABC commentary team with Alan McGilvray and myself. He achieved what will probably be an all-time record for a commentator. He became the first grandfather to comment on his grandson playing in a Test. It was in fact Ian Chappell's first Test match. I was the commentator when Australia's fifth wicket fell at 383, Doug Walters having been caught by Jim Parks off David Brown for nought.

Down the steps from the George Giffen Stand emerged the youthful Ian Chappell, aged twenty-two, and I suddenly realised what a unique opportunity this offered. Vic was at the back of the box during his rest period and I signalled to him to come and take my place, although it was not his turn to do commentary. I was able to say, 'Now for the first time in any Test match here is a grandfather to comment on the very first ball his grandson receives in Test cricket. Come on in, Vic.' And so it happened, though for the life of me I cannot remember what happened to the first ball. At any rate Ian was not out to it, as he went on to make seventeen.

Vic was most grateful for being given the chance. He had been a fine cricketer, a hard-hitting bat and superb close fielder. He also made an inspiring leader when he captained Australia in South Africa in 1935–6, Australia winning the series 4–1. He was a great sportsman who played cricket in the right way. What he would have thought of some of the antics which have happened on the field in more recent years I dread to think – especially as his grandson Ian was concerned in quite a few of the more unsavoury incidents!

Pearson Surita

Pearson Surita came from Calcutta, where in addition to his cricket, he was a judge at the races. He had a benign, friendly face with a slightly surprised look on it. He spoke slowly with rather a posh accent and laughed easily with a pleasant chuckle. He knew his cricket and was most helpful to us with his knowledge of Indian names and customs.

His sense of direction was perhaps not all that it should be. On the England tour of India in 1981–2, just before close of play one day, he and Don Mosey were having an argument about which way the pitch at Eden Gardens faced. Pearson, who of course knew the ground better than most people, insisted that it faced one way; Don the other. Sitting in the studio back home I was inclined to back Don, because if Pearson was right at the time when they were broadcasting the sun was setting in the north! I am assured by those who have been to India that it is the same there as everywhere else – it does actually set in the west. But even when he visited us in our box at Lord's the following summer, Pearson was still insistent that he was right.

Roy Lawrence

I worked with Roy Lawrence both over here and in the West Indies. He was a kind, gentle person and an excellent commentator, with a detailed knowledge of West Indian cricket. He lived in Jamaica, but during the 1970s came over to Great Britain and lived in Harrogate. But when there was a change of government and things became more settled, he returned to Jamaica in 1981. His worst moment on the air must have been during the tear-gas riots at Sabina Park during Colin Cowdrey's tour of 1967–8. I was with him in the commentary box as the bottles began to be hurled on to the field.

When the police used the tear-gas they miscalculated the wind and the gas was blown across our box and the press box, and after a few spluttering and gasping moments we had to give up trying to describe the scene and returned listeners to the studio. When the riot had stopped and the gas had cleared Roy made a most moving apology on behalf of West Indian cricket, especially as the trouble had been on his beloved Sabina Park. He unashamedly broke down, and it was one of the most dramatic broadcasts at which I had ever been present.

On a lighter note, he admitted that he once opened a broadcast in 1960 with: 'Well, it's another wonderful day here at Sabina Park with the wind shining and the sun blowing gently across the ground'!

Tony Cozier

The other West Indian commentator with whom I have enjoyed working both here and in the West Indies is Tony Cozier, for whom, strangely, I have no nickname. In contrast to Roy Lawrence he is a forceful character and a lively and enthusiastic broadcaster, not afraid to speak his mind. Even if it doesn't always make perfect sense. During one Test match he announced: 'Botham has a chance of putting everything that's gone before behind him'!

Perhaps more than any other overseas commentator he has

had to defend his country's team against criticism, given I hope in a friendly fashion, by the majority of the *TMS* team. Of course, this criticism has nothing to do with the standard of the West Indians' cricket. How could it, when they have frequently proved themselves so superior to England, and have undoubtedly been the outstanding team in the world of Test cricket?

The criticism has been given because of the slow over rate of their bowlers and the excessive number of bouncers which they have tended to bowl. Coming from an Englishman it must sound rather like sour grapes but I personally feel it is justified. On the other hand it has been largely compensated for by the magnificent stroke play of their batsmen, and the awe-inspiring speed of their bowlers – they have no need to bowl so many bouncers.

At any rate Tony has a simple answer to all such criticism. Look at the results, he says. The West Indian record speaks for itself. The slow over rate does admittedly rob the spectators of a considerable number of overs a day. But look at the entertainment they get watching these fast bowlers in action, and seeing so many wickets tumble quickly during a day. As for the bouncers, he says, that is entirely in the hands of the umpires, and they have the necessary powers to stop them if they think they are deliberately intimidating. Tony puts his case over very well in a perfectly friendly way but quite rightly feels he should defend his country.

He is a very hard worker, writes for the newspapers and travels with the West Indies team on their tours abroad. When in Great Britain he manages to play some club cricket, and on the Monday mornings regales me with his successes behind the timbers. We always look forward to welcoming him to the box whenever the West Indies visit this country. He is an expert on all West Indian cricketers and their records, although I am not so sure about his knowledge of their cricket grounds. 'The Queen's Park Oval is exactly as its name suggests,' he told us once, 'absolutely round!'

Alan Richards

Another overseas commentator with whom I have had the pleasure of working is Alan Richards from New Zealand. He is a cheerful, friendly person and an excellent all-round commentator. He is an Auckland man and extremely versatile in his sports. He played cricket for the provincial side at Eden Park and also played soccer in the winter, and became a director of North Shore United – a First Division club. He has also been a racehorse owner and a keen follower of the Turf, both flat racing and trotting.

So far as cricket commentary is concerned he came over here for the New Zealand tours of 1978 and 1983, and also for the Prudential World Cups of 1979 and 1983. He has been to every cricketing country where the game is played at International Cricket Conference level. Alan had an unforgettable experience in Pakistan in the mid-1970s. He was a member of the Pakistan Radio commentary team for simultaneous transmission in Pakistan and to New Zealand. He followed one of the local commentators and after doing his twenty-minute stint, handed over to another Pakistani commentator. To Alan's horror the next twenty minutes were entirely in Urdu, so that his New Zealand listeners were left completely in the dark as to what was happening!

He has some mixed memories of his Test match commentaries. His first experience as a cricket commentator coincided with New Zealand's first ever Test victory against the West Indies in 1956, but some of his other sixty-five Tests were not so happy.

He was at the microphone at Eden Park in 1975 when a lifting ball from Peter Lever struck Ewen Chatfield. Chatfield collapsed and swallowed his tongue and would probably have died had not England's physiotherapist, Bernard Thomas, dashed out and given him the kiss of life. Alan says this was the most difficult ten minutes of commentary he has ever had to do. But an incident at Christchurch in 1980 was not much better, when West Indian Colin Croft deliberately banged into umpire Fred Goodall, causing a hostile demonstration from the incensed crowd. Alan's job was made more difficult because his commentary was being relayed to the Caribbean and he had to be very careful in what he said.

Perhaps his most unpleasant experience was at Melbourne in 1981, when, with New Zealand requiring six runs to win off the last ball, Australia's captain Greg Chappell instructed his brother Trevor to bowl an underarm grub all along the ground. Alan – like every sportsman all over the world – was horrified at this unsporting action, so foreign to cricket. He wisely just gave the facts without expressing his opinion, and handed quickly over to his Australian colleague Ian Brayshaw and left him to say what everyone was feeling.

In soccer he was the first English-language commentator to visit China, where he went twice to cover World Cup qualifying games. He did not find commentary there particularly easy, with Chang passing to Wong who beat Ling and then passed to Teng who headed the ball to Pu who back-heeled to Gu who slipped it to Ma whose shot at goal accidentally hit his colleague Ping in the back!

On his arrival in Peking in 1975 Alan was asked through an interpreter, 'Mr Richards, has New Zealand suffered badly under the imperialist English aggressors?' Alan immediately thought of the day at Eden Park in 1955 when England had bowled out New Zealand for a record low Test score of twenty-six, but decided to answer, 'No.'

Alan must be one of the only commentators in the world to have described both World Cup cricket *and* football.

8 Test match Special

M Y OWN BROADCASTING CAREER underwent an important development when in 1963 I was appointed the first-ever BBC Cricket correspondent. I continued all my commentary (still at that time exclusively for television) but I was also partly allied to the News Department. Whereas in the past they used to read out reports of Test matches from the tapes, now that they had their own correspondent, they decided to risk taking live reports straight from the ground into the news. They considered it a risk because a news bulletin has to be the exact length allotted to it – usually ten minutes – to the nearest second. They were naturally worried about trusting a commentator to do exactly the time they asked for, generally a minute but on occasions as little as thirty or forty seconds. This report also often had to be given whilst the commentator was already describing play on Radio 3 or, in the case of overseas matches, on some other channel. But to their admitted amazement it worked, even over the thirteen thousand miles to Australia, and it is now an everyday event.

From my first overseas tour in 1958 until I retired as a member of the staff in 1972 I was lucky enough to do seven such tours for the BBC covering MCC visits to all the Test-playing countries except India, where at that time the poor communications made live broadcasting back to Great Britain not worth the while. In addition I also commentated on two other tours not involving England. One was for ABC when Australia played the Rest of the World in 1972, and the other for SABC during South Africa's last Test series, which they played against Australia in South Africa in 1970.

Since the mid-1960s I had shared my Test match commentaries between television and radio. Charles Max-Muller was then Head of Radio OBs and had been responsible for my being made BBC Cricket Correspondent in 1963. He rightly felt that with that title I should not just be used by television. So from 1965 up to 1969 I had been doing three Tests each season for television, and two for radio, with John Arlott and myself interchanging between the two. Though sorry to be away from television I was honoured to be allowed to join the ball-by-ball commentary teams of *Test match Special*, which had been going since 1957. It was quite difficult to change one's technique from Test to Test, trying not to talk too much at one, and then having to talk non-stop at the other.

Since the war the radio commentators had included Rex Alston, Jim Swanton, John Arlott, Alan Gibson, Robert Hudson and Neil Durden-Smith. In addition there was always a visiting broadcaster from the country which was touring England. Summarisers had included Arthur Gilligan, Alf Gover, Freddie Brown and Norman Yardley. But by 1970 Rex Alston had retired and Robert Hudson had left his commentary seat for the administrative job of Head of Radio OBs – taking over from Charles Max-Muller. The 1970 set-up was to be chosen from John Arlott, Alan Gibson, Neil Durden-Smith and a visiting commentator, with Freddie Brown and Norman Yardley still the summarisers.

It was on my return from an enjoyable two months away in South Africa that I got the biggest shock of my broadcasting career. The first person I ran into on my return was Neil Durden-Smith. He said how sorry he was that I was no longer going to do the cricket commentary for television. He must have been surprised by the look of shock and bewilderment on my face, because this was the first I had heard of it. I went to see Robert Hudson – my new boss – who confirmed that he had been told of the change. He said he was sorry for me but delighted for the sake of *Test match Special* as he wanted me to become a regular member of that team. This kind invitation certainly softened the shock, because it was undoubtedly a blow to my pride.

I must emphasise that I have never questioned the right of BBC Television to get rid of me and I understood their reason for doing so. The commentary team of Peter West, Jim Swanton, Richie Benaud, Denis Compton and myself had become a happy group of friends who enjoyed our cricket and hoped that viewers did the same. It was natural that we probably gave an 'amateurish' atmosphere to the box with too many jokes and friendly asides and back-chat.

By 1970 I think BBC Television felt that they wanted a more 'professional' approach. No more jokes, no more camera shots of extraneous attractions like the member fast asleep or the bored blonde reading a book. They wanted the commentator to stick to the cricket only, and quite obviously the best people to do this would be ex-Test players. So the new regular commentary team became Richie Benaud and Jim Laker with Peter West remaining as linkman and interviewer. Denis Compton and Ted Dexter were the main summarisers, to be joined later by Mike Smith, Brian Close, Ray Illingworth, Tom Graveney and even Geoff Boycott when not playing. After a few seasons Denis Compton decided to drop out, feeling frustrated by the restrictions put on his natural exuberance and love of a laugh.

My transfer to *Test match Special* in 1970 was the start of what have been some of the happiest years of my life. *TMS* is a rather unique institution. In fact the BBC itself has called it a 'new art form'. This, I have always felt, is rather overdoing it. But it is certainly a different type of broadcasting to anything that has been done before. I have to admit that it is since I joined in 1970 that it has become more different, and that I must bear some of the responsibility for this. In view of the success of *TMS* this may sound boastful. But in fact there is a section of listeners who disapprove of our way of broadcasting. They are, luckily for us, a minority, but we do recognise that they would prefer the old straightforward method of commentary without all the funnies and the cakes. They obviously have a case, but from the wonderful reaction which we get from so many people we feel that we are doing what the majority enjoy.

The change in *TMS* has been gradual but it is still founded on the original concept of providing the listener with an accurate, colourful, and lively description of a day's cricket, bearing in mind also that cricket *can* be dull and does need the occasional injection of fun to maintain the listeners' attention.

The conditions under which we work are not ideal, being often too cramped, too crowded and too hot. One would expect this to make the commentators niggly and touchy but somehow we never seem to mind. Our boxes are far better than they used to be. In the ideal box five of us can sit in a row which allows for the commentator, the summariser, Bill Frindall, the next commentator and anyone who has popped into the box for an interview.

About half an hour or so before play is due to start I usually find time to pop in and say good morning to the umpires. If one of them is Dickie Bird I tell him that the weather forecast is bad and that there will undoubtedly be some awkward and unpopular decisions to make about the light later in the day.

This gets him thoroughly worried. But as he is at his happiest when the cares of the world are on his shoulders, I feel I have done some good.

During the day, however, I stay in the box for most of the time. Some go out for a breather or a gossip with friends, others who may be writing for a paper wander off to the press box. But somehow I like to stay at the scene of action in case I miss some vital piece of play. The sponsors kindly provide us with lunch boxes, though on occasions we go for a picnic with family or friends or to one of the many boxes or tents which are features of the modern Test ground. It all adds up to a marvellously relaxing day, doing something one enjoys in the company of friends. How lucky I have been to have had such convivial and compatible colleagues, and I am grateful to them all for the way they have put up with my pranks and puns.

John Arlott

John Arlott did more to spread the gospel of cricket than any other man alive. For thirty-four years his rich, gruff, Hampshire burr spanned the world. He took cricket into palaces, mansions, cottages, crofts, mud huts and, for all I know, igloos. He rightly became the voice of cricket and more imitated than any other commentator. Although he started his working life as a clerk in a mental hospital, followed by nine years in the police where he rose to detective-sergeant, he was basically a poet. He could do naturally what we lesser mortals had to work at – paint pictures with words. The sound of his voice alone conjured up visions of white flannels on green grass, and the smell of bat oil and new-mown grass. But his powers of description with the ever apt phrase enabled the listener to 'see' the scene he was describing. He always tried to imagine that he was talking to a blind person and coloured his commentary accordingly.

One of the classic commentaries of all time was his hilarious description of the Lord's ground staff removing the covers off the square at Lord's. They took at least twenty minutes and John never missed a trick, covering every detail of what was going on. He also gave a very fine word picture of the streaker at Lord's in 1975. I know if I had been doing it I should have gone too far – 'two balls going down the pitch at the same time' – that sort of thing. But John struck exactly the right note.

He also had the enviable gift of being able to produce the apt witty comment on the spur of the moment. 'Bill Frindall,' he informed the listeners once, 'has done a bit of mental arithmetic with a calculator!' When he was with the MCC in South Africa the MCC captain, George Mann, was clean bowled by the slow left arm South African bowler 'Tufty' Mann. It was an unplayable ball, pitching on the leg stump and taking the off-bail. Without a moment's hesitation John said: 'Mann's inhumanity to Mann!'

He had always adored cricket and with his retentive memory soon became one of the great cricket historians. How good he was as a player I am never quite sure. But he did travel round with the Hampshire team before the war, and once at Worcester actually fielded as twelfth man for them in a county match. He was also a great listener and throughout his career cultivated the company of the county cricketers all over England – wherever he was commentating. He was not afraid to ask, and so learned much about the technique and skills of the game.

He also made many friends among the first-class cricketers and this had a happy sequel when they elected him President of the Cricketers' Association. This was a tribute and an honour and it was an office he continued to hold after his retirement from broadcasting cricket.

We all have to have our piece of luck and his chance came in 1946 when India was touring England – the first tourists since the war. After leaving the police John had become a poetry producer for the Far Eastern Service and they selected him to follow the Indians round the country, in order to send nightly reports on the matches back to India. It was soon obvious that cricket had made a find and Lobby chose him to commentate along with Rex Alston and Jim Swanton. From then until he retired he was a member of the radio commentary team at every Test played in this country.

He was a home-lover and very much a family man so he did not tour with MCC as much as Rex Alston or, later on, myself, Christopher Martin-Jenkins and Don Mosey. In fact he paid just one visit each to the three main cricketing countries, Australia, South Africa and the West Indies.

He was an emotional, kind and compassionate man, not ashamed to cry if he was affected that way – and incidentally he had more than his fair share of personal tragedy. He was also witty, much enjoyed conversation and could tell a funny story very well. This he usually did before play started after he had recovered from his exertions of climbing up to the commentary box. He always arrived hopelessly out of breath and more often than not mopping his brow with his handkerchief. He loathed the heat and several of us suffered rheumatic pains in the back through his insistence on having the commentary-box door open, so as to produce a through draught.

His commentary was in the Lobby mould, describing the action until the ball was dead and then adding a piece of 'colour' until the next ball was bowled. In the same way that Neville Cardus had largely created the characters of those old Yorkshire and Lancashire professionals, so John built up the physical appearance of the cricketers – deep-chested, raw-boned, broad-shouldered were frequent adjectives. He would be fascinated by trousers too tight or shirts billowing in the breeze. The umpires in their funny hats and caps were easy game for him. But he never restricted himself to just the cricket. Like I do, he saw a game of cricket as something more than whether the ball was doing this or that. He would comment on the action going on all round the ground with a slight penchant for the pigeons feeding in the outfield. It was wonderful stuff and brought the cricket match alive.

But of course broadcasting cricket was only part of his life, albeit a very important part. He was a man of many talents and an expert on books, wine, aquatints and glass. To visit his home was like going to a very hospitable museum. In his spare time he had amassed a wonderful collection of all those things he knew about and loved. His main hobby was drinking wine but over the years he put more back into his cellar than he and his friends ever drank. And that is saying a lot! I never went to his new home at Alderney after he retired but in Alresford he made use of the old cellars of the one-time pub in which he lived. It was full of every type of wine from the old, rare and priceless to the sort which you or I would keep for a very special party. If you were his guest he would remember what was your favourite wine and there would be a bottle waiting for you in front of your place at the table.

It's no secret that in the commentary box we do have the occasional glass of champagne or wine which so many kind people send to us. In the old days this would have been unthinkable. In fact when I first joined *Test match Special* I had never had any such refreshment during broadcasting hours. But John gradually introduced the idea of taking a little red wine with his lunch, and then somehow lunch used to get earlier and earlier! So that is just one of the legacies which he left behind him, and now the occasional popping of a cork in the background is usually a sign of lunch or close of play approaching.

John's cricket library was one of the largest and best private collections in the world. I say 'was', because before moving to Alderney he had to get rid of a lot of his books, only keeping the rarest and best. And in addition to cricket he had valuable first editions on other subjects.

Besides being such an expert collector John was a prolific writer, whether reporting cricket or commenting on wine for the *Guardian* or writing on average one or two books every year. It was also the accolade for any book on cricket to have a foreword by John Arlott. He must have written hundreds. It always amazed me how he could maintain this output and still find the time and energy to commentate. For many years he did his full stint of commentating and then at close of play went off to write his piece for the *Guardian*. But in the last five years or so he used only to do three commentary periods and finished by three o'clock, so that he could go off to the press box to write.

This would be enough for most men. But on Sundays he shared the BBC 2 Television commentary with Jim Laker on the John Player League. This would often mean travelling a hundred miles or more from the Test match, and having to be back fresh for *Test match Special* on Monday. One thing he told me once surprised me. He always took the first stint on BBC 2 from 2.00 to 3.00 pm. Then he would do the first stint after tea, from about 4.30 to 5.30 pm. He would then go home or back to wherever the Test match was. This meant that he had never actually seen the finish of any of the John Player matches on which he had been commentating.

At the beginning of the 1980 season John announced that it was to be his last as a Test match commentator – I remembered he had commentated on *every* Test played in England from 1946 onwards. He explained, 'I'm going while people are still asking me *why* I'm going rather than thinking, "why doesn't he go?"' A salutary lesson for all of us – especially for me at my time of life! In other words, although *he* didn't say so, he was going out at the top. The result was a series of dinners and presentations which went on non-stop throughout the summer

– everyone wanted to give him a farewell dinner – and they did! How he stood up to it I don't know but somehow he arrived fit and well for what would be his last day – the fifth day of the Centenary Test at Lord's.

Some unwise radio reporter tried to interview him as he arrived puffing as usual at the top of the stairs. Whilst he opened the morning session there were cameramen perched in dangerous positions filming him through the window of the commentary box. There were film lights inside the box, and rows of champagne bottles sent by admirers. It was a unique day for a unique person. We couldn't really believe it all in the box – after 3.00 pm there would be no more John Arlott on *Test match Special*. He got through the morning session in his usual good form, in between opening cables and letters, and celebrating in the way he knew best. We were all dreading his final twenty-minute stint, which was due to start at 2.30 pm.

We all gathered in the box – it was packed – no one wanting to miss this historic moment in broadcasting history. The clock moved up towards 2.50 pm and as he started what was to be his last over, we all expected him to begin a series of thank yous and farewells to the listeners. But no such thing happened. He finished the over without one single mention of his departure and then when the last ball had been bowled calmly said, 'And after Trevor Bailey it will be Christopher Martin-Jenkins.'

There was a second or two's silence and then we all stood up and clapped. John got up and slowly left the box as Alan Curtis announced to the crowd over the public address system, 'Ladies and gentlemen! John Arlott has just completed what will be his last ever Test match commentary for the BBC.' The reaction was wonderful. The crowd applauded, the Australians and the two England batsmen turned round and clapped, and the members on the top balcony applauded and clapped John on the back as he threaded his way through them to disappear from sight. It was a dramatic and heart-rending display by the cricket world at the headquarters of cricket saying goodbye to an old friend who had been their favourite commentator for thirty-four years. What a triumph and what an exit. John's timing as ever had been impeccable. And a final accolade. At the end of the season MCC made him an Honorary Life Member – and no cricketer could wish for better than that.

John retired to his lovely house in the Channel Isles where he wrote and drank with the many friends who went over there to visit him. He made the occasional foray to the mainland for broadcasts, interviews or television commercials. He still wrote on wine for the *Guardian*. And for the first time ever he was able to listen to the *Test Match Special* which he did so much to create. We miss him tremendously for his friendship and convivial companionship. The programme misses him too for his expertise, wit and unique style of commentating.

John Arlott died in December 1991. Strangely, except for one day at Old Trafford in 1989 to open the Neville Cardus stand, he never went back to a Test match. I suspect that as he listened to *TMS* he must sometimes have felt that Johnston had gone too far with one of his appalling puns or schoolboyish leg-pulls. If he did think so, I hope he forgave me. Because in our different ways we have both loved cricket. And he could always console himself that – unlike me – he never in all his cricketing life made a gaffe.

Henry Blofeld

I have said that we are all different in the commentary box, and no one is more different than Blowers. In appearance he looks rather like a mad professor, with his horn-rimmed spectacles and long flowing hair. He normally speaks extremely fast, and this is reflected in his broadcasting. His style has been described as 'frenetic', and his voice certainly becomes excitable whenever the play warrants it. But there is a sense of tremendous enthusiasm in all that he says. Once, when a fielder missed an easy chance, he declared: 'It's a catch he'd have caught 99 times out of 1000!' While at another Test he said: 'He's standing on one leg – like a horse in a dressage competition!'

The box is never dull when Blowers is on the air. His descriptions of play are blended with a collection of non sequiturs depending on what his particular fancy is at the moment. Sometimes he is 'bus happy', sometimes it is pigeons or any bird he can see, and he also has a penchant for butterflies.

In 1982 at the Oval there was a helicopter rally somewhere, and he caught 'helicopteritis'. They *were* particularly tempting as they were flying from west to east over the Thames at the Vauxhall End, and he soon got into double figures totting up their runs. And of course at Old Trafford the trains passing through Warwick Road Station are an irresistible temptation.

His 'busitis' was at its best (or worst!) one day at Lord's when he religiously reported every bus passing the Nursery End in Wellington Road: 'X comes up to bowl and the ball is played quietly to mid-off as a bus comes into sight. And as Y walks back to his mark I can see another red bus, followed by two more . . .' And so it went on. He has such a thing about buses that at the Oval in 1982 he said, 'Here comes a *good-looking* bus!'

For a countryman he is not too sure of his birds, though he usually gets the pigeons and seagulls right. But, as a listener pointed out in a letter, Henry should know that they are not pecking the outfield for *worms*. I suppose his classic was at Headingley one year, when he claimed to spot a butterfly *walking* across the pitch! I would like to add that he said that it had a slight limp, but he didn't go that far.

I suppose he creates more amusement and giggles among ourselves in the box than any other commentator. But he takes our gentle chaffing extremely well and proceeds unruffled to describe the play, which he does with professional accuracy. Not surprising really, because he himself briefly played first-class cricket, and for many years since has travelled round the cricketing world commentating, reporting and writing on all the Test matches wherever they are played during the winter.

As a young boy he went to Sunningdale Preparatory School, where the headmaster was a friend of mine. He soon reported to me that he had a brilliant wicket-keeper called Blofeld in his first eleven. He was by far the best the school had ever had and played for four years in the eleven. From there Blowers went to Eton where he got into the first eleven at the age of fifteen, a very rare feat in such a big school. In 1957 – his third and last year – he was appointed captain. Everyone who went to play against the school came away praising the ability of Blowers behind the stumps. Here – in the opinion of Ben Barnett, the old Australian wicket-keeper – was an England player of the future. But sadly one day just before the Eton and Harrow match, he was involved in a terrible accident. He was having a bicycle race against his friend and vice-captain Edward Lane Fox, from Agars Plough to Upper Club – two playing fields at Eton. They were separated by the road to Datchet, and as Blowers – in the lead – cycled across it, he struck a Women's Institute bus and was flung for yards down the road. He suffered appalling head injuries, and so could not play in the match at Lord's, and his life was in the balance for some time.

But somehow he made a miraculous recovery and in 1959 went on to win a cricket blue at Cambridge as a batsman. He has played good class club cricket since then and can always be proud that he kept wicket for his native Norfolk at the age of sixteen. He could also boast – but I have never heard him do so – that he was one of only three schoolboys to make a hundred at Lord's against the Combined Services. The other two were Peter May and Colin Cowdrey. So he was in good company. And he made it a double at Lord's, when in 1959 he made 138 for Cambridge in their match against MCC, an innings described by *Wisden* as a 'fine century'.

Blowers was a good stroke player but he never scored as fast as he talks. He gets twice as many words into a one-minute report as anyone else. And even when we have our discussions during the rain he speaks at machine-gun pace. He usually looks straight ahead of him and once he gets stuck into a subject, the words flow and it's difficult for anyone else to get a word in edgeways – and that's saying something in our box!

Blowers is delightful company, full of stories and anecdotes which are so full of details of time and place, that they do tend to go on a bit! Many of them are about his adventures on his trips abroad where at various times he appears to have been mugged, arrested, threatened by a cricket captain, and left standing stark naked in a hotel corridor.

In the early 1980s he became a cult with the Hillites at Sydney. Henry Blow-Fly they called him and there was even a Henry Blow-Fly Fan Club. He used to go across to the Hill to talk to them. As you will have gathered, talking plays a big part in his life, which is why he is such a good commentator and welcome member of the *TMS* team. His most endearing habit is the way in which he apologises for *everything*. No matter if it is not his fault; the box resounds with 'Sorry, sorry' when he is around. I firmly believe that if one accidentally shoved him off Beachy Head, he would be saying 'Sorry, sorry' as he fell towards the rocks below. Manners Makyth Man is the Winchester motto, not Eton's. But it applies to Blowers.

Christopher Martin-Jenkins

Jenkers is the man of many voices, and his mimicry and impersonations come up to the highest professional standard. Indeed
at one Lord's Taverners' Lunch he spoke first and produced
many of his impersonations, not just of sportsmen and television personalities, but also of politicians. He brought the
house down and made things very difficult for the star imper-
sonator who had to speak after him. He can do almost anyone,
even me! But he is shy about doing it in front of me, though I
did once catch him taking off my rather ridiculous hyenalike
laugh.

I first met him when he was still a schoolboy at Marlborough
where he was two years in the first eleven. He was captain in
his second year but alas Marlborough were beaten at Lord's by
Rugby, though Jenkers himself made 99, thus missing by one
the chance to join his fellow commentators Blofeld and Lewis
as a century-maker at Lord's. That was in 1963, the year in
which I became the BBC's first cricket correspondent. I received
a letter from him during the summer term asking for my advice
on how to become a cricket commentator (I still get letters
asking the same question). I asked him to come up to the BBC
to meet me and, so he reminds me, I gave him lunch in the
BBC Club in the old Langham Hotel. I did my best to encourage
him, and told him – as I tell everyone – to get a tape-recorder
and go out and describe anything and everything. Obviously a
cricket match would be ideal. But the object is to say to oneself:
'I will now talk non-stop for fifteen minutes, and imagine that I
am trying to describe what I am seeing to a blind man' (one
who has *gone* blind, not been *born* blind, which makes a visual
explanation more or less impossible).

He went up to Cambridge where, although he failed to get
a cricket blue, he and his brother became famous for their
impersonations, rather in the style of Tony Fayne and David
Evans. He did, however, play for Surrey's second eleven but
with his goal still the same after five years. He wanted above
everything else to be a cricket commentator. There are
hundreds of young boys who have the same dream but, since
there are only about ten cricket commentators who can achieve
Test match status at one time, it is a more-or-less impossible
dream. You must have luck, which is just what Jenkers had. In
1968 Jim Swanton appointed him Assistant Editor of the

Cricketer and for two years he was able to live cricket, absorbing the atmosphere, getting to know all the players and administrators, and learning how to report and write about cricket.

It was an invaluable schooling and in 1970 he had no difficulty in getting a job in the BBC Radio Sports Department of OBs, where he continued to learn about reporting and commentating on cricket, but now as a broadcaster, and not as a writer. In 1972 I retired as a member of the BBC staff and so had to relinquish the job of cricket correspondent. After a year's gap, Jenkers was appointed in my place and did the job for seven years, before going freelance in 1980, and becoming Editor of the *Cricketer*.

Those seven years were for him in some ways immensely satisfying, but in another way extremely frustrating. He went on all the tours with the MCC and broadcast commentary back to this country. In addition there came more and more demands from the News on Radio 4 and the many sports bulletins on Radio 2 for one-minute reports on the Tests and other games. Unfortunately he became so good at doing them that when he was back here in the summer he found he was being given all the reports to do, and very little commentary.

But gradually people came to realise what a good commentator he is, as well as a reporter, and he is now a fully-fledged member of the commentary team. After Don Mosey retired from the BBC staff, Jenkers took over for a second spell as BBC cricket correspondent from 1985–91, before leaving the job and the *Cricketer* to become cricket correspondent of the *Daily Telegraph*.

He is clear and articulate and to start with he had a very young voice in contrast to the more mature voices of some of his colleagues.

This *should* have been an advantage, but strangely in cricket – as opposed to the faster moving games like soccer and rugby – listeners tend to be a bit suspicious of youth. 'What does *he* know about it? He sounds too young to know . . .' But Jenkers overcame this because of his accurate and perceptive description of the play, and his immense background knowledge of the administrative set-up, the laws and regulations, and details of the players themselves. As Editor of the *Cricketer* he was at the hub of affairs and was often 'in the know', in contrast to someone like myself who no longer does cricket reports and news interviews.

He can also boast the slimmest figure in the commentary box. He is tall, lean and willowy with a jaunty walk and often looks as if he might be blown over by a strong wind! He is invaluable in our many discussions because he has strong views which he is happy to defend and argue about.

He is really a priceless asset to the BBC, should the latter ever wish to economise drastically. He could, on his own, carry out a day's commentary so that the listeners would think that we were all in the box taking our turn every twenty minutes. He can imitate the summarisers as well. I really think he could get away with it, though it might be a bit exhausting.

The more I write about my colleagues the more I realise that I am on my own as a gaffe-maker. None of them seems to make the mistakes or double entendres that I do. I did however catch Jenkers once during the summer of 1982. We had been talking about a man in the crowd with a bald head. I can't remember the reason. Anyhow, Jenkers tried to refer to him on one occasion and instead of calling him, as he intended, 'Our bald-headed friend,' he said, 'Our bald-freddied hen'! Still, he has many years ahead of him and he will probably do better than that!

In spite of his slender frame he has great energy and an enormous capacity for work. On all his tours, in spite of commentating all day and doing interviews and reports at all hours of the day, he used to write a book on the tour in question, which meant that while others were relaxing after a well-earned dinner, he would be upstairs tapping away at his typewriter behind closed doors. His editorials in the *Cricketer* were always full of sound sense and judgement and he has been a firm advocate of the right way in which cricket should be played.

If he has a failing it could be that he tends to give our producer Peter Baxter a heart attack whenever he is due to take over commentary. He is seldom waiting in the box but hurriedly appears just as the other commentator has said, 'Over now to Christopher Martin –.' Oh, and one other thing I nearly forgot. Anyone who is in the box when he is commentating is advised to put cotton wool in their ears, against the moment when a batsman is out or there is some dramatic action on the field. On these occasions Jenkers' high-pitched shout is the envy of every drill sergeant at the Guards Training Depot at Caterham!

Don Mosey

My tendency to give people nicknames is a fairly harmless habit which I hope gives more amusement than annoyance. Even when I was in the Grenadier Guards during the war our mess sergeant became 'Uncle Tom', my technical clerks were 'Honest Joe' and 'Burglar Bill' – and so on. And what's more the regular peacetime Grenadier officers so far forgot their tradition of strict discipline that they too used the nicknames. The success of a nickname depends on whether it sticks. Three of my own favourites were 'Melon' (for the Australian Test cricketer D. J. Colley), 'The Hatchet' (for an officer friend called Berry) and 'Nymph' (for umpire David Constant).

This brings me to The Alderman – the name with which I saddled Don Mosey some years ago. People often asked us how it came about, whilst agreeing that the title suited him well. It started when a broadcast of the Radio 2 quiz-game *Treble Chance* was going out from the Lancaster Town Hall. Don was organising the broadcast on behalf of BBC North Region, and he seemed to me to fit in well with all the dignified trappings of the Mayor's Parlour and Council Chamber. So from that moment I elected him The Alderman, which he gracefully accepted ever afterwards.

He was another of our *TMS* team who by his character and background brought contrast to our commentaries. He lived in Morecambe and his office was in Manchester. Both in Lancashire. But forget that – he was a Yorkshireman born in Keighley, who played his first League cricket match at the age of eleven. So, incidentally, did Brian Close and they both made eleven not out on their debut. He then combined playing rugby and cricket with reporting sport for the press and could boast one performance which rivalled anyone else's best in the commentary box. In one game he made 100 in forty-five minutes and took 7 for 28 including a hat trick. He was an opening bat and fast bowler and after the war, when he served in India, he played League cricket and in benefit matches whenever his journalistic duties allowed.

After reporting for the *Daily Express* and then writing on county cricket for the *Daily Mail*, he came to the BBC in Manchester, combining producing with broadcasting. In addition to cricket, he commentated on rugby and golf. He sometimes had the pleasure of describing the play of his son Ian, one of the country's top golf professionals. Don had hoped that Ian would play cricket for Yorkshire, and to make sure sent his wife Jo back to Yorkshire from Nottingham *three months* before the birth!

Don had all the characteristics of a true Yorkshireman. This meant that he was blunt, honest, obstinate and said exactly what he thought. He tried to be a perfectionist in all he did, setting himself a very high standard. As a result he found it difficult to tolerate inefficiency in others, so that when he spoke his mind he was bound to offend some people. He saw most things in black or white, and eschewed compromise, determined to defend his principles whatever the cost. He was the complete traditionalist – Queen and Country, strict standards of behaviour and discipline, and, needless to say, orthodox three-day cricket as opposed to the limited-over competitions.

There was a perfect example of his innate traditionalism during the summer of 1982. He was an ardent devotee of the D'Oyly Carte Gilbert and Sullivan operas. With his friend Phil Sharpe at the piano he could sing his way through all the songs. When the American version of *Pirates of Penzance* opened at Drury Lane I saw it and thought it was a wonderful production – lively, fast-moving, with magnificent choreography and a brassy band as opposed to the rather thin orchestrations of D'Oyly Carte. It was really more of a pantomime than an opera. I implored him to go and see it if only to compare it with the traditional presentation. But he was adamant, and refused to go. It was sacrilege to interfere with something which had been such a success for so many years.

I have devoted quite a bit of space to trying to portray Don's character, because it was all reflected in his commentary. His style was laconic and conversational with a very precise choice of words. Although during one match he announced: 'This is David Gower's hundredth Test. And I'll tell you something. He's reached his hundredth Test in fewer Tests than any other player.'

He did not flow non-stop and get too excited, as some of us do. He reported calmly what he saw, and if he approved or disapproved he would say so. Once again out came the Yorkshire honesty. If he was bored he would admit it, and would not try to build up something which didn't exist. He had a deep knowledge of cricket based partly on his own playing experience, but even more on his close association and friendship with many of the first-class players – especially with the Yorkshire players like Brian Close, Freddie Trueman and Ray Illingworth. A rare combination of skills and tactical sense.

He toured all the Test-playing countries with one important exception – Australia, and that was probably the biggest disappointment of his life. He had gradually built up to what was to be the pinnacle of his broadcasting career. On his other tours his reports had been typically honest about the hotels, the food, the broadcasting conditions and the travel. His weekly newsletter was a model description of places visited and the goings-on of the England team. But inevitably some of his criticisms – no matter how true – offended some people. As, for instance, from India during the England tour of 1981–2 when he admittedly was not too complimentary about some of the conditions. But ironically he had been stationed in India as a soldier, and loved the country. This was evident in many of his reports but it was the words of criticism that stuck in people's minds.

Anyhow, the BBC did not send him to Australia in 1982–3, and this was a body blow to him. Underneath the tough Yorkshire crust was an extremely sensitive and emotional man. The reason for the BBC's decision was largely because of a change of policy in broadcasting from Australia. Previously the BBC had sent out its own commentator to join the ABC commentary team, whose output was then relayed back to England. But due to complicated contractual difficulties the BBC now had to set up their own broadcasting unit and the commentary team was made up of those already in Australia for their various newspapers and magazines, such as Henry Blofeld, Tony Lewis and Chris Martin-Jenkins. All small comfort I'm afraid for the Alderman.

Don was a terrible giggler, and the slightest thing seemed to set him off. This tempted one to play tricks on him as we did once when he was in the commentary seat and had just received a card from Peter Baxter instructing him to 'welcome world service'. This he did and went on with his commentary. A few minutes later we put another card in front of him. 'welcome listeners in the VIRGIN islands, and explain that their position is some considerable distance from the Isle of MAN.' This of course had the desired effect.

Edgbaston was an unlucky ground for The Alderman. Whenever we were broadcasting from there Cyril Goodway, the chairman, kindly came along and stood in front of our box to take orders for pre-lunch drinks. He made various signs through the glass which we all understood, and he then noted down our requirements. On the first occasion Don broadcast with us at Edgbaston he knew nothing of this very civilised custom. He was on the air when Cyril appeared as usual at about 12.30. 'Oh,' said The Alderman. 'I can't see what's going on. Some stupid idiot is making ticktack signs at me through the window. He must be crackers.' We hurriedly wrote an explanation on a piece of paper but it was a poor return to Cyril for all his kindness over the years!

Don flattered himself on the use and derivation of words, so a few years ago I introduced him to a word game which I learned before the war in the office of our family coffee business. Don and I used to play it during intervals or sometimes when we were both resting between commentary periods. We received lots of letters asking us how it was played, and after several failures by me to explain it properly, I asked Don to devise an understandable explanation. This is it.

All that is required for the word game is two people, each with pencil and paper. *Each* draws a plan of twenty-five squares, thus:

Player A says a letter – any letter of the alphabet – and *both* players place that letter in any square of their choice on the plan. Player B then chooses a letter and again *both* players write the letter into their plan. The idea is to build up words across and down the plan. Carry on giving letters in turn until twenty-four of the twenty-five squares are filled on both plans. The final square is then filled using *any* letter of each individual player's choice. Score ten for a five-letter word, five for a four-letter word, one for a three-letter word.

Any score over eighty is very, very good – over seventy very good, over sixty good, and over fifty fair. It's actually very skilful with lots of ploys such as slipping in an x, z or q to embarrass your opponent. Try it sometime – but to save arguments, have a dictionary handy. I was always amazed that, in spite of all his knowledge of the English language, I was usually in the lead at the end of the season.

Don was appointed BBC cricket correspondent in 1984, for his final year as a member of the BBC staff before going free-lance. Then in 1991 he published his autobiography *The Alderman's Tale*, in which he was highly critical of what he called 'the public schoolboy' element on *TMS*. His last commentary with us was during the 1991 England v Sri Lanka Test match at Lord's, when Jonathan Agnew made his début as a *TMS* commentator. But whatever may happen in the future, I hope he will always continue to send me those rude seaside postcards from Morecambe.

Bill Frindall

Bill's is the easiest nickname to explain. He has a black beard and is undoubtedly a wonder, so 'The Bearded Wonder' came quite naturally. He is the vital part of the commentary machine. All we commentators are easily expendable and replaceable. But it would be hard to replace the B. W. He came into broad-casting in 1966, following the sad death of the *TMS* scorer Arthur Wrigley, just over a month after the end of the 1965 cricket season. He started scoring for the Temple Bar CC at the age of ten. After six years in which he began to learn about the history of cricket and its records, he then played club cricket. He is an enthusiastic tearaway fast medium in-swing bowler, and a sound batsman who bats lower than he thinks he should. He does not have much spare time during a busy summer, but on any day when he is not in the box, he will be playing cricket somewhere. He is much in demand for Sunday charity matches and organises his own tours abroad to places like Malta and Singapore. Woe betide me on the Monday of a Test match if I forget to ask him over the air how he got on in his Sunday game.

He was in the RAF for six years and then was about to start life in the City as a life assurance inspector, when he heard the news of Arthur Wrigley's death. He had been keeping his own statistical records of first-class players for some time, and had studied the scoring methods of those three original BBC scorers (as they were called in those days), Arthur Wrigley, Roy Webber and Jack Price.

Bill has never been lacking in confidence and immediately decided to apply for the job as a replacement for Arthur. He came up to the BBC to see the cricket producer Michael Tuke-Hastings, and myself as cricket correspondent. We were struck by his confidence and obvious knowledge of cricket. But perhaps we were even more impressed by the layout and the neatness of the sample score-sheets which he brought with him. We had no doubt that he was our man and he was given a contract for the 1966 season, without our even seeing another applicant.

There must have been many people who would have liked the job, though it meant giving up the whole of the summer to scoring in the Tests and county matches. But he was prepared to take the risk, and has been the regular statistician on *TMS* ever since. Note the new title, which is well earned. His scoring is vitally important and he has evolved a fairly complicated format based on the original Wrigley–Webber method. It tells the commentator all he wants to know – where each stroke has gone, the exact time anything has happened, the number of balls received off each bowler, the changes in the weather, details of all the extras, delays for the ball going out of shape, the statistics of the streaker and so on.

He is usually first in the box every morning, bringing with him an amazing collection of books, pens, pencils, rubbers, calculator, a thermos, a cushion and three stopwatches. The cushion is vital because whereas we can get up and stretch our legs after our twenty-minute stints, he is stuck to his chair for the whole two-hour session. How he manages to concentrate for that length of time and do all the things he has to do against a fairly chaotic background of chatter, laughter and requests for information, I just don't know. He can do at least three things at once, including signing autograph books which are often thrust under his nose just as he is about to record the end of an over on his elaborate score-sheet. Those three stopwatches are important too. They hang on hooks in front of him, the one on the left showing the batting time of the batsman on the left of the main scoreboard; the centre one for the overall time of the innings; and the right-hand one for the other batsman. At the start or close of play at any interval you can, if you listen carefully, hear three distinct clicks as he presses each watch as the first ball is bowled or the umpires take off the bails.

Bill can answer any question about individual cricketers, their records, results of past Test matches and so on. He carries round with him a collection of books, many of which he has compiled himself. He may not be able to answer a question immediately, but he knows exactly where to look and in a few seconds all is revealed. While he is searching for the answer he has to keep the score, and sometimes to pull his leg we ask him how many balls there are left in the over, just as he is delving into some enormous tome. After catching him out once or twice he now regularly replies *'approximately'* two or three or whatever it may be.

But he does not just wait for us to ask him questions. The B. W. comes to each Test armed with up-to-date figures of any possible record that could be broken during that Test. His microphone is only switched up when one of us asks him a deliberate question, so when he is trying to attract attention listeners can only hear his frantic whispers in the background. He will nudge the commentator to show that he is 'broody' and has some priceless piece of information or sometimes he will pass a note saying something like: '. . . If Bloggs hits another four he will have scored more boundaries in a Test hundred than any other Englishman.'

When he does this while I am on the air I often bait him and say, 'I'm not too sure – my memory is not very good – but I think that if Bloggs hits another four he will have scored more boundaries . . . I'll just ask Bill Frindall to check up in his books.' It usually succeeds in getting a rise out of him, probably displayed by a big snort. He is an inveterate snorter whenever anything amuses him, which seems to be quite often!

Trevor Bailey and Fred Trueman

Trevor Bailey and Fred Trueman both retired as the expert summarisers on Test match Special at the end of the 1999 cricket season.

Trevor Bailey is the longest-serving member of the present *TMS* team, having made his first broadcast in 1965 and, for a change, I was not responsible for his nickname of 'The Boil'. He acquired it when playing football for Leytonstone with his great friend and fellow Essex player Doug Insole. The crowd was largely made up of cockneys and they used to encourage him with shouts of 'Come on, Boiley' – hence The Boil.

For more than twenty-five years he has been one of the 'experts' in the box, and no one could be more qualified to that title. Captain of Dulwich College, Cambridge blue (1947–8), Secretary and Captain of Essex, and sixty-one Tests for England, achieving the rare double of 2,290 runs and 132 wickets. In addition he took thirty-two catches and was one of the finest all-rounders who ever played for England. Most people will remember him for his many back-to-the-wall defensive innings, and his famous forward defensive stroke. He liked winning but even more he loathed to lose and saved England on many occasions, the one which most people remember being the stand between him and Willie Watson at Lord's in 1953 against Australia. So in addition to 'The Boil' he was also known as 'Barnacle' – something which sticks and is very difficult to remove.

He has become a really professional broadcaster and is one hundred per cent reliable. He can fill in at a moment's notice, keep talking when nothing is happening, and is always ready to rescue a commentator when, as it has occasionally happened, he is incapable of speech because of laughter. The Boil's voice has a slightly nasal drawl with a chuckle never far away. He can be sarcastic but always does his best to be on the players' side. He knows what it is like out there in the middle. However, he does make the odd gaffe. 'The first time you face a googly,' he told us once, 'you are going to be in trouble if you've never faced one before'!

He is a severe critic of bad tactics, bad behaviour and bad cricket. As a player he was always a shrewd tactician with an inside knowledge of his opponents' weaknesses. He speaks his mind about what he thinks are captains' mistakes, and always deplores a player reacting badly to an umpire's decision, or gesticulating or swearing at an opponent.

This is not to say that he himself was not above a bit of gamesmanship, which is very different to cheating. For instance he would have no hesitation in bowling down the leg-side as he did to save the game at Headingley against Australia in 1953. He himself has defined bad cricket as 'a night-watchman trying to hit a six, a seam bowler who fails to bowl a reasonable line and length, or a very late call which leaves the other batsman stranded in the middle of the pitch . . .'

He tends to talk in short staccato sentences like Mr Jingle in *The Pickwick Papers* which has given him yet another nickname in the box – Mr Jingle. He will say: 'Fine bowler. Good line and length – moves it either way – never tires – good cricketer – like him in my side.' He also, like all of us, has his favourite adjective or adverb. His is 'literally', and he has been logged as saying: 'His tail is literally up'; '. . . it's a tense moment for Parker who is literally fighting for a place on an overcrowded plane to India'; 'Tavaré has literally dropped anchor.'

On a tour or in the box he is a splendid companion, who enjoys a party more than most. He has a delightful, slightly cynical sense of humour and sometimes in triumph comes out with an even worse pun than any of mine. He is also a good feed for some of the jokes we make in the box. I remember once asking him, 'What do you call a Frenchman who is shot out of a cannon?' He repeated the question in full as every music-hall straight man always did: 'I don't know, what *do* you call . . . etc.' I was then able to answer: 'Napoleon Blownaparte,' at which he broke with tradition and laughed.

He is a joy to work with because you know he will never let you down or be lost for something to say. His broadcasting is like his batting – safe, reliable, unhurried, provocative at times, and gives the listener a sense of security. With him in the box we have the feeling that we cannot lose.

Life in the commentary box has never been the same since Freddie Trueman joined The Boil as our other regular expert summariser. He is outsize in everything – his figure, his personality, his pipe and his stories. Like another great Yorkshireman, Sir Harold Wilson, Fred has an astonishing memory. His knowledge of cricket, its records and its players is phenomenal. He and I do our best to stump each other with quiz questions. I am easy meat but I can very rarely catch him out. He played his cricket with such astute tacticians and technicians as Hutton, Illingworth and Close and he has obviously stored everything he saw or heard in his 'little grey cells'. He might in fact have made a great captain, and can at least be proud of his achievement in 1968. In the absence of Brian Close he captained Yorkshire against the Australians at Sheffield and Yorkshire beat them for the first time since 1902 by an innings and sixty-nine runs.

Fred is down-to-earth in everything he says and I must say

is extremely fair. He will praise or criticise as the occasion warrants and express himself strongly in either case. During one Test match he declared: 'Anyone foolish enough to predict the outcome of this match is a fool!'

He is undoubtedly a bit puzzled by some of the modern cricket tactics and has a favourite phrase: 'I don't know what's going off out there.' And I must admit that I often agree with him! He is at his most critical about the modern fast bowlers, particularly as regards their actions and their fitness. Inevitably it may seem to some listeners that he is looking at the past through rose-coloured spectacles. But if anyone is honest – as of course every Yorkshireman is – he or she must agree that the standard of play in first-class cricket *has* dropped, except for fielding, throwing and running between the wickets.

Fred, as you can imagine, is never lost for words or the apt phrase and his sense of humour comes through in all he says. He also enjoys the simple jokes that are often sent in to us:

Brian: If you were stark naked out in a snowstorm, what animal would you like to be, Fred?
Fred: I dunno, Johnners, let's have it.
Brian: A little otter.
or
Brian: Who was the ice-cream man in the Bible?
Fred: All right. I'll buy it.
Brian: Walls of Jericho.

After I had told this joke a listener wrote in to me and asked, 'What about Lyons of Judah?'

Fred undoubtedly adds great weight to our commentary team. He can speak with the confidence of a man who took 307 Test wickets. He brings a strong northern flavour to contrast with the more southerly tones and attitudes of all of us in the box, except for Don Mosey. I know that Fred loves every minute of his time with us. We enjoy having him too and value all his cricketing knowledge and experience, although we are never *quite* sure what he is coming out with next. Of one thing, though, we can be sure. He will always be creating a smoke-screen with his vast pipe or Lew Grade cigars. The resulting smell is pretty pungent, so we call Fred's cigars 'Adam and Eve' – every time he's Adam, we Eve! But it is a small price to pay, and he wouldn't be Fred without them.

I am sure that after reading this book some of you will say, 'Oh, he hasn't mentioned so-and-so.' And you will be quite right. I have only written about other commentators with whom I have had the pleasure of working in OBs. Ever since I left the BBC in 1972 there has been a steady influx of new commentators, especially in the worlds of soccer, rugby and athletics. I have met and worked with many of them in various sports programmes but not on an outside broadcast, as I have really only been concerned with cricket and the Boat Race, as far as sports commentary is concerned.

I would like to wish all those commentators – as well as the ones whom I have mentioned – as much happiness, fun, enjoyment and job satisfaction as I have had during my broadcasting life. Commentators are a unique band. There are very few of us, and in spite of the travel, long hours, the stresses and the working conditions – often too cramped, too hot or too cold – we should all be extremely grateful for having such a wonderful job. People *do* sometimes complain, forgetting how lucky they are and that there are so many millions of people far worse off than themselves. Perhaps this story will remind them.

There was a young parachutist about to make his first jump from an aeroplane, and he was naturally very nervous and scared. His instructor tried to calm him down and told him that there was nothing to worry about.

'Just remember,' he said, 'when I give you a push count five and then pull the top ring on your parachute. *If*, by any chance, nothing happens, don't panic. Just count another five, and then pull the bottom ring. This will open your reserve parachute, and you will sail gracefully down to earth. Nothing to worry about at all.'

The learner was still shivering with fright but when they were at the right height and place, the instructor told him, 'Right, I am going to push you out now. Don't forget. Count five – top ring – count another five – bottom ring. And whatever you do, don't panic. Off you go. Good luck.'

With that, he pushed the learner out of the plane. The young man remembered what he had been told. He counted five, pulled the top ring and waited for something to happen. Nothing did. So again he remembered what he had been told. He counted another five and confidently pulled the bottom ring. But again – this time to his horror – nothing happened.

His pace increased and he was dropping at an alarming rate down to earth, when he suddenly spotted someone coming *up* towards him. It was a man in a peak cap and overalls, carrying a large spanner.

The parachutist – now in a complete state of panic – shouted at this man as he shot upwards towards him:

'Help! Help! Do you know anything about parachutes?'

'No, I'm afraid I don't,' replied the man in the peak cap as he shot past him. 'And what's more, I obviously know bugger all about gas boilers!'

PART II:
GUIDE TO CRICKET

9 Test matches – Six of the Best

THE FIRST EVER TEST MATCH was played at Melbourne between Australia and England in March 1877. Test matches were originally of three days' duration, but can in fact be any length of three days or over as agreed between the two countries playing. For instance in Australia between the wars, Tests were played to a finish; others in England have been four days, and there was the famous *timeless* Test at Durban in 1939 which ended in a draw after ten days because MCC had to catch the boat home!

I am now going to select what I consider to have been the six best out of the more than 250 Test matches on which I have commentated since 1946. I'm going to cheat a bit, though, and actually choose seven Tests. As the hors d'oeuvre I must include one at which I did not commentate. But how I wish that I had been there! I refer to the one and only tie ever to have happened in Test cricket.

AUSTRALIA v WEST INDIES – BRISBANE, 1960

In view of its fairy-tale finish perhaps the most remarkable thing about it was that up to noon on the last day it was just a very good game of cricket which, it seemed, after a hard struggle, Australia would win fairly easily. West Indies won the toss and batted first, making 453 with Sobers scoring a magnificent 132. Australia replied with 505 of which O'Neill made 181 – his biggest Test score – supported by Bobby Simpson with 92. In West Indies' second innings, Alan Davidson, who had taken five wickets for Australia in the first innings, again bowled superbly and thanks largely to his taking another six wickets West Indies were all out for 284 after half-an-hour's play on the fifth and final day of the match. This meant that Australia only had to score 233 to win at a rate of about 45 runs per hour – an easy task on paper even though Wes Hall did take a long time to bowl his overs.

They started disastrously, losing Simpson and Harvey for a mere 7 runs, and soon after lunch they were 57 for 5 with O'Neill, McDonald, and Favell all out. A stand of 35 between Mackay and Davidson took the score to 92 for 6 when Mackay was bowled by Ramadhin, and the Australian captain, Benaud, joined Davidson with only Grout, Meckiff and Kline to come. The odds had swung West Indies' way. At tea, the score was 110 for 6 and Australia needed 123 to win at a run a minute with four wickets in hand – quite possible, but it still looked like a West Indies victory.

Davidson and Benaud thought otherwise. They hit the bad balls for four and ran like stags between the wickets, turning ones into twos and half runs into quick singles. The game swung completely Australia's way and with ten minutes to go they needed only nine runs to win with Davidson and Benaud still going strong. It then looked as if Australia had this first Test in the bag. But now – as they say – read on!

Sobers bowled a ball down the leg-side to Benaud who pushed it for a single – eight to win. Davidson took another run off Sobers and so gave Benaud the strike – seven to win. Another ball pitched on the leg-stump and Benaud thought he would pinch another quick run by pushing it wide of Joe Solomon at forward square leg. But as he called for one and ran, Solomon threw in from side-on and hit the stumps with Davidson a yard out at the wicket-keeper's end. So Davidson was run out for his highest score in Test cricket – a fine 80 – and Australia with three wickets in hand still needed seven runs to win.

Wally Grout came in, played two balls from Sobers and then scored a single off the seventh ball of Sobers' over. Six to win and with Benaud failing to score off the last ball of the over, Grout was left at the striker's end to face Hall in what was certain to be the last over of the match as there were now only four minutes to go.

Hall went slowly back to his mark to start his long run – at that time by far the longest in the world. It was obviously essential for Grout to give Benaud the strike and as the first ball struck him somewhere on the body, the ball dropped at his feet and Benaud scampered up the pitch with Grout in considerable pain somehow reaching safety at the other end.

Five to win. Seven balls to go and Hall proceeded to bowl a

very fast bumper which Benaud tried to hook for four and so level the scores. But the ball hit his glove and he was well caught behind the wicket by Gerry Alexander. Benaud out for a captain's 52, still five runs to make for victory, now only six balls left and Ian Meckiff – no great shakes as a batsman – the next man in. He played the first ball without scoring, and missed the second which went through to Alexander standing a long way back. Grout, backing up, called Meckiff and they just managed a bye, with Alexander returning the ball quickly to Hall who threw it, but missed the stumps at the bowler's end. Four runs to win, with four balls left.

Hall next bowled a good length ball to Grout and it flew off the top edge of his bat to Kanhai at backward square leg. But to the horror of every West Indian present, Wes Hall following through fast, dashed for the catch himself and missed what would have been an easy enough catch for Kanhai. The batsman had taken one run, so now it was three balls to go and three runs to win.

Meckiff hit the next ball from Hall up in the air over mid-wicket and it looked a certain four and victory for Australia. But the grass in the outfield had not been mown that day and Conrad Hunte ran round the boundary and was able to pick up the ball which stopped a foot or so from the boundary. The batsmen had run two and were going for the third which would win the match, but in one fell swoop, Hunte picked up the ball and threw it eighty yards straight over the top of the stumps to Alexander. Grout flung himself at the crease but he was out – by a cat's whisker.

What a throw! What speed and accuracy! Just imagine the excitement. As the batsmen had run two, the scores were now level and one run was wanted for victory by Australia with two balls to go. This was Hall's eighteenth over of the innings and he must have been almost dropping. But he tore up to the bowling crease and bowled a fast one on the stumps to Kline who pushed it to forward short leg and ran. Once again Solomon was the fielder and once again – incredible to relate – he picked up and threw down the stumps from side-on with Meckiff just short of the crease. A roar, and up went the umpire's finger. Possibly the greatest, certainly the most exciting Test match had finished in a tie and I doubt if any of the twenty-two players would have wished for any other result.

FIRST TEST MATCH
Played at Brisbane, 9, 10, 12, 13 and 14 December
Match tied

WEST INDIES

C C Hunte	c Benaud b Davidson....	24	c Simpson b Mackay.....	39
C W Smith	c Grout b Davidson.......	7	c O'Neill b Davidson......	6
R B Kanhai	c Grout b Davidson.......	15	c Grout b Davidson.......	54
G S Sobers	c Kline b Meckiff...........	132	b Davidson	14
†F M M Worrell	c Grout b Davidson.......	65	c Grout b Davidson.......	65
J S Solomon	hit wkt b Simpson.........	65	lbw b Simpson	47
P D Lashley	c Grout b Kline.............	19	b Davidson	0
‡F C M Alexander	c Davidson b Kline........	60	b Benaud	5
S Ramadhin	c Harvey b Davidson.....	12	c Harvey b Simpson......	6
W W Hall	st Grout b Kline	50	b Davidson	18
A L Valentine	not out	0	not out	7
Extras	(lb 3, w 1).....................	4	(b 14, lb 7, w 2)	23
Total	....	453	....	284

AUSTRALIA

C C McDonald	c Hunte b Sobers...........	57	b Worrell	16
R B Simpson	b Ramadhin	92	c sub b Hall	0
R N Harvey	b Valentine......................	15	c Sobers b Hall	5
N C O'Neil	c Valentine b Hall..........	181	c Alexander b Hall	26
L E Favell	run out	45	c Solomon b Hall	7
K D Mackay	b Sobers	35	b Ramadhin	28
A K Davidson	c Alexander b Hall	44	run out	80
†R Benaud	lbw b Hall........................	10	c Alexander b Hall	52
‡A T W Grout	lbw b Hall........................	4	run out	2
I W Meckiff	run out	4	run out	2
L F Kline	not out	3	not out	0
Extras	(b 2, lb 8, nb 4, w 1).......	15	(b 2, lb 9, nb 3)...............	14
Total	....	505	....	232

BOWLING									FALL OF WICKETS			
AUSTRALIA	O	M	R	W	O	M	R	W	WI	E	WI	E
Davidson	30	2	135	5	24.6	4	87	6	1st	1st	2nd	2nd
Meckiff	18	0	129	1	4	1	19	0	1st 23	84	13	1
Mackay	3	0	15	0	21	7	52	1	2nd 42	138	88	7
Benaud	4	3	93	0	31	6	69	1	3rd 65	194	114	49
Simpson	8	0	25	1	7	2	18	2	4th 239	278	127	49
Kline	17.6	6	52	3	4	0	14	0	5th 243	381	210	57
O'Neil					1	0	2	0	6th 283	469	210	92
WEST INDIES												
Hall	29.3	1	140	4	17.7	3	63	5	7th 347	484	241	226
Worrell	30	0	93	0	16	3	41	1	8th 366	489	250	228
Sobers	32	0	115	2	8	0	30	0	9th 452	496	253	232
Valentine	24	6	82	1	10	4	27	0	10th 453	505	284	232
Ramadhin	15	1	60	1	17	3	57	1				

† Captain   ‡ Wicket-keeper

Umpires: C J Edgar and C Hoy

ENGLAND v AUSTRALIA – THE OVAL, 1953

Whenever I am asked which is my most memorable moment in Test cricket I invariably choose the last ball of the final Test between England and Australia at the Oval in 1953. The first four Tests had all been drawn but in this fifth and final Test, England, under a professional captain in Coronation year, won the match and the series and so regained the Ashes which Australia had held since 1934 – a period of nineteen years. As you can imagine, there were tremendous scenes of enthusiasm at the end of the game. I shall never forget the sight of Edrich and Compton fighting their way back to the pavilion through the converging crowd, though in fact it was only possible to follow their progress from their bats held aloft rather like two submarine periscopes.

For the fifth time in the series, Australia's captain, Hassett, won the toss, and England went into the field with an extra bowler – May and Trueman coming in for two batsmen, Watson and Simpson. But in spite of the Oval pitch's reputation for taking spin, Australia left out Benaud and had no genuine spinner in their side, something which later they were to regret.

Right from the start Bedser and Trueman bowled superbly and, helped by two showers which freshened up the pitch, soon had half the Australian side out for 118. But thanks to some splendid big hitting by Ray Lindwall, who made 62, Australia recovered and their last five wickets added 157 to give them a total of 275. England batted for two overs in the first evening before bad light stopped play. Hutton was nearly out off a bouncer from Lindwall. He snicked it on to his cap which slowed it down so that it dropped short of the slips. But in the process it knocked off his cap, which nearly hit the stumps, when, of course, he would have been out 'hit wicket'.

On the second day – Monday – England fared badly against Lindwall and Johnston, and in spite of a typical 82 from Hutton and a useful 39 from May, they finished with 235 for 7 with Bailey fighting back. Next morning, supported first by Trueman, then by Bedser, Bailey went on to make 64 and thanks to a last wicket partnership of 44 between him and Bedser, England finished 31 runs ahead.

This proved to Hutton that the pitch was growing easier and would no longer help the quicker bowlers. So when Australia went in and had only scored 19 runs, Hutton brought on his famous Surrey spinners, Laker and Lock. From that moment on Australia were in terrible trouble. An hour later they had lost five wickets for 61, only 30 runs ahead, thanks to Lock's great accuracy and Laker's spin. Ron Archer with a thrilling 49 tried to hit them out of trouble with a six and seven fours but the innings ended with the score at 162, Lock and Laker taking five and four wickets respectively. With three possible days and fifty minutes left for play (a sixth day could be used if necessary) England needed only 132 to win. Hutton was run out going for a second run when the score was 24 but at the close of play Edrich and May were still together and England needed only 94 to regain the Ashes.

There was tremendous tension and excitement on that last morning at the Oval and the runs came extremely slowly – only 24 in the first hour. Then, with the score at 88, May was out and in came Denis Compton to join his Middlesex 'twin' Bill Edrich. Slowly they added 35 runs and then at about 2.45 pm Hassett conceded defeat by putting himself on to bowl. Four runs were scored off his over and so with five runs needed he called to his vice-captain, Arthur Morris, to bowl his slow left-arm chinamen from the pavilion end. A single to Edrich, then Compton played the next two balls with exaggerated care – the crowd were on tenterhooks and they shouted encouragement and crowded round the boundary edge waiting to rush on to the field.

Then Morris bowled one of his off-spinners outside the leg stump. I was commentating on television at the time. 'This is it!' I thought, as I saw Compton play his famous sweep. But no! He hit it all right but the ball was magnificently fielded by Alan Davidson at backward short leg. Loud cheers and groans – the uproar was now continuous. The fifth ball was the same as the previous one – a slow off-break outside the leg stump. This time Compton made no mistake and hit the ball hard down towards the gas-holders.

Whether it ever got there I don't think anyone knows – ball and fielders were enveloped by the crowd and up in our television box, overcome by excitement and emotion, I was only able to shout hoarsely 'It's the Ashes, it's the Ashes.' By bowling those last five balls, Arthur Morris became the most televised Test bowler ever! From then on they were used as a demonstration film sequence in every television and radio shop in the land and were played for hour after hour, day after day. Such is fame!

FIFTH TEST MATCH
Played at the Oval, 15, 17, 18, 19, 20 and 21 August
England won in four days by 8 wickets

AUSTRALIA

Batsman	1st innings		2nd innings	
†A L Hassett	c Evans b Bedser	53	lbw b Laker	10
A R Morris	lbw b Bedser	16	lbw b Lock	26
K R Miller	lbw b Bailey	1	c Trueman b Laker	0
R N Harvey	c Hutton b Trueman	36	b Lock	1
G B Hole	c Evans b Trueman	37	lbw b Laker	17
J H de Courcy	c Evans b Trueman	5	run out	4
R G Archer	c and b Bedser	10	c Edrich b Lock	49
A K Davidson	c Edrich b Laker	22	b Lock	21
R R Lindwall	c Evans b Trueman	62	c Compton b Laker	12
‡G R A Langley	c Edrich b Lock	18	c Trueman b Lock	2
W A Johnston	not out	9	not out	6
Extras	(b 4, nb 2)	6	(b 11, lb 3)	
Total		275		162

ENGLAND

Batsman	1st innings		2nd innings	
†L Hutton	b Johnston	82	run out	17
W J Edrich	lbw b Lindwall	21	not out	55
P B H May	c Archer b Johnston	39	c Davidson b Miller	37
D C S Compton	c Langley b Lindwall	16	not out	22
T W Graveney	c Miller b Lindwall	4		
T E Bailey	b Archer	64		
‡T G Evans	run out	28		
J C Laker	c Langley b Miller	1		
G A R Lock	c Davidson b Lindwall	4		
F S Trueman	b Johnston	10		
A V Bedser	not out	22		
Extras	(b 9, lb 5, w 1)	15	(lb 1)	1
Total		306	(for 2 wkts)	132

BOWLING

ENGLAND	O	M	R	W		O	M	R	W
Bedser	29	3	88	3	...	11	2	24	0
Trueman	24.3	3	86	4	...	2	1	4	0
Bailey	14	3	42	1	...				
Lock	9	2	19	1	...	21	9	45	5
Laker	5	0	34	1	...	16.5	2	75	4
AUSTRALIA									
Lindwall	32	7	70	4	...	21	5	46	0
Miller	34	12	65	1	...	11	3	24	1
Johnston	45	16	94	3	...	29	14	52	0
Davidson	10	1	26	0	...				
Archer	10.3	2	25	1	...	1	1	0	0
Hole	11	6	11	0	...				
Hassett					...	1	0	4	0
Morris					...	0.5	0	5	0

FALL OF WICKETS

	A 1st	E 1st	A 2nd	E 2nd
1st	38	37	23	24
2nd	41	137	59	88
3rd	107	154	60	
4th	107	167	61	
5th	118	170	61	
6th	160	210	85	
7th	160	225	135	
8th	207	237	140	
9th	245	262	144	
10th	275	306	162	

† Captain ‡ Wicket-keeper

Umpires: D Davies and F S Lee

ENGLAND v WEST INDIES – LORD'S, 1963

I shall never forget the dramatic climax of the second Test at Lord's in 1963 between England and the West Indies. At the BBC it is famous as the Test which stopped the television News – literally. Because of the tremendous excitement at the finish I was told by our producer to say that we would stay at Lord's and not go over to Alexandra Palace for the usual 5.50 News – something quite unheard of at the BBC where the News is sacred. In fact someone up at Alexandra Palace must have had itchy fingers or perhaps disliked or knew nothing about cricket, for after listening to an over of commentary and not getting the finish they had expected, they quietly faded us and started the News – only to be swamped by telephone calls from irate viewers, one of whom happened to be the Director of BBC Television himself. So back they hurriedly came and viewers were able to share in one of the most thrilling finishes ever.

But right from the start the match was a winner – first one side was on top, then the other and so it went on for five days. England brought back Derek Shackleton at the age of thirty-eight and, captained by 'led Dexter, lost the toss. Frank Worrell chose to bat and Conrad Hunte hit the first three balls of the match off Freddie Trueman for four apiece. What a start! Poor Freddie was perhaps handicapped by a slippery run-up as rain had delayed the start. But for the rest of the day England were on top. At lunch the West Indies' score was only 47, Shackleton moving the ball all over the place but without any luck. Kanhai played attractively for 73, and Sobers, 42, and Solomon, 56, shared useful stands with him. But at the close of play West Indies were only 245 for 6, five of the wickets falling to Trueman, none to the unlucky Shackleton. But he made up for it the next morning, taking three wickets in four balls to finish off the West Indies' innings for a total of 301.

Then Charlie Griffith struck two early blows for the West Indies and with Edrich and Stewart out, England were 20 for 2 when Ken Barrington joined Ted Dexter. There followed a masterful display of power-driving and hooking by Ted Dexter. He lashed the fiery fast bowling all over the field. He reached his 50 in 48 minutes and hit ten fours in 81 minutes off 73 balls before being lbw to Sobers for 70. I give these details because for me this is still the best short Test innings I have ever seen. Dexter and Barrington had added 82 in an hour. But Cowdrey and Close failed and it was left to Barrington's 80 and Parks' 35 to help England to 244 for 7 at close of play. The pattern was much the same as the West Indies' innings on the day before. But in spite of a brave 52 not out by Freddie Titmus England were all out for 297 on the Saturday morning, four runs behind and with Charlie Griffith finishing with bowling figures of 5 for 91.

At the start of the West Indies' second innings the game swung right round once more in England's favour, Trueman and Shackleton dismissing five West Indies' batsmen for 104. Surely England were on top now? Yes, but by the close of play a fine partnership by Basil Butcher and Frank Worrell took the West Indies' score to 214 for 5 – a more than useful lead of 218 in a match where the bowlers were on top of the batsmen. But on Monday morning the see-saw started again and the West Indies' innings closed for 229 – the last five wickets falling for only 15 runs in six overs. Butcher made a great 133 and he and Worrell had added 110. Once again Trueman had done most of the damage, taking 5 for 52, giving him 11 for 152 in the match, supported by Shackleton with figures of 4 for 72.

So with just under eleven-and-a-half hours left to play, England needed 234 to win. Although such a total wouldn't be reached without a fight, there was all the time in the world and at this point English hopes were high. But as happened so often in this match they were soon to be dashed. Stewart, Edrich and Dexter were quickly out and England were 31 for 3, leaving 203 runs still needed when Cowdrey joined Barrington. Hall was bowling very fast and short and the ball was lifting danger-ously. The two batsmen stuck it bravely but when he had scored 19, Cowdrey received a cracking blow on the bone just above the left wrist and had to retire hurt.

The score was then 72 and an X-ray revealed that the bone was broken and the wrist was straightaway put into plaster. At that time no one knew whether Cowdrey would be available to resume batting or not, being sufficiently optimistic not to look so far ahead. But in bad light Barrington was playing one of his best Test innings, showing unusual aggression (he hit Gibbs for two sixes in one over) and with Close took the score to 116 for 3 when the light became too bad at 4.45 pm and play was abandoned for the day.

So England still needed 118 to win with six wickets in hand plus Cowdrey to keep one end up, if necessary. But Tuesday

131

was dark and wet, and play could not start until 2.20 pm. So now with Hall and Griffith averaging no more than fourteen overs per hour, time suddenly became an important factor, and England's chances were not helped by a very different Barrington from that of the day before. He made only 5 runs in 55 minutes and at the end of the first hour only 16 runs had been scored, which left 100 needed for victory in a possible 125 minutes. Close and Parks took the score to 158 and at tea the score was 171 for 5 with 63 runs needed in 85 minutes – still perfectly possible, but we kept reminding ourselves that with Cowdrey injured it was really 171 for 6 and that at the rate Hall and Griffith were bowling the run rate needed was at least $3^1/_2$ per over.

After tea Titmus and Trueman fell to successive balls from Hall, and with Allen as his partner Close began to charge down the pitch against the fast bowlers. He was trying to knock them off their length and although he scored some runs on the leg-side, it was too dangerous a tactic to last and he was caught down the leg-side by wicket-keeper Murray. Close had made seventy valuable runs and had batted with great courage, finishing up with his body a mass of bruises. And so with nineteen minutes left England were 219 for 8 when Shackleton joined Allen to try and get the fifteen runs needed for victory. They managed to sneak seven of these before Hall paced out his long run back to the pavilion to start the last over of the match. Six balls left. Eight runs needed. Allen and Shackleton were both *normally* good for twenty or so runs. I say normally because this occasion was far from that. They knew that at a pinch Cowdrey would come out to act as non-striker but (with a broken wrist) could hardly be expected to stand up to the thunderbolts of Hall.

The tension on the ground was unbearable. English supporters in the crowd were hushed; West Indians were shouting encouragement to their heroes – especially big Wes. The eyes and ears of Great Britain were also sharing in the scene through television and radio. Hall must have had memories of that final over at Brisbane as he set out on his long run. No score off the first ball, one run to Shackleton off the second and another to Allen off the third. Frank Worrell, the captain was calming and encouraging his side just as he had done at Brisbane, 'Relax fellows, relax.' He, as ever, looked the most relaxed of all as he stood quietly at forward short leg. Six runs were needed and only three balls left, so Shackleton clearly had to do something. He pushed the ball in front of him on the leg-side and called for a run. The ball went straight to Worrell who, true to his maxim, did not panic. He saw the thirty-eight-year-old Shackleton setting off for the bowler's end and made a quick decision. He wouldn't throw at the stumps – Wes Hall wasn't behind them anyway. He may or may not have remembered that he too was aged thirty-eight. Anyway, he backed himself to outsprint Shackleton and, turning with the ball, ran to the bowlers' end, knocking off the bails a split second before Shackleton arrived breathless at the crease. So Shackleton was run out and Cowdrey had to come in to join Allen.

Six runs still wanted, two balls to go. So in theory any of four results was possible but I don't believe that Allen ever intended to go for the runs. Had he scored an odd number, Cowdrey would have had to face a ball as a left-hander holding the bat with the right hand only. Of course you may ask why Allen didn't try to hit a six off the last ball. But be honest. Would you have done so? At all events he played the last two balls from Hall with a dead bat and the match was a draw – one of the greatest since cricket began and proof that for a game to be great one side needn't necessarily win. I think that both teams were equally happy to settle for a draw and so too, I think, were the spectators. Both sides deserved to win, neither deserved to lose.

SECOND TEST MATCH
Played at Lord's, 20, 21, 22, 24 and 25 June
Match drawn

WEST INDIES

C C Hunte	c Close b Trueman	44	c Cowdrey b Shackleton	7
E D A McMorris	lbw b Trueman	16	c Cowdrey b Trueman	8
G S Sobers	c Cowdrey b Allen	42	c Parks b Trueman	8
R B Kanhai	c Edrich b Trueman	73	c Cowdrey b Shackleton	21
B F Butcher	c Barrington b Trueman	14	lbw b Shackleton	133
J S Solomon	lbw b Shackleton	56	c Stewart b Allen	5
†F M M Worrell	b Trueman	0	c Stewart b Trueman	33
‡D L Murray	c Cowdrey b Trueman	20	c Parks b Trueman	2
W W Hall	not out	25	c Parks b Trueman	2
C C Griffith	c Cowdrey b Shackleton	0	b Shackleton	1
L R Gibbs	c Stewart b Shackleton	0	not out	1
Extras	(b 10, lb 1)	11	(b 5, lb 2, nb 1)	8
Total		301		229

ENGLAND

M J Stewart	c Kanhai b Griffith	2	c Solomon b Hall	17
J H Edrich	c Murray b Griffith	0	c Murray b Hall	8
†E R Dexter	lbw b Sobers	70	b Gibbs	2
K F Barrington	c Sobers b Worrell	80	c Murray b Griffith	60
M C Cowdrey	b Gibbs	4	not out	19
D B Close	c Murray b Griffith	9	c Murray b Griffith	70
‡J M Parks	b Worrell	35	lbw b Griffith	17
F J Titmus	not out	52	c McMorris b Hall	11
F S Trueman	b Hall	10	c Murray b Hall	0
D A Allen	lbw b Griffith	2	not out	4
D Shackleton	b Griffith	8	run out	4
Extras	(b 8, lb 8, nb 9)	25	(b 5, lb 8, nb 3)	16
Total		297	(9 wkts)	228

BOWLING

ENGLAND	O	M	R	W		O	M	R	W
Trueman	44	16	100	6	...	26	9	52	5
Shackleton	50.2	22	93	3	...	34	14	72	4
Dexter	20	6	41	0	...				
Close	9	3	21	0	...				
Allen	10	3	35	1	...	21	7	50	1
Titmus					...	17	3	47	0
WEST INDIES									
Hall	18	2	65	1	...	50	9	93	4
Griffith	26	6	91	5	...	30	7	59	3
Sobers	18	4	45	1	...	4	1	4	0
Gibbs	27	9	59	1	...	17	7	56	1
Worrell	13	6	12	2	...				

FALL OF WICKETS

	WI	E	WI	E
	1st	1st	2nd	2nd
1st	51	2	15	15
2nd	64	20	15	27
3rd	127	102	64	31
4th	145	115	84	130
5th	219	151	104	158
6th	219	206	214	203
7th	263	235	224	203
8th	297	274	228	228
9th	297	274	228	228
10th	301	297	229	

† Captain   ‡ Wicket-keeper   Umpires: J S Buller and W E Phillipson

WEST INDIES v ENGLAND – GEORGETOWN, GUYANA, 1968

I felt I must include in this book my most agonising draw, that is a match saved by England after a long-drawn-out struggle when all had seemed lost. An Australian writing a similar book would be sure to pick the Fourth Test v West Indies at Adelaide, 1961, when their last pair, Mackay and Kline, held out for an hour and fifty minutes to draw the match. Two Tests immediately came to my mind. First the Lord's Test of 1953 when England needed 343 to win, lost three quick wickets for 12 and with nearly five hours left were 73 for 4 when Trevor Bailey joined Willie Watson for their famous backs-to-the-wall stand of 163 for the fifth wicket. This undoubtedly saved England and I well remember the nail-biting tension of that long, hot summer afternoon.

But somehow there always seemed *some* hope that England would be able to draw. Unlike the fifth Test at Georgetown, Guyana on the MCC Tour of the West Indies in 1967–8. That Test was the climax of a hard, tough and thrilling series, where England, under Colin Cowdrey, so nearly won the first Test and almost lost the second after a bottle-throwing and tear-gas riot. After a dull draw in the third Test, England won the fourth after a sporting declaration from Gary Sobers. So you can imagine that when they came to play the last Test, one up in the series, they were determined not to be beaten whatever happened. And yet how near they came to disaster in a tremendous six-day battle.

West Indies won the toss on a slowish pitch and made 414, Kanhai and Sobers in a 250 partnership scored 150 and 152 respectively, and John Snow claimed four wickets. When England batted, Boycott made a typical century and with Cowdrey (59) added 172. But when Lock was joined by Pocock, England were 259 for 8 and it looked as if the series was going to slip from their grasp. Lock, however, hit magnificently and with Pocock defending stubbornly (he was nearly an hour-and-a-half without scoring), they added 109 for the ninth wicket – an English record against West Indies. Lock finished with 89 – the highest score of his first-class career – and England's total of 371 meant that they were 43 runs behind.

Except for a brilliant 49 by opening batsman Nurse and another great but more subdued innings of 95 not out by Sobers, the West Indies' batsmen in their second innings couldn't cope with John Snow. In seven balls, after lunch on the fifth day, he dismissed Nurse, Lloyd and Camacho, and then later came back just before the close to clean-bowl King, Hall and Gibbs. So Sobers ran out of partners and failed by five runs to score two hundreds in the match. West Indies were all out for 264 and England on the last day needed 308 runs to win. Boycott and Edrich got them off to a good start by quickly scoring 30 off the fast bowlers. But then on came Gibbs and Sobers to bowl spin and England collapsed in dramatic fashion, Gibbs taking four wickets for four runs in four overs. Sobers trapped Edrich with his googly, then Boycott, Graveney, Barrington and d'Oliveira all fell to Gibbs and England were 41 for 5 with just under four hours left.

Cowdrey was joined by Knott and although these two had batted superbly through the tour, I think every Englishman present at this moment saw only one result – a West Indies' victory and, with it, all Cowdrey's hopes and endeavours crashing to the ground. But somehow he and Knott stayed there against the wiles of Gibbs and Sobers who bowled over seventy overs between them in the innings. In an attempt to flurry the batsmen they got through their overs at a breathless pace, sacrificing somewhat their accuracy and direction in the process. Both batsmen used their pads more than one normally likes to see, but I must admit that at that stage I was prepared for them to do anything to survive, so long as it was legal! However, with 70 minutes still to go Cowdrey was lbw to Gibbs for 82. By a mixture of hitting the bad balls for four and keeping out the good balls they had added 127. But 70 minutes was a long time for tail-enders to last against the class spin of Gibbs and Sobers. Snow, who seemed to play *every* ball with his pads lasted 35 minutes before he, like Cowdrey, eventually misjudged the line and was lbw for a sterling 1.

Lock, somewhat desperate, lasted only eight minutes and Pocock for ten, being unluckily given out 'caught' first bounce. All this time, Knott was defending sternly but hitting anything loose and wide of the stumps for four – especially with his favourite cut. Pocock was out amidst scenes of unbelievable excitement and shouting from the now frenzied crowd. The last man in, Jeff Jones, had one ball from Gibbs to play and seemed to be in a complete daze. After all, his career batting average in first-class cricket was at that stage 4.09, so you can hardly blame him! Furthermore, he had been sitting watching this tense struggle all day and at close of play the night before could hardly have expected to be called on to play such a vital role! Anyway, with our hearts in our mouths we watched him lunge out with his pads at Gibbs and survive that one ball. Then Knott played an immaculate maiden over from Sobers. There was just time for one over and the result of the series depended on Jeff Jones.

The shouts from the crowd were deafening and it was impossible to give a fluent and coherent commentary. But somehow – and don't ask me how many times he hit the ball with his bat – Jeff Jones played out that last over, surrounded by the whole of the West Indies side. He might have let the ball hit his bat once but I mustn't exaggerate! But there he was 'not out' at the close of play, and gallant little Alan Knott had batted for nearly four-and-a-half hours for 73 not out, which remarkably contained no fewer than fifteen fours, so sure was his defence and so expert his dispatch of any bad ball. It is an innings he will never forget and certainly I don't want to go through such prolonged agony ever again.

FIFTH TEST MATCH
Played at Georgetown, 28, 29, 30, March, 1, 2 and 3 April
Match drawn

WEST INDIES

S M Nurse	c Knott b Snow	17	lbw b Snow	49
G S Camacho	c and b Jones	14	c Graveney b Snow	76
R B Kanhai	c Edrich b Pocock	150	c Edrich b Jones	22
B F Butcher	run out	18	c Lock b Pocock	18
†G S Sobers	c Cowdrey b Barrington	152	not out	95
C H Lloyd	b Lock	31	c Knott b Snow	1
D A J Holford	lbw b Snow	1	b Lock	3
‡D L Murray	c Knott b Lock	8	c Boycott b Pocock	16
L A King	b Snow	8	b Snow	20
W W Hall	not out	5	b Snow	7
L R Gibbs	b Snow	1	b Snow	0
Extras	(lb 3, w 2, nb 4)	9	(b 1, lb 2, w 1, nb 3)	7
Total		414		264

ENGLAND

G Boycott	c Murray b Hall	116	b Gibbs	30
J H Edrich	c Murray b Sobers	0	c Gibbs b Sobers	6
†M C Cowdrey	lbw b Sobers	59	lbw b Gibbs	82
T W Graveney	c Murray b Hall	27	c Murray b Gibbs	0
K F Barrington	c Kanhai b Sobers	4	c Lloyd b Gibbs	0
B L d'Oliveira	c Nurse b Holford	27	c and b Gibbs	2
‡A P E Knott	lbw b Holford	7	not out	73
J A Snow	b Gibbs	0	lbw b Sobers	1
G A R Lock	b King	89	c King b Sobers	2
P I Pocock	c and b King	13	c Lloyd b Gibbs	0
I J Jones	not out	0	not out	0
Extras	(b 12, lb 14, nb 3)	29	(b 9, w 1)	10
Total		371	(9 wkts)	206

BOWLING

ENGLAND	O	M	R	W		O	M	R	W
Jones	31	5	114	1	...	17	1	81	1
Snow	27.4	2	82	4	...	15.2	0	60	6
d'Oliveira	8	1	27	0	...	8	0	28	0
Pocock	38	11	78	1	...	17	1	66	2
Barrington	18	4	43	1	...				
Lock	28	7	61	2	...	9	1	22	1
WEST INDIES									
Sobers	37	15	72	3	...	31	16	53	3
Hall	19	3	71	2	...	13	6	26	0
King	38.2	11	79	2	...	9	1	11	0
Holford	31	10	54	2	...	17	9	37	0
Gibbs	33	9	59	1	...	40	20	60	6
Butcher	5	3	7	0	...	10	7	9	0

FALL OF WICKETS

	WI	E	WI	E
	1st	1st	2nd	2nd
1st	29	13	78	33
2nd	35	185	84	37
3rd	72	185	86	37
4th	322	194	133	39
5th	385	240	171	41
6th	387	252	201	168
7th	399	257	216	198
8th	400	259	252	200
9th	412	368	264	206
10th	414	371	264	

† Captain   ‡ Wicket-keeper   Umpires: C Jordan and C Kippins

ENGLAND v AUSTRALIA – THE OVAL, 1968

My next choice is another Test which England won, thanks largely to the efforts of a volunteer ground staff who made it possible for play to be restarted on the last day when it appeared that a cloudburst had robbed England of a well-deserved victory. This was the fifth Test against Australia at the Oval in 1968. After losing the first Test, England were robbed of victory by bad weather in at least two of the following three, so that they had to win at the Oval to level the series. Cowdrey won the toss and England made 494 thanks to Edrich (164) and d'Oliveira, who made 158. D'Oliveira had been recalled to the England side at the last moment and until this fine attacking innings he had not been on many people's list for the forthcoming MCC tour of South Africa. The subsequent row which led to the cancellation of the tour is now cricket history.

Lawry was top scorer for Australia in their first innings with 135, but they were all out for 324 – 170 behind, due to some fine fast bowling by Snow and Brown who each took three wickets. But time was slipping away for England – it was already after lunch on the fourth day – and if they wanted to have a chance of winning they had to score runs quickly. This they did being all out for 181 in three hours – all the main batsmen flinging their bats at the ball. Australia therefore needed 352 to win in six-and-a-half hours. That evening they lost both Lawry and Redpath. On the fifth morning the sun was still shining, as it had done throughout the match but there were ominous dark clouds gathering around the Oval. Underwood got Chappell and Walters, and Snow caught Sheahan off Illingworth, Inverarity being the only Australian batsman to show any real confidence. He and Jarman were together at lunch when Australia's score stood at 86 for 5.

With three-and-a-half hours left, it looked odds on an England victory. But during the lunch interval there was a colossal cloudburst. Within half an hour the whole ground was a lake and, though the hot sun reappeared at 2.15 pm, no one seriously thought there would be any more play in the match. No one, that is, except Colin Cowdrey and the groundsman Ted Warne. Cowdrey *paddled* out to inspect the damage and miraculously the big lake changed slowly into a number of mini-lakes as the water began draining away. Then Ted Warne and his ground staff, supported by a large number of volunteers from the crowd, got to work with blankets, mops, squeegees and brooms. Incredible to relate, the umpires decided play could restart at 4.45 pm, which meant that Australia had to survive for 75 minutes or England take their last five wickets in that time. Inverarity and Jarman defended stoutly for 38 minutes. The pitch was dead and Cowdrey switched his bowlers from end to end and crowded the batsmen with close fielders – all to no avail.

Then came the breakthrough which England needed. Cowdrey brought on d'Oliveria and in his second over he got a ball to hit Jarman's off-stump as he stretched forward and Australia were 110 for 6 with 35 minutes to go. For the next half an hour we were to watch some of the most gripping cricket which I personally have ever seen. Underwood at once came on in place of d'Oliveira, the fielders crowded even closer round the bat and the pitch which had had hot sun on it for nearly three hours began to come to life. Underwood got lift and turn, and batting, though not impossible, must have been a nightmare. Mallett and McKenzie were well caught by Brown at forward short leg in Underwood's first over of his new spell – 110 for 7, 110 for 8 and about 25 minutes left. In came Gleeson smiling cheerfully as usual, even in this crisis for his country. He actually shook hands with some of the close fielders as he took up his stance at the wicket! He lasted gallantly for nearly a quarter of an hour before being bowled by Underwood.

The score was 120 for 9 as Connolly strode out to join Inverarity with ten minutes left. Inverarity had been in for four hours but only six minutes before time his concentration lapsed for once and he played no stroke at a ball from Underwood which didn't turn as much as he expected and struck him on the pad. There was a shout from everyone in the England side – the *farthest* fielder only ten yards from the batsman. Without hesitation up went umpire Charlie Elliott's right arm and Inverarity was out for 56 and Australia for 125. England had won on the post by 226 runs.

It will look an easy enough victory in the record books but an unsuspecting reader will never know how close it was. England had a lot for which to thank Underwood as he finished with figures of 7 for 50. But there is no doubt that their greatest debt was to the anonymous band of voluntary 'driers-up' who helped Ted Warne and his men to make a playable cricket ground out of a lake.

FIFTH TEST MATCH
Played at The Oval, 22, 23, 24, 26 and 27 August
England won by 226 runs

ENGLAND

J H Edrich	b Chappell	164	c Lawry b Mallett	17
C Milburn	b Connolly	8	c Lawry b Connolly	18
E R Dexter	b Gleeson	21	b Connolly	28
†M C Cowdrey	lbw b Mallett	16	b Mallett	35
T W Graveney	c Redpath b McKenzie	63	run out	12
B L d'Oliveira	c Inverarity b Mallett	158	c Gleeson b Connolly	9
‡A P E Knott	c Jarman b Mallett	28	run out	34
R Illingworth	lbw b Connolly	8	b Gleeson	10
J A Snow	run out	4	c Sheahan b Gleeson	13
D L Underwood	not out	9	not out	1
D J Brown	c Sheahan b Gleeson	2	b Connolly	1
Extras	(b 1, lb 11, w 1)	13	(lb 3)	3
Total		494		181

AUSTRALIA

†W M Lawry	c Knott b Snow	135	c Milburn b Brown	4
R J Inverarity	c Milburn b Snow	1	lbw b Underwood	56
I R Redpath	c Cowdrey b Snow	67	lbw b Underwood	8
I M Chappell	c Knott b Brown	10	lbw b Underwood	2
K D Walters	c Knott b Brown	5	c Knott b Underwood	1
A P Sheahan	b Illingworth	14	c Snow b Illingworth	24
‡B N Jarman	st Knott b Illingworth	0	b d'Oliveira	21
G D McKenzie	b Brown	12	c Brown b Underwood	0
A A Mallett	not out	43	c Brown b Underwood	0
J W Gleeson	c Dexter b Underwood	19	b Underwood	5
A N Connolly	b Underwood	3	not out	0
Extras	(b 4, lb 7, nb 4)	15	(lb 4)	4
Total		324		125

BOWLING

AUSTRALIA	O	M	R	W		O	M	R	W
McKenzie	40	8	87	1	...	4	0	14	0
Connolly	57	12	127	2	...	22.4	2	65	4
Walters	6	2	17	0	...				
Gleeson	41.2	8	109	2	...	7	2	22	2
Mallett	36	11	87	3	...	25	4	77	2
Chappell	21	5	54	1	...				
ENGLAND									
Snow	35	12	67	3	...	11	5	22	0
Brown	22	5	63	3	...	8	3	19	1
Illingworth	48	15	87	2	...	28	18	29	1
Underwood	54.3	21	89	2	...	31.3	19	50	7
d'Oliveira	4	2	3	0	...	5	4	1	1

FALL OF WICKETS

	A 1st	E 1st	A 2nd	E 2nd
1st	28	7	23	4
2nd	84	136	53	13
3rd	113	151	67	19
4th	238	161	90	29
5th	359	185	114	65
6th	421	188	126	110
7th	458	237	149	110
8th	468	269	179	110
9th	489	302	179	120
10th	494	324	181	125

† Captain ‡ Wicket-keeper

Umpires: C S Elliott and A E Fagg

AUSTRALIA v ENGLAND – SYDNEY, 1971

Commentating on winning the Ashes at the Oval in 1953 is a moment I shall never forget but one which I was lucky enough to be able to repeat when England regained the Ashes in the seventh Test at Sydney in February 1971. Once again – this time on radio – I was able to describe the final ball which brought the Ashes back to England, so I must include this final Test also in my selection. Even without that special quality which the Ashes gives to Test matches this was one of the most tense and closely fought Tests I have ever seen and like all really great games the fortunes of the two sides changed almost hourly throughout the five days.

To the relief of the England camp, Australia dropped Lawry and failed to select McKenzie. Had they played I feel sure the result would have been different. This is not a criticism of their new captain, Ian Chappell, who did a very good job and, on winning the toss, put England in to bat. England were without Boycott who had broken his arm, and on a lively pitch in a humid atmosphere had only scored 11 for 1 wicket at the end of the first hour. Luckhurst, for once, failed. Had McKenzie been bowling he must have taken some wickets. As it was, the inexperienced opening pair of Lillee and Dell bowled too short and were very wild in their direction.

Even so, England struggled for most of the day. Edrich made 30 and Fletcher 33, but with d'Oliveira out for 1 they were 69 for 4 when Illingworth came to the wicket to play yet another of his rescue-act innings. Hampshire went for 10, but Knott lasted over an hour for a useful 27. By this time the two spinners Jenner and O'Keeffe were bowling really well. The pitch was taking spin and the innings closed for 184 with Illingworth eighth man out, bowled by Jenner's googly for the top score of 42. Jenner and O'Keeffe each took three wickets, and Chappell's gamble had come off in spite of the poor support from his fast bowlers. But Illingworth was luckier with his. Both Snow and Lever took a wicket in the half-hour left for play, and at the close Australia were 13 for 2 with both Eastwood and Stackpole out.

There was a hard tussle the next morning and in the two hours before lunch Australia added 71 and lost the wickets of night-watchman Marsh and their captain, Ian Chappell. But after lunch Walters and Redpath added 63 in the first hour.

Walters led a charmed life, being missed at slip off Underwood and at deep third man by Underwood off Willis. It also looked as if Knott had stumped him when he took a ball in front of the stumps off a mishit from Walters who was out of his crease. But it was great cricket to watch and a fascinating battle between the footwork of Redpath and Walters and the flight and change of pace of Underwood. He got them both in the end, Walters going yards down the pitch only to be stumped and Redpath giving a catch to the bowler when he had made 59. At tea the score was 165 for 6 representing a considerable drop in the scoring rate – only 18 runs coming in the second hour. O'Keeffe was soon out after tea, and with Greg Chappell and Jenner together the new ball was taken.

Then followed the famous 'walk off' incident. I was broadcasting at the time so most of what happened is clear in my mind. For the rest I have checked and double-checked what happened out in the middle. I have set out the facts below so that you can judge for yourself and make up your own mind what you would have done had you been the captain in Illingworth's place – always remembering that you had a chance to sit back and think whereas he had to act on the spur of the moment.

The first two overs with the new ball were bowled by Snow and Lever with no suspicion of a bouncer. With the seventh ball of the third over, Snow, however, did bowl a bouncer at Jenner who ducked into it, was hit on the back of the head, collapsed, and had to be carried off. The crowd naturally enough booed and shouted, roaring their disapproval of Snow. While the new batsman Lillee was on his way out to the wicket, Lou Rowan, the umpire at Snow's end, told Snow that he should not have bowled a bouncer at a low-order batsman like Jenner. Snow became incensed at this and asked Rowan in not too polite a way whose side he thought he was on. Umpire Rowan then seemed to lose his temper and in what appeared to be an emotional decision, promptly warned Snow under Law 46 Note 4(IV) for persistent bowling of short-pitched balls. Then it was Illingworth's turn to protest at what he considered a wrong interpretation of the law. How could one bouncer come under the heading of persistent? Unfortunately, in the heat of the moment, Illingworth also became annoyed and was seen by thousands on the ground and tens of thousands on television to wag his finger at Lou Rowan. What in fact he was trying to indicate was that Snow had only bowled 'one' bouncer. He was not trying to admonish the umpire.

Amid a storm of booing – I've seldom heard such a noise on a cricket ground – Snow completed his over by bowling one ball at Lillee. He then turned to go off to his position at long leg. When he had got halfway there some beer cans were thrown in his direction from the small Paddington Hill to the left of the Noble Stand. Snow turned back and returned to the square where Illingworth told the umpires that he would not go on playing until the field was cleared of the cans. The team sat down whilst this was being done by the ground staff. After a few minutes the ground was clear and Snow set off again for long leg.

I remember saying on the air at the time that I thought the whole incident was going to end happily as members in the Noble Stand and people on the Hill started to applaud Snow and a man stretched out over the railings to shake hands with Snow. Snow went up and shook hands but a tough-looking spectator who had obviously 'had a few' then grabbed hold of Snow's shirt and started to shake him. This was the signal for more cans and bottles to come hurtling on to the field, narrowly missing Snow. Willis ran up and shouted something to the crowd. Then Illingworth came up, saw the bottles flying and promptly signalled to his team to leave the field.

The two batsmen and two umpires stayed on the square. Then the two umpires made their way to the pavilion – the first time they had left the square since the trouble started. Rowan made it plain to Illingworth that if he did not continue he would forfeit the match and an announcement was made that play would be resumed as soon as the ground had been cleared, not only of the cans and bottles but also a number of spectators who had clambered over the fence. This, in fact, took only ten minutes and Illingworth led his men back thirteen minutes after leading them off. In the remaining forty minutes, the England side somewhat naturally seemed to have lost their zest, and Chappell and Lillee added 45 runs so that Australia finished the day at 235 for 7 – a lead of 51.

That was the incident as I saw it, though it is true to say that opinions differ about what exactly did happen. I said at the time, and I still believe, that Illingworth was right to lead the side off. Not only was it becoming dangerous with bottles flying around, but this action so stunned the crowd that the throwing stopped immediately and play was very soon restarted. In other similar circumstances in the West Indies, the fielding side had stayed on the field and play had to be abandoned for the day. There was, of course, no excuse for Illingworth to argue in such a demonstrative manner with the umpire. He has since publicly said he was sorry he acted as he did and also concedes that he should have gone back to the square and warned the umpires that he was taking his team off. But he had to make a quick decision and it is surprising that neither umpire left the square at any time to go to deal with the incident at the trouble spot.

Illingworth and Snow have also been criticised for Snow's return to long leg after the first lot of cans had been thrown at him. There are two views about this. As captain, you either take the peaceful way out and give way to force and threats or you stick to your right to place your fieldsmen where you like. And finally, Snow was criticised for going up to the fence and accepting the proffered handshake. Who can say what the reaction would have been if he hadn't? I apologise for dealing at such length with this unhappy incident and now you must judge for yourselves. Meanwhile, let's get back to the cricket which continued on the Sunday morning.

Lillee was out to the first ball of the day, caught by Knott off Willis, who two overs later bowled Greg Chappell behind his legs for a fighting 65. Jenner came in at the fall of the first wicket, showing no after-effects from his injury and he made a bright 30 before being last man out, bowled by Lever. Australia were all out for 264, giving them a lead of 80 runs, and in the 70 minutes before lunch, Luckhurst and Edrich put on 60 with the former playing some brilliant strokes. He was out soon after lunch for 59, Fletcher made 20 and by tea England had made very slow progress to reach a score of 130 for 2. Two more wickets, Edrich 57 and Hampshire 24, fell before the close when England were 228 for 4 – leading by 149 runs. They owed a lot to d'Oliveira and Illingworth who stayed together for the last hour-and-a-half and added 64. But next morning Illingworth was soon lbw to Lillee for 29 and d'Oliveria caught in the slips off Lillee for 47. Only 34 runs came in the first hour – Knott making 15 of them. England had still not anywhere near enough runs.

However, Lever and Snow each hit out scoring 17 and 20 respectively, but when England were all out for 302, they had lost their last six wickets for only 73 runs – O'Keeffe with three wickets again looking the most dangerous Australian bowler. Australia needed 223 runs to win in fifteen-and-a-half hours (a sixth day could be used if necessary) – an easy enough task most people thought, even though Australia had not got the steadying influence of Lawry.

They made a bad start – Snow yorking Eastwood for 0 in the first over. But then came tragedy for England. Stackpole hit a short ball from Lever high in the direction of long leg. Snow ran in to make the catch but came too far. He turned to try to make the catch before the ball went over the boundary but somehow overbalanced and caught the little finger of his bowling hand in the fence and broke it. He went off in great pain with the bone protruding through the skin – a horrid sight. Umpire Lou Rowan signalled six although in fact the ball had hit the fence and had not gone full pitch over it. This was the testing time for England, already without their best batsman and now cruelly robbed of their best bowler.

But Illingworth outwardly remained as calm as usual, though what he was thinking one can well imagine. Were the Ashes going to slip away from him after all? But the team rallied round him magnificently, Lever soon got Ian Chappell for 6, Illingworth himself had Redpath caught for 14 and bowled Stackpole, sweeping, for yet another fine innings of 67. At the close of play, Australia were 123 for 5 with Chappell and Marsh the not-out batsmen. The other wicket to fall had been Walters who again showed his dislike of fast bowling. This time he played an incredible shot – an upper cut – off a short ball from Willis and was caught chest-high on the boundary in front of the pavilion at third man! So with two days to go if necessary, Australia needed exactly 100 to win and it was really anybody's match, with the Australians tending to think England would win, and vice versa.

Once again the England side backed up Illingworth superbly and he himself, in his longest bowling spell of the series, bowled magnificently. Underwood bowled Marsh, hitting desperately across the line, for 16, and the score was 131 for 6. Knott stumped Chappell off Illingworth – 142 for 7, but O'Keeffe put up a stout defence and had been in for nearly an hour when Illingworth brought on d'Oliveira who virtually finished off the match. He dismissed O'Keeffe and Lillee in successive balls and though Dell saved the hat-trick and hung on with

Jenner for twelve tense minutes, at 12.37 pm it was all over and the Ashes were ours. Jenner snicked a ball on to his pads and it flew to Fletcher at silly point who made the catch and the England team made straight for their captain, Illingworth, and carried him off the field.

England had won by 62 runs and what a wonderful cricket match it had been. It was of course a personal triumph for Illingworth who led his team magnificently in the field, encouraging and sustaining their morale. In addition he had borne the brunt of the bowling after Snow went off and his second innings figures of 20–7–39–3 did much to win the match. But it was also essentially a team effort and I shall always be glad that I was there to share their happiness in their hour of triumph on bringing back the Ashes to England after twelve years.

THE SEVENTH TEST MATCH
Played at Sydney, 12, 13, 14, 16 and 17 February
England won by 62 runs

ENGLAND

Batsman	First Innings		Second Innings	
J H Edrich	c G Chappell b Dell	30	c I Chappell b O'Keeffe	57
B W Luckhurst	c Redpath b Walters	0	c Lillee b O'Keeffe	59
K W R Fletcher	c Stackpole b O'Keeffe	33	c Stackpole b Eastwood	20
J H Hampshire	c Marsh b Lillee	10	c I Chappell b O'Keeffe	24
B L d'Oliveira	b Dell	1	c I Chappell b Lillee	47
†R Illingworth	b Jenner	42	lbw b Lillee	29
‡A P E Knott	c Stackpole b O'Keeffe	27	b Dell	15
J A Snow	b Jenner	7	c Stackpole b Dell	20
P Lever	c Jenner b O'Keeffe	4	c Redpath b Jenner	17
D L Underwood	not out	8	c Marsh b Dell	0
R G D Willis	b Jenner	11	not out	2
Extras	(b 4, lb 4, w 1, nb 2)	11	(b 3, lb 3, nb 6)	12
Total		184		302

AUSTRALIA

Batsman	First Innings		Second Innings	
K H Eastwood	c Knott b Lever	5	b Snow	0
K R Stackpole	b Snow	6	b Illingworth	67
‡R W Marsh	c Willis b Lever	4	b Underwood	16
†I M Chappell	b Willis	25	c Knott b Lever	6
I R Redpath	c and b Underwood	59	c Hampshire b Illingworth	14
K D Walters	st Knott b Underwood	42	c d'Oliveira b Willis	1
G S Chappell	b Willis	65	st Knott b Illingworth	30
K J O'Keeffe	c Knott b Illingworth	3	c sub. b d'Oliveira	12
T J Jenner	b Lever	30	c Fletcher b Underwood	4
D K Lillee	c Knott b Willis	6	c Hampshire b d'Oliveira	0
A R Dell	not out	3	not out	3
Extras	(lb 5, w 1, nb 10)	16	(b 2, nb 5)	7
Total		264		160

BOWLING

AUSTRALIA	O	M	R	W	O	M	R	W
Lillee	13	5	32	1	14	0	43	2
Dell	16	8	32	2	26.7	3	65	3
Walters	4	0	10	1	5	0	18	0
G Chappell	3	0	9	0				
Jenner	16	3	42	3	21	5	39	1
O'Keeffe	24	8	48	3	26	8	96	3
Eastwood					5	0	21	1
Stackpole					3	1	8	0
ENGLAND								
Snow	18	2	68	1	2	1	7	1
Lever	14.6	3	43	3	12	2	23	1
d'Oliveira	12	3	24	0	5	1	15	2
Willis	12	1	58	3	9	1	32	1
Underwood	16	3	39	2	13.6	5	28	2
Illingworth	11	3	16	1	20	7	39	3
Fletcher					1	0	9	0

FALL OF WICKETS

	WI	E	WI	E
	1st	1st	2nd	2nd
1st	5	11	94	0
2nd	60	13	130	22
3rd	68	32	158	71
4th	69	66	165	82
5th	98	147	234	96
6th	145	162	251	131
7th	156	178	276	142
8th	165	235	298	154
9th	165	239	299	154
10th	184	264	302	160

† Captain   ‡ Wicket-keeper   Umpires: T F Brooks and L P Rowan

ENGLAND v AUSTRALIA – HEADINGLEY, 1981

My sixth and final choice must be this remarkable Test which England won by 18 runs. It is true to say that no Test match in my time has had a bigger effect on the cricketing public. There was drama before it even started. England, under the captaincy of Ian Botham, narrowly lost the first Test at Trent Bridge largely due to a spate of dropped catches. The second Test at Lord's was drawn with Botham making a 'pair' and promptly resigning the captaincy.

So the third Test at Headingley saw Mike Brearley return as captain of England. Everyone was wondering how Botham would react to playing under someone else and whether Brearley could help him recapture the all-round form which he so sadly seemed to have lost.

So far as Brearley was concerned it was not a very encouraging start. He lost the toss and Australia batted first making 401 for 9 declared. But Botham salvaged *his* reputation by taking 6 for 95. Brearley's misfortunes continued. England were all out for 174 of which he made 10, and when England followed on he was again out for a small score – 14. England were soon 135 for 7 with Botham still there firing on all cylinders, but with England still 92 runs behind with just three wickets to fall.

From then on the fairy-tale of this amazing Test changed from fantasy to sensational fact. Graham Dilley joined Botham. They had a short conference and are said to have decided that the only solution to such a desperate situation was to give it 'a bit of humty'. In other words they were going to attack and try to dominate the Australian bowlers. And how well they succeeded. Dilley is a left-hander, very strong and by nature a clean hitter. At the other end was Botham now in a ferocious mood and playing some highly unorthodox but brilliantly effective strokes. Together for the eighth wicket they added 117 in 80 minutes – only 7 short of an English record against Australia.

The bowling was in disarray, and when Dilley was finally bowled by Alderman for 56 – at that time his highest first-class score – Botham was joined by Chris Old. These two added another 67 runs and at close of play England were 351 for 9, Willis somehow lasting out for 45 minutes. They now had the slender lead of 124 runs but what a dramatic change from the position three hours earlier. Botham was 149 not out – a fantastic innings. His hundred included one six and nineteen fours – 82 runs in boundaries. That speaks for itself and confirmed for many of us that he is the finest hitter of a cricket ball that we have ever seen.

But back to the drama of the final day. Botham managed to hit one more four before Willis was out for one of the best two's he has ever scored! Australia needed only 130 runs to win, so perhaps it was not so surprising that Lillee and Marsh accepted Ladbroke's generous odds of 500–1 against an England victory!

England's batting recovery had been sensational enough. But what was to follow was even more unbelievable. Brearley started off with Botham bowling downhill from the Kirkstall Lane end and with Willis trundling uphill and upwind from the Football Stand end. This worked, because Botham soon got Wood caught by Taylor behind the wicket and Australia were 13 for 1. But then nothing happened for over an hour. Dilley was tried, Old replaced Botham, and Australia progressed steadily to 56 for 1 – only 74 runs needed for victory with nine wickets in hand.

Brearley then switched Willis to the Kirkstall Lane end. It was like a magician waving his wand. Willis began to bowl faster than we had ever seen him. He produced prodigious bounce out of this fairly placid pitch. As a bowler he was transformed and accomplished the finest bowling performance of his career. It was fantastic cricket. The crowd began to roar, life in Great Britain came to a halt. Every television set and radio in the country must have been tuned in to hear the Australian wickets tumbling at an extraordinary rate, 56 for 1 soon became 75 for 8, six of the wickets falling to Willis. There was a short desperate stand of 35 between Lillee and Bright which took the score up to 110, and Australia must have begun to think that they would just manage to snatch a victory, which by all reasonable expectations, should have been theirs the previous afternoon. But Willis was still inspired. He took the last two wickets to finish with his best ever analysis of 8 for 43 and England had won by 18 runs. It must certainly rank as the most astonishing turnaround in any Test match. It was impossible to take it in at the time. It was all so incredible.

It was clearly Botham's and Willis's match and thanks to them Brearley had succeeded in creating a new spirit of enthusiasm throughout the country. Cricket became the main talking point whenever people met. Two more amazing performances by Botham (5 for 11 at Edgbaston, and 118 in 123 minutes including six sixes at Old Trafford) enabled England to win the series 3–1 and so retain the Ashes.

THIRD TEST MATCH
Played at Headingley, 16, 17, 18, 20 and 21 July
England won by 18 runs

ENGLAND

Batsman	1st dismissal	1st	2nd dismissal	2nd
G Boycott	b Lawson	12	lbw b Alderman	46
G A Gooch	lbw Alderman	2	c Alderman b Lillee	0
†J M Brearley	c Marsh b Alderman	10	c Alderman b Lillee	14
D I Gower	c Marsh b Lawson	24	c Border b Alderman	9
M W Gatting	lbw Lillee	15	lbw Alderman	1
P Willey	b Lawson	8	c Dyson b Lillee	33
I T Botham	c Marsh b Lillee	50	not out	149
‡R W Taylor	c Marsh b Lillee	5	c Bright b Alderman	1
R G D Willis	not out	1	c Border b Alderman	2
G R Dilley	c and b Lillee	13	b Alderman	56
C M Old	c Border b Alderman	0	b Lawson	29
Extras		34		16
Total		174		356

AUSTRALIA

Batsman	1st dismissal	1st	2nd dismissal	2nd
J Dyson	b Dilley	102	c Taylor b Willis	34
G M Wood	lbw b Botham	34	c Taylor b Botham	10
T M Chappell	c Taylor b Willey	27	c Taylor b Willis	8
†K J Hughes	c and b Botham	99	c Botham b Willis	0
G N Yallop	c Taylor b Botham	58	c Gatting b Willis	0
A R Border	lbw b Botham	8	b Old	0
‡R W Marsh	b Botham	28	c Dilley b Willis	4
R J Bright	b Dilley	7	b Willis	19
D K Lillee	not out	3	c Gatting b Willis	17
G F Lawson	c Taylor b Botham	13	c Taylor b Willis	1
T M Alderman	not out	0	not out	0
Extras		32		18
Total (9 wkts dec.)		401		111

BOWLING

AUSTRALIA	O	M	R	W		O	M	R	W
Lillee	18.5	7	49	4	...	25	6	94	3
Alderman	19	4	59	3	...	35.3	6	135	6
Lawson	13	3	32	3	...	23	4	96	1
Bright					...	4	0	15	0
ENGLAND									
Willis	30	8	72	0	...	15.1	3	43	8
Old	43	14	91	0	...	9	1	21	1
Dilley	27	4	78	2	...	2	0	11	0
Botham	39.2	11	95	6	...	7	3	14	1
Willey	13	2	31	1	...	3	1	4	0
Boycott	3	2	2	0	...				

FALL OF WICKETS

	WI 1st	E 1st	WI 2nd	E 2nd
1st	12	55	0	13
2nd	40	149	18	56
3rd	42	196	37	58
4th	84	220	41	58
5th	87	332	105	65
6th	112	354	133	68
7th	148	357	135	74
8th	166	396	252	75
9th	167	401	319	110
10th	174		356	111

† Captain ‡ Wicket-keeper

Umpires: B J Meyer and D L Evans

PART III:
IT'S BEEN A PIECE OF CAKE

10 Happy Memories

I SUPPOSE MOST OF US from time to time sit back and reflect on our lives. I know I do, and every time I feel a little ashamed that the game of cricket has played such a large part in mine. First of all following the scores in the papers, then reading some of the many books. Playing it, of course, and merely watching it as a spectator, and finally for well over half of my life earning some of my living by commentating on it. All that time spent on just a game! Or is it something more than that? Many of us believe that it is. More than anything else in my life it taught me to try to work and play with others, and to be a member of a team. I was taught the importance of improving my own performance by practice, dedication and discipline; and to accept the umpire's decision, to win or lose gracefully and to take the inevitable disappointments with a smile. These are the ideals and I am not boasting or pretending that I have ever lived up to them, but they do explain the phrase 'it's not cricket'.

Far more indelible than memories of games played or watched are the happy recollections of countless friendships resulting entirely from a mutual love of cricket. I was lucky to collect a growing band of friends as I progressed through life. School, university, business, the war and club cricket provided many of them. And then, beyond my wildest dreams, when I joined the BBC in 1946 and became a commentator, Test and county cricketers gave me *their* friendship. I shall always treasure this. Here was I, a humble (?!) club cricketer accepted by the greats in the game. It has made my time in the commentary box a supremely happy one, and I shall always be grateful to them, and to all my colleagues in the commentary box.

One great bonus which cricket has given to the world is its humour and its literature. More stories are told about its characters, and more books have been and are being written about it, than of all other games put together. It is something which makes it unique in sport and enables those of us past our playing days to relive matches and to meet and learn about all the players which cricket has produced.

I have commentated on more than 250 Test matches either on television or on radio. So I feel the time is right for me to try to portray, and to pay tribute to, some of the players and characters, and to try to recapture the tremendous pleasure which their skills and performances have given to me. With two exceptions I will only write about those on whom I have personally commentated. They are my own personal choice, and inevitably other people's favourites will be left out. I don't suppose they will mind, but if they do I am sorry. There is a limit to the size even of a cricket book, however.

I have chosen fifty. I am very conscious of the fact that I have left out many fine players, especially from overseas – such as Michael Holding and Malcolm Marshall. I have also had to leave out some of my good companions on tours, who provided so much fun and laughter as we travelled round the world together – people like David Brown, Robin Hobbs, Ramon Subba Row, 'J. T.' Murray, Peter Parfitt and Peter Richardson.

Finally, the title of the book. It is not meant to sound conceited, as if I am boasting that my commentator's job has been easy. It merely refers to the somewhat bizarre association that I have had with chocolate cakes. It all started some ten years ago when a kind lady sent me a chocolate cake on my birthday, during a Test match at Lord's. I perhaps unwisely thanked her over the air. Since then gifts of all sorts have flooded into the box: bottles, sweets, biscuits and of course cakes galore – usually chocolate. On some occasions they are works of art. For instance, last year I was given by some friends in Cardiff a colour reproduction in icing of the famous picture of Lord's in the early 1900s, which hangs in the Memorial Gallery at Lord's! It depicts a rather rotund fielder stopping a ball in front of the small stand which used to be on the left of the pavilion, where the Warner Stand now is. Walking on the edge of the boundary is King Edward VII with Queen Alexandra on his arm, and sitting in the stand is the easily recognisable figure of Lily Langtry!

So what do we do with all the cakes? Some we eat, or share with our television colleagues, our engineers and our many casual visitors to the box. The one I have mentioned above was too good to eat, and it is still in my freezer in St John's Wood. I am also glad to say that we often send those we cannot eat to local children's hospitals. With my thanks to the many hundreds of people who have sent in cakes, I hope they – and you too – will now appreciate the title!

The first I can remember of anything to do with cricket was when I was aged about six, and an old Oxford blue called H. G. Tylecote lived in the village of Offley where we had our home. He used to come and coach my eldest brother Michael on our tennis court, and I was allowed to do a spot of fielding. Two years later I went to boarding school at Eastbourne, and it was there that I 'became' Patsy Hendren. My brother was J. W. Hearne (young 'Jack'), and we used to play needle matches in the nets. So I think it makes sense to give my hero pride of place in the batting order of my favourites, and he is one of the two exceptions of the fifty on whom I never commentated.

I have always regretted that I never commentated on a Hendren innings. This also applies to other great cricketers whom I watched before the war – not that I did much watching in the years from 1921 to 1939. Whenever I could, I preferred to play instead, but I was lucky to be at school in Eastbourne from 1921 to 1925, and we used to go to the Saffrons to see H. D. G. Leveson-Gower's eleven against both Oxford and Cambridge. I remember famous names like A. P. F. Chapman, the three Ashtons (G., H., C. T.), Rev. F. H. Gillingham, R. H. Bettington, G. E. B. Abell, the two Gilligans (A. E. R., A. H.), T. C. Lowry, M. D. Lyon, G. T. S. Stevens, K. S. Duleepsinhji and F. B. R. Browne.

The latter had the nickname of 'Tishy', because just before he delivered the ball he crossed his legs. The 'Tishy' came from a mare of that name who used to cross her legs when jumping and, not surprisingly, fell a number of times. There was a rather rude joke at the time which said that she had crossed her legs and fallen at Becher's in the Grand National because she had spotted the Rector of Stiffkey in the crowd on the other side of the fence. Stiffkey was a village in Norfolk and there was a cause célèbre involving the Rector and a number of London prostitutes. F. B. R. was a master at St Andrew's school, which could also boast of J. L. Bryan on its staff. Naturally they were always a good side and normally beat us except when D. R. S. Bader (the famous Douglas) was in our eleven. He could be relied on to make a hundred more often than not. This great airman-to-be was a popular figure at my school, Temple Grove, because whenever he *did* make a hundred we were excused evening prep. Writing down all these names reminds me of a fairly useless skill which I have always had. I am very bad at remembering names but I'm a wizard at initials and would gladly choose 'Initials of First-class Cricketers' as my specialist subject on *Mastermind*.

But I digress. Back to the Saffrons, where I seem to remember a number of fancy caps, including the Harlequins. I must have seen Yorkshire play there once, because I distinctly remember Herbert Sutcliffe with his sleek black hair hooking a six over long leg.

From 1923 we lived in Dorset for a couple of years, before moving to Herefordshire. In July 1924 our tutor took me and my brother in the sidecar of his motorbike to watch Hampshire play Notts at Bournemouth. We sat by the sightscreen and watched a bald, red-faced Arthur Carr, in a cream silk shirt with a knotted handkerchief round his neck, driving with great power. Alec Kennedy, the fast-medium bowler, had a beautifully smooth run up to the wicket, and standing at mid-off was the considerable figure of Lionel Tennyson. I was especially interested in the wicket-keeper Livsey, who in addition to keeping wicket was also Tennyson's butler. Personally, after six hours crouching behind the stumps, I wouldn't have felt like waiting at table! On this occasion I didn't see Philip Mead bat. I only saw him walking from slip to slip at the end of each over with his shambling farmer's gait. I was lucky enough to see him bat a few years later and can confirm this classical description of him by a very dear friend – the late 'Crusoe', R. C. Robertson-Glasgow:

> Having settled his whereabouts with the umpire, he wiggled the toe of his left boot for some fifteen seconds inside the crease, pulled the peak of a cap that seemed all peak, wiggled again, pulled again, then gave a comprehensive stare round him as if to satisfy himself that no fielder, aware of the task ahead, had brought a stick of dynamite. Then he leaned forward and looked down at the pitch, quite still. His bat looked almost laughably broad.

Great stuff. Can you wonder that Crusoe was my favourite cricket writer? I met him first at a dinner at the Club in Trinity, Oxford, in 1933, when he gave his famous rendering of 'Eskimo Nell'. No one has ever done it better!

I once played with Lord Tennyson when, through Alec

Douglas-Home (later Lord Home), I was asked to play for the Lords and Commons against Westminster at Vincent Square. Tennyson came into the dressing room with an enormous portmanteau. He opened it up and revealed a batch of bottles – whisky, gin, wine and so on. 'Help yourselves, gentlemen,' he said, 'and if you care to give me an order afterwards I shall be only too pleased that it is delivered to your house.' The only other person I know who used to sell his wares in the dressing room was Godfrey Evans, who would bring a small case full of attractive marcasite jewellery in which he was financially interested.

And whilst on the subject of jewellery, there was a splendid character who used to haunt the Yorkshire grounds. He carried in his pocket a small soft leather bag full of the most priceless jewels. Goodness knows what they were worth, but he used to come up to our commentary box and display the dazzling rings and bracelets. Why he was never mugged I don't know. Perhaps he was – I haven't seen him for over twenty years. He always used to have a good story, and once told me: 'I'm very worried about the three Ms.' 'The three Ms?' I asked. 'What on earth are they?' 'Oh,' he said, 'the Missus, the maid and the mortgage. They're all three overdue!'

Whilst still in Dorset I had a tremendous thrill – I actually saw the great Jack Hobbs play, alas the only time that I did. It was in a charity match at Bridport in 1924, and so far as I can remember he made 17. I can still picture one magnificent square cut which he played, though my vision was somewhat clouded by the smoke of a foul-smelling pipe smoked by either J. T. Brown or J. Tunnicliffe, the great Yorkshire opening pair. They were sitting in front of me and I don't know which one was the offender. But they were first-class cricketers and I forgave them anything.

After the war I was lucky to meet Jack, and no nicer nor more modest man can ever have played cricket; he had a delightful sense of humour and a twinkle in his eye. I used to visit him when he retired to Hove.

In 1925 we moved to Herefordshire, so were in easy reach of Cheltenham and Worcester. In 1926 I saw my first ever touring team, and got my first sight of those baggy green Australian caps. They were playing Gloucestershire at Cheltenham. I had read a lot about the fast bowling of Jack Gregory and was duly impressed with his speed and long run up to the wicket. A chap called Ellis was keeping wicket in place of Oldfield, and one ball from Gregory was so fast that he could only get his left hand to it and his glove came off. The crowd were cheered by a lively second innings of 32 by their burly captain, Lt.-Col. D. C. Robinson. Brig.-Gen. Poore of Hampshire (1898–1906) was once asked in the 1930s how he would have dealt with Harold Larwood. 'I'd have charged him,' he replied. Well, Lt.-Col. Robinson obviously had the same idea as he advanced down the pitch to meet Gregory's expresses. He missed some, snicked some and hit some, but it was highly entertaining while it lasted. I have fleeting memories of Dipper, Sinfield, Parker and Goddard, but none of Hammond because he didn't play for Gloucestershire that year. He had picked up a virus in the West Indies and was in a nursing home throughout the summer.

We were lucky to see the Australians batting, and it was the small figure of C. G. Macartney – green floppy cap pulled low over his eyes – who caught my attention with his late cutting. And I realise now how lucky I was not only to see Gregory, but also the gnomelike Clarrie Grimmett with his round-arm action spinning out the Gloucestershire batsmen. (He took 11 wickets in the match.) I met him and interviewed him in the 1960s at Adelaide. He was obviously very bitter that he had not been selected to tour England with Don Bradman's team in 1938. On figures alone he had reason to be. In the winter of 1935–6 he had toured South Africa and in five Tests took 44 wickets for 14.59 apiece, which still remains the highest for Australia in any Test series. The following winter Gubby Allen's team visited Australia and, surprisingly, Grimmett did not play in a single Test, his place being taken by another leg-spinner, F. A. Ward, and later by the left-arm chinaman bowler L. O'B. Fleetwood-Smith. Both these were selected to tour England in 1938 with very limited success, Ward taking 0 for 142 in the one Test in which he played, and Fleetwood-Smith 14 wickets – but at a cost of over 50 runs per wicket. So it rather looks as if there was a clash of personalities somewhere.

We paid quite a few visits to the lovely Worcester ground nestling in the shadow of the Cathedral. It was the time of Major M. F. S. Jewell and M. K. Foster, one of the seven Foster brothers who all played for Worcestershire. My special favourite was Tarbox (C. V.) because of his unusual name. And of course there was Fred Root with his new leg theory bowling – giant in-swingers with a posse of fielders in the leg trap. He was no more than fast-medium so was never as dangerous as Larwood. My stepfather decided to copy him, and you should have seen the looks on the Much Marcle village side when he directed six of them to crowd round the bat on the leg-side. They were not only in danger from the usual village sloggers but also from my stepfather's 'deliveries', which tended to stray wide of the leg-stump and head straight for the cluster of short legs. He was soon persuaded to give it up!

I also paid two visits to Taunton: the first time in 1925 to see Yorkshire play Somerset. I can remember nothing of the game except that during the lunch interval I saw Abe Waddington and Maurice Leyland walking across the ground to the lunch tent. I rushed after them to get their autographs and to my great disappointment they refused. I inwardly cursed them at the time but I now realise why they did so – and it's a tip I would pass on to all young autograph-hunters. Never ask a cricketer for his autograph when he's on the way to lunch. He only has forty minutes and his mind is concentrated on only one thing – his stomach!

My second visit was far luckier. It was in 1932 and I saw K. S. Duleepsinhji make 90 in what was I think his last first-class innings. I can picture him now – dark, slim, rather frail but with exquisite timing. J. C. (Farmer) White was wheeling away over after over at one end with his accurate slow left arm, but time and time again Duleep danced down the pitch and hit him over or past mid-on. A sight to treasure.

Tuesday, 1 July 1930 will always be a red-letter day in my cricket life. It was the day I saw my first Test match. It was the fourth and last day of the second Test match against Australia at Lord's. Some of the 'twenty-two' (second eleven) at Eton were entertained in one of the old Tavern boxes by an old blue called 'Sonny' Mugliston. He was a remarkable and rather unique sportsman. He got a cricket blue at *Cambridge* in 1907 and 1908 and also played seven matches for Lancashire during that period. But here comes the unusual part. At soccer he played left back for *Oxford* and the Corinthians and also represented *Oxford* at golf. How he divided his time between Cambridge and Oxford is not revealed.

Anyway, he was a friendly and generous host and we arrived in time for an excellent lunch. We then saw the second half of Percy Chapman's great innings of 121. At lunch England were

262 for 5, still needing 42 to make Australia bat again, and with a slight chance of saving the game. Gubby Allen was batting with Chapman but was lbw to Grimmett for a hard-hit 57. Chapman, who might have been out before he had scored (a skier dropped between V. Richardson and Ponsford), proceeded to hit out at everything and hit three sixes off Grimmett bowling from the Nursery End. I can still see them – towering on-drives into the far corner of the Mound Stand. There was tremendous excitement when he reached his first – and only – Test hundred. And then a short time afterwards he was facing Fairfax from the Pavilion End when he snicked a ball to Oldfield behind the stumps.

Believe it or not, he told our cricket master, Nick Roe, whom he saw later in the pavilion, that he had swallowed a bluebottle! Enough to get anyone out! Otherwise he might have gone on and saved the match, but as it was Australia only needed 72 to win, and after a short panic when they lost three wickets for only 22 runs they won by seven wickets. Walter Robins put on early and took two quick wickets, but the one I can remember is D. Bradman caught Chapman bowled Tate 1. It was really a hat trick for me as it was the first time I saw Bradman bat, the first time I saw Tate bowl, and it was the best catch I had ever seen up to then. Bradman had made a brilliant 254 in the first innings and we were all longing to see him bat. He tried to cut a ball from Tate, however, and although he hit it right in the middle only inches off the ground, Chapman scooped the ball up in the gully. Naturally we were disappointed at not seeing more of Bradman, but it really was a tremendous catch.

Chapman at the time was at the peak of his career – as captain of England he had regained the Ashes at the Oval in 1926, followed by his successful 4–1 tour of Australia in 1928–9. He was the ideal schoolboy's hero – tall, with curly hair and a chubby smiling face, and a brilliant hitter and fielder with enormous hands. I had seen him playing at the Saffrons for Cambridge against Leveson-Gower's eleven, and he was usually in the covers, swooping in on the ball.

From that day at Lord's, although he made 45 in the next Test, things began to go wrong for Chapman. To general surprise he was dropped from the fifth Test at the Oval, Bob Wyatt taking over as captain. No one was more surprised or disappointed than Chapman himself. The *Daily Mail* published an article by him which hit the headlines: 'Why have I been dropped?' by Percy Chapman. He had a point because he had averaged over 40 in the series and Wyatt had never played against Australia. One phrase in Chapman's article sticks in my mind: 'My friends are good enough to say that my batting is still as good as ever.' But typically he sent a telegram wishing Wyatt good luck.

That winter he captained England on an unsuccessful tour of South Africa, both for England and for himself. He had been selected for the tour before he was dropped at the Oval and this must have made things very awkward for him. He continued to play his type of attractive cricket throughout the early 1930s, proving a popular captain of Kent until he gave up at the end of 1936. He was becoming more and more involved in his job of selling whisky, and it gradually dragged him down. The debonair smiling personality, the born leader, the striker of sixes and the outstanding fielder of his generation became a sad figure. I used to see him after the war at Lord's. I would pass the time of day but I never got to know him well. Quite one of the saddest days of my life was when I saw him being carried to a taxi outside the back door of the pavilion. I try to shut out that memory and just remember that July day in 1930 when he scored his only Test hundred at Lord's and gave immense pleasure to a schoolboy who looked on him as a godlike figure.

But cricket in general has only happy memories for me, so let's start on the tributes to my chosen fifty players who have given me so much pleasure during my commentaries in Test matches.

11 Patsy Hendren, Don Bradman, Wally Hammond

Patsy Hendren

AFTER I 'BECAME' HENDREN in 1921, I noticed one day an advertisement in a paper. It showed a picture of Hendren batting, and underneath said: 'Why not take Wincarnis like Patsy Hendren of 26 Cairn Avenue, Ealing W5?' Just think of putting Ian Botham's private address in a paper for all to see! Anyway, there it was, and I immediately wrote off asking Patsy for his autograph, neglecting to enclose a stamped addressed envelope. After a few days, back came a piece of foolscap paper with three of his autographs. They looked something like this:

E. Palsy Hendre<u>n</u>.

Note that the t was not crossed, and the two lines under the n. His kindness made a deep impression on me. My signature today is still:

Brian Johnsto<u>n</u>.

My next indirect connection with him was in 1926 after England had won the Ashes at the Oval. There was no commentary point over the radio then, so at the end of the match Patsy was rushed by taxi to Broadcasting House to give a summary of the game. I can still remember the words in which he described the exciting scenes in front of the pavilion: 'The crowd was real glad and all was merry and bright.'

From then on I followed his career closely until he retired in 1937. Each morning I would find the sports page and see how many he had made. He seldom let me down. Early in his career, before I adopted him, he had had some hiccups in Test matches and was said not to have a Test match temperament. But he finished up with a Test average of 47.63 – just .09 behind Boycott (!) and ninth in the batting averages of all England Test batsmen. In other areas of first-class cricket there is no question as to where he stood. Altogether he scored 57,611 runs, beaten only by Hobbs and Woolley; 170 hundreds, beaten only by Hobbs; and an overall average in his career of 50.80, with only six other batsmen averaging more. So what was so special about him both as a player and as a man?

He had every stroke in the book from the late chop or cut, the square cut and an off-drive between cover and extra cover. He drove fiercely and was the best hooker of his time. He was – as befitted a professional footballer who played on the wing for Brentford – very fast between the wickets and always tried to take a quick single off his first ball. He was small by modern standards, with very strong wrists and forearms, and his twinkling feet and magnificent 'arm' made him an outstanding fielder in the deep. In later years he fielded closer to the wicket, either at slip or crouching at short leg with his hands cupped and his bottom sticking out.

As a man he was cricket's most lovable clown, who never went too far. When batting he seemed to be in permanent conversation with the wicket-keeper, judging by the laughter of all those lucky enough to be fielding near to the wicket. He had an ugly puglike face and made remarks with a deadpan look. His favourite expression when telling a story was, 'Oh dear, oh dear.' He enjoyed pulling the leg of batsmen and would often chase a ball and stoop to pick it up when still ten yards or so short of it. He would even turn round and pretend to throw the ball. When he saw the batsmen hesitating he would run on and pounce on the ball, throwing it back low and fast over the top of the stumps.

After the war I used to go and sit with Patsy when he was scoring for Middlesex. He told me once of the occasion on Arthur Gilligan's tour of 1924 when Patsy was fielding out in the deep just under the Hill. A batsman hit a steepling catch to him. Up and up it went and Patsy tried to position himself underneath. As he did so a voice from the Hill shouted: 'If you drop that catch, Patsy, you can sleep with my sister.'

I asked him what happened. 'Oh dear, oh dear,' he said. 'As I hadn't seen his sister, I decided to make the catch.'

He also told me that he was once sitting in a train when a

very pale man with a white silk scarf wound round his neck got into the carriage. He looked so ill and miserable that Patsy took pity on him and asked him what was the matter.

'Oh,' croaked the man, 'it's terrible. My club side was playing in the final of a competition. The opposition, with one wicket in hand, needed two runs to win off the last ball of the match. The batsman shied it in the air and it came to me at deep mid-on. They had run one by the time the ball came down – it was an absolute sitter – and I dropped it. They then ran another and won the match. My team mates will never forgive me.'

'Oh,' said Patsy jocularly, trying to cheer the poor man up, 'if I'd done that, I'd have cut my throat.'

'I have done,' whispered the man hoarsely.

Patsy was a lovable man, who gave pleasure to thousands both with his antics and performances on the field, and with his humour and sense of fun off it. He was my first real hero. I think I made a good choice.

Don Bradman

Back now to that July day at Lord's in 1930 when I saw for the first time the greatest run-making machine cricket has ever known. Early in the afternoon I had seen his brilliant running, picking up and throwing from the deep. Then, when Australia batted, down the pavilion steps he came, in green baggy cap walking ever so slowly with measured strides – using his bat as a walking-stick. Whenever I saw him bat after that he invariably did the same, sometimes looking up at the sky – accustoming his eyes to the light. He failed on this occasion and it was not until 1938 that I saw him bat again – at Lord's in the second Test when he made 102 not out and in the third Test at Headingley, 103.

Why was he so great? Before I try to answer that, I'll stagger you with some of his outstanding figures. He only played in 52 Tests, and in 80 innings scored 6,996 runs with 29 hundreds at an average of 99.94! He only needed to score four in his last Test innings at the Oval to give him an average of 100.00 exactly, and his 7,000th run in Test cricket.

Of these 52 Tests, 37 were against England, with five home Tests each against South Africa, the West Indies and India. The only *overseas* Tests he played were against England. Just imagine what his Test record would have been had he toured the other countries, and had Australia played New Zealand, Pakistan and Sri Lanka as they do today.

His overall figures are even more astonishing: 338 innings for 28.067 runs at an average of 95.14 with 117 hundreds – in other words, he made a hundred every three times he went in. His 117 hundreds include 452 not out, four other scores over 300, and thirty double-centuries. Enough said. I hope you feel duly staggered!

So what had he got that set him on a plane above all other run-getters both past and present?

First, I think his character. He was a perfectionist. Whatever he did, he wanted to achieve as near one hundred per cent perfection as possible. He was not ashamed to learn from others. In fact, he told me he was never coached but used to watch and copy the great Australian and English batsmen he saw as a young man. Then there was his insatiable love of batting and making runs, rivalled only in latter days by Geoff Boycott. People like Jack Hobbs often used to get themselves out after they had made a hundred, but not Bradman. And to help him he had the sort of dedicated concentration which is necessary to achieve the really big scores. Like Hanif, Gavaskar and Boycott, he could shut himself away from what was going on around him.

He had an amazing quickness of eye, which enabled him to see the ball that fraction earlier, and so enable him to get early into position and play the ball that much later than most batsmen. I believe that when he had his eyes tested his eyesight proved to be excellent but not phenomenal. Incidentally, I always regret that the portrait of Bradman in the pavilion at Lord's has him wearing spectacles – as he does today.

Then there was his general athleticism: he was a fast runner and mover with a boxer's footwork. The combination of his eye, concentration and his footwork meant that he could play *all* the strokes. He was strong, with powerful forearms, so was especially good off the back foot with his cutting and hooking. Equally, he would dance down the pitch and drive the ball, but very seldom in the air. He decided early on that by keeping the ball along the ground he would eliminate one way of getting out.

He was a great placer of the ball, a good judge of a run and always ran his first run very fast. He told me once in an interview that he attributed much of his successful placing of the ball to his memory. Before each ball he would glance quickly round the field and note where each fielder was positioned. He would then – *before he received the ball* – decide where if possible he would hit it – no matter what its length – either on the offside or onside. In other words, he memorised the empty spaces. No wonder he kept the score-board ticking over so fast. In fact – and I'm sticking my neck out – I would say that he must have been the fastest scorer of all the great Test batsmen. The main difference between him and someone like Geoff Boycott was that Bradman's aim was to dominate the bowlers and to get on top. He wanted to dictate the play. Boycott, on the other hand, was prepared to 'sit it out' and concentrate on *not* getting out.

There was otherwise a certain similarity between the two in that cricket came first in their lives. They were both loners who would be happier in their hotel rooms, conserving energy and resting, rather than being 'one of the boys' and enjoying a fun social life.

A justifiable criticism of Bradman was that he was not as good a player on bad wickets as Hobbs, Sutcliffe, Hammond and Hutton had been. To this he used to reply that Walter Lindrum did not make his big breaks on bad billiard tables. He expected and got the best. So it could be fairly said that Bradman was not prepared to get 'stuck in' and try to defend against the turning ball on a rain-affected wicket. A perfect example of this was the second Test at Lord's in 1934 where Hedley Verity took 15 wickets for 104 runs in the match. Bradman proceeded to take the whole thing rather light-heartedly and for once even hit the ball in the air, actually hitting seven fours in his first innings of 36.

His success, and the adulation and extra money that came his way, did not always make Bradman popular with his fellow players (you could say the same about Boycott), but I met Bradman many times, especially in Australia, and found him a cheerful, friendly and outspoken character. He was quick to argue his point and, what's more, knew all his facts and figures. When I first commentated for the Australian Broadcasting Commission at Sydney we used to have a small box in the Noble Stand and immediately below our open window was a row of seats reserved for the Australian selectors. He could hear every word we said and would often turn round and laugh or gesticu-late at any comment with which he did not agree.

In another more recent interview I asked him whether, if he were playing today, he would have worn a helmet, and to my surprise he said yes. I pointed out to him that he had never worn one against Larwood, but he stuck to his point. Personally I think he was merely trying to be kind to the modern batsmen, but he denied this.

He was seldom caught out in conversation, though in his admirable researches Irving Rosenwater worked out that Bradman was caught out *on the field* in 58 per cent of his dismissals, compared with 26 per cent bowled. Finally, of course, Bradman was a fine leader of men and one of the greatest tacticians ever. He captained Australia twenty-four times, and to my mind there has been no better Test match captain.

To end I must go back to just before 6 pm on 14 August 1948 at the Oval for the fifth Test against Australia. From the pavilion emerged Don Bradman to play his last ever Test innings. In the television commentary box Roy Webber had advised us that the Don only needed to make four runs to bring his Test match average to exactly 100.00. He was given a tremendous and emotional reception by the packed crowd, who stood and cheered him all the way to the wicket. As usual he walked to the wicket ever so slowly. As he approached the square Norman Yardley called for three cheers from his England team, who had all gathered on the pitch. Some shook him by the hand.

Bradman quietly took his guard, apparently unmoved by all the emotional scenes. There was a hush from the crowd as Hollies ran up to bowl from the Vauxhall end. Bradman played the first ball quietly on the offside. The next pitched on a perfect length on or just outside the off-stump. Bradman pushed forward as if to play it as a leg-break, but it was a perfectly disguised googly. It touched the inside of his bat and he played on. Bowled for 0 in his last Test innings. The cheers as he turned and walked slowly back to the pavilion were as loud as when he came in. Not, I like to think, because the crowd were pleased that England had got his wicket, but rather as the best way possible to say goodbye to the greatest run-getter of all time.

Just three final comments on this dismissal:

1. A film was made of the series and showed Bradman being bowled by Hollies with Hollies bowling *round the wicket*. This he did *not* do on this occasion. I believe that what happened was that the camera got Bradman being bowled, but had not shot Hollies as he ran up. So they must have gone to the film archives and found an old shot of Hollies who happened – bad luck to them – to be bowling round the wicket. I don't think many people noticed it. But I had to do the commentary on the film and was very conscious of a fake picture.

2. In interviews in later years I asked the Don whether he had missed the ball because his eyes were full of tears at his tremendous reception. He denied it emphatically, but then he would – he was nothing if not tough. But I still don't believe that he could have been unaffected.

3. The other question I asked was whether he knew that he only needed four more runs to bring his Test career average to 100.00. He told me with a twinkle in his eyes that he had had no idea, but that if he had done, he might perhaps have taken a wee bit more trouble!

Wally Hammond

I was lucky enough to see Wally Hammond play. I saw him make his superb 240 against Australia at Lord's in 1938, and his 76 in the Headingley Test in the same year. As a commentator I was also privileged to describe two of his innings against India eight years later in 1946. Unless you saw Hammond it is difficult to comprehend how great a player he was, though his figures prove a certain amount. In all first-class cricket: 50,551 runs, average 56.10; 167 hundreds; 732 wickets and 819 catches. In Tests: 7,249 runs, average 58.45; 22 hundreds. He also took 83 wickets and made 110 catches.

The simple fact is that he was head and shoulders above his contemporaries in England. He dominated English cricket throughout the late 1920s and the 30s. Even after the war he headed the batting averages in 1946 with an average of 84, for the eighth season in succession – an all-time record.

He was a marvellous athlete and successful in whatever game he played. He had a commanding presence and there was an aura of majesty in the way he walked to the wicket.

'Like a ship in full sail,' R. C. Robertson-Glasgow once wrote. He was strong and beautifully built, and like a boxer was light on his feet. His most famous stroke was his square cover drive, and his back strokes, even in defence, were dreaded by fielders at mid-off and mid-on.

He played with a light bat, so was a perfect late-cutter, and also produced an unorthodox stroke down to long leg, more of a paddle than a sweep. They used to say that he was not so strong on the leg-side, but it must be remembered that in his day most bowlers bowled a line on off-stump or just outside, so he didn't get all that much practice! He was, though, to prove occasionally vulnerable to Bill O'Reilly, who with his bounce concentrated on Wally's leg-stump.

As a bowler he was not unlike Maurice Tate, with a good action and plenty of pace off the pitch. He took a short run but bowled at a brisk medium pace. At first slip he was in the top class alongside names like Woolley, Gregory, Miller, Simpson, Cowdrey, Sharpe, Chappell (Greg) and Botham. He made it all look so ridiculously easy. I don't ever remember seeing him fling himself at the ball. He just seemed to stand there and pouch the ball – often putting it in his pocket after he had made the catch.

When he became an amateur in 1938 he captained England twenty times, including two overseas tours to South Africa and Australia. He was an efficient captain on the field without being great. Off the field – especially on tours – he tended to go his own way, and rather left the team to their own devices. As I have said, I was the television commentator for the two London Tests against India. It's difficult to believe it now, but I never spoke to him nor interviewed him during that time. It just didn't happen in those days. No interviews on the prospects of a match, at the close of play nor even at the end of the game. Like actors and actresses of that era, cricketers were more remote from their public and not as overexposed as they are today.

For one who had dominated the scene for so long, the twilight of Hammond's career was rather sad. He had that very successful post-war season in 1946, followed by an unsuccessful tour of Australia both for himself and his team, but he did score 79 in his final Test – against New Zealand in Christchurch. He then, except for two appearances in 1950 and 1951, retired from first-class cricket, and eventually settled in South Africa, where he became coach at the University of Pietermaritzburg.

It was in Durban in 1964 that I spoke to him for the very first time. I was covering Mike Smith's MCC tour for the BBC and one day went down to the Kingsmead ground in Durban to see them practise. I spotted a lone figure leaning over the back of a stand which was alongside the nets. He was looking down on the players practising below. I recognised him immediately and introduced myself. He couldn't have been more charming and quite obviously still took a great interest in cricket, especially in the MCC team. I alerted Mike Smith, who immediately asked Wally to come down to the nets, where he remained with the team for the rest of the practice.

That night in the lounge of the hotel I saw the great man surrounded by the MCC team, who were hanging on to his every word as he reminisced about the past. It was a happy ending to what I always felt was rather a sad life after he had given up cricket. The players were thrilled to meet him and it must have given him much pleasure and satisfaction to be the centre of their admiration and obvious hero-worship. That was in December 1964, and he died in July 1965 at the age of only sixty-two. I shall always remember him from a photograph of him playing his famous cover drive, from a yard outside his crease, with his dark-blue handkerchief showing out of his trouser pocket, and Bertie Oldfield crouching down behind the stumps. He was in the perfect position for the stroke as he followed through with his bat. It must have been a four.

12 Len Hutton, Denis Compton, Alec Bedser, Arthur Morris

Len Hutton

I N 1952 LEN BECAME the first professional to be appointed captain of England in this country. In 1956 he was the first professional to be made an honorary member of the MCC and the second professional to be knighted (Jack Hobbs was the first in 1953). And how well he wore the mantle. He became the wise old man of cricket, whose judgement and comments were respected throughout the cricket world. For two years – 1975–6 – he served as a selector, but otherwise he kept largely in the background except for his presidency of Scarborough CC and the Forty Club.

He was no committee man but, until his death aged seventy-four in 1990, he could be seen at most Tests in this country, and other big cricket occasions, confidentially whispering words of wisdom into somebody's ear. He had a dry wit and spoke quietly with a twinkle in his eye. He remained a fine reader of the game and a good judge of players. He usually ended his often enigmatic remarks with a 'see what I mean?'

I only saw him play once before the war, and that was in the Lord's Test in 1938, when he only made 4 and 5 against Australia. This followed his 100 exactly at Trent Bridge and the next innings he played was his world record 364 at the Oval, later beaten by Gary Sobers's 365 not out against Pakistan in 1958. I listened to that great cricket commentator Howard Marshall describing Hutton's innings in his commentary from the Oval.

At that time Len was a lean and rather fragile figure, with a hungry look. Indeed, throughout his career his health was never really one hundred per cent. He suffered a further handicap during the war when as a PT instructor he damaged his left arm in a fall, and ever afterwards it was a shade shorter than his right. This *should* have affected his batting, but it never appeared to do so.

He was a complete stylist with every stroke and the most correct of all post-war batsmen, with the possible exception of Barry Richards, who was at least his equal. Unlike most overseas batsmen he was a magnificent player on bad pitches, and his immaculate defensive technique matched that of Hobbs, Sutcliffe and Hammond. He tended to play spinners from the crease, and although he had every stroke in the book, I didn't often see him hook. I remember best his exquisite off-drive, which was pure perfection with everything in the right place. He had a phlegmatic temperament, was determined and, outwardly at least, appeared unaffected by the battering he so often had to face as an opening batsman against the likes of Lindwall and Miller.

The one exception to this was the Lord's Test against Australia in 1948 when he – like most of the others – did not seem to 'relish' Lindwall's short-pitched bowling, and took a lot of knocks on the body. As a result – for the only time in his career – he was dropped by the selectors for the next Test. But when he came back he scored 81 and 57 at Headingley, and 30 (the only double figures in England's 52 all out) and 64 at the Oval – both top scores for England.

Len was one of England's most successful captains. He won the series against India in 1952, regained the Ashes after nineteen years at the Oval in 1953, drew 2–2 against the West Indies in 1953–4 and then kept the Ashes in Australia in 1954–5. Captaincy seemed to drain his strength, however. He found the pressures too much, and in the end, on the 1954–5 tour of Australia, it began to affect his batting. When he returned triumphantly to England he was immediately appointed captain for all five Tests against South Africa, but he contracted lumbago, Peter May took over the captaincy, and Len never played another Test. At the end of that season he retired from first-class cricket, having only been able to play in ten matches for Yorkshire because of ill-health. Quite simply, he had had enough.

Not only was Len a successful Test captain but he was also a fine tactician, especially in the way he could detect a batsman's weakness, and set the field accordingly. Probably because of the fierce fast bowling he himself had to face, he always wanted as many fast bowlers in his side as possible. He believed –

correctly – that in Tests it is generally fast bowlers who win the matches. One of his ploys in the field was perhaps not so acceptable, however. He was the first to slow down the over-rate as a tactic to spare his fast bowlers. Ever since then the slow over-rate has been the curse of Test cricket, and has robbed the paying spectators of many overs each day. Nowadays, in most Test series regulations decree a minimum of overs to be bowled each day.

Earlier I mentioned Hutton's wit. Denis Compton told me that during a torrid time at Lord's in the 1953 Test, Hutton and he were facing a terrible barrage from Lindwall and Miller. At the end of an over Len beckoned Denis for a mid-wicket conference. 'What tactics is he going to suggest?' thought Denis. All Len said was, 'There must be better ways of earning a living than this,' and then walked back to face the next over.

To sum up, Len was certainly one of the best ever opening batsmen in Test cricket, and was probably the equal of Hobbs and Sutcliffe on bad wickets. And if you ask any cricketer to write out his world eleven of all time, I think you will find that more often than not, one of the opening batsmen will be Len Hutton.

Denis Compton

By 1936 Patsy Hendren was soon due to retire and I was looking for another 'hero' to take his place – preferably from Middlesex. It didn't take me long to make my choice. In the Whitsun match at Lord's that year against Sussex, number eleven in the Middlesex side was a young eighteen-year-old from the Lord's ground staff playing his first first-class match. He had a last-wicket partnership with Gubby Allen, but was finally given out lbw for 14. He told the story of how Gubby said to the umpire, Bestwick: 'He wasn't out.' 'I know he wasn't, Mr Allen, but I am dying to have a wee!' replied Bestwick.

Young Denis Compton had arrived, and I saw him a week later make 87 against Northants, an innings which even then showed his class and the originality of his strokes.

So I 'adopted' him as my replacement for Patsy, who retired at the end of 1937, when he made a duck in his last innings for Middlesex. In the same year Denis played in his first Test against New Zealand at the Oval, where as a possible augury of things to come he was *run out* for 65. But on this occasion it was *not* his fault – just bad luck that a hard hit by Joe Hard-staff was deflected on to the stumps at the bowler's end, with Denis out of his crease. I didn't see him play in a Test until 1938 against Australia at Lord's, where in the second innings he came in at number seven, with England in real trouble at 76 for 5. He had made a hundred up at Trent Bridge in his first Test against Australia, and here at Lord's he batted with tremendous confidence, and as a twenty-year-old showed all his strokes in an attacking innings of 76 not out. I congratulated myself on making such a perfect choice as my replacement for Patsy.

I suppose that no cricketer of *any* generation could have given more pleasure to more people than Denis did. He was the cavalier of cricket with the dancing feet, unorthodox in attack but strictly orthodox in defence. The highlight of his career was the glorious summer of 1947 when he thrilled the war-weary and cricket-starved crowds with two records which are still unbroken – 18 hundreds and 3,816 runs in one season. Not that he himself worried about statistics. He was the enter-tainer supreme who just loved to play cricket. He would dance down the pitch to the slow bowlers and sometimes to the fast bowlers as well.

His favourite strokes were the late cut or 'chop', the square cover drive, the on-drive, the hook and his own special sweep down to fine leg. The latter got him out occasionally but he made a lot of runs with it. At the Oval once I saw him fall over when trying to sweep, but he still managed to hit the ball for four as he lay flat on the ground. Like Bradman, he did not often hit the ball in the air. During the tea-interval at Lord's in a match against Hampshire someone chided him about this. He promptly went out after tea and hit Derek Shackleton's first ball over mid-off for six into the pavilion.

Two points need stressing about Denis. First of all, his flair and the brilliance of his stroke-play was supported by perfect defensive strokes. So he was the complete batsman, fully capable of coping on a difficult or turning pitch. Secondly, there was his tremendous courage when facing Lindwall and Miller. There were no helmets in those days. He had to rely on a good eye, sound judgement as to whether to duck or hook and, most important of all – guts. The best example of this was at Old Trafford in 1948 when he was struck over the eye by a ball which flew off his bat as he tried to hook a no-ball bouncer from Lindwall. After being stitched up and a short rest he returned to make a fine 145 not out.

His running between the wickets has become legendary. He was certainly the worst judge of a run of any top-class batsman I have ever seen. His partners used to say that a call from Compton was just a basis for negotiation. He once achieved a hat-trick of run-outs in his brother Leslie's benefit match. To make matters worse one of the victims was the beneficiary himself! Denis did go on to make 72 not out on a turning wicket, but he admits that his brother wasn't too pleased with him on his way back to the pavilion.

As one might expect from an outside left who won an FA Cup Winner's medal with the Arsenal in 1950, he was a fine fielder and catcher. Had he not made so many runs, he would, I'm sure, have become a more regular wicket-taker with his left-arm chinamen and googlies. Even so, he managed to take 622 wickets in his career, including 25 in Tests. His googly was not all that easy to detect and when I kept wicket to him in charity matches, he used to kindly give me a signal when it was coming.

To sum up Denis: he was a casual character, forgetful of appointments and sometimes late. He often had to borrow other players' bats, trousers, socks and even boxes, because he had lost or forgotten his. He was handsome and debonair, and the women loved him. So did he the women! For years his face was on every advertising board in the country boosting Brylcreem. In the advertisement his hair was immaculately brushed, though on the field of play it fell all over his face. He nearly missed out on this lucrative contract because he used to receive hundreds of letters which he seldom had time to open. One day an agent called Bagenal Harvey offered to go through the mail and answer when necessary. Amongst the pile of letters he found one from Brylcreem offering Denis the contract.

His vagueness and forgetfulness are legendary. He was invited to a leaving party by J. J. Warr in 1987. The time and venue was 6.30 pm at the Royal Exchange on a Wednesday. Denis arrived at 5.30 pm at the Stock Exchange on the previous Tuesday!

1988 saw many celebrations of his seventieth birthday including a splendid banquet at the Inter-Continental Hotel.

Over six hundred guests were there including 'anyone who is anyone' in cricket and the football world. At the start of the dinner the chairman, George Mann, rose to welcome the guests, with an empty chair on his left. He had just begun his speech when in rushed a rather dishevelled Compton – last man in – late as usual. At least he came to the right place on the right day.

There has always been a slight mystery about the exact year of his birth. *Wisden* have got it right now as 1918, but when Denis was fifty a large party was given for him by a number of friends. They were busy drinking his health when the telephone rang and it was for Denis. He went to answer it and came back looking rather forlorn. 'Who was it?' they asked, 'It was my mother,' said Denis. 'She says I am only forty-nine!'

He had a wonderful sense of humour and for ten years or so on television he made a delightful companion in the commentary box. As a summariser he was a kind critic, and an enthusiastic advocate of attacking cricket and sporting behaviour on the field. I have one complaint against him, however. His laugh was rather loud in the commentary box and often made a perfectly innocent remark sound a dirty one. For instance, once at Worcester I said: 'Barry Richards has just hit one of d'Oliveira's balls clean out of the ground.' Nothing wrong in that in cricket terms, you might think. But a guffaw from Denis Compton completely changed its meaning!

His career was plagued by knee trouble, caused by injuries when he played football for the Arsenal. Unfortunately, he did not have the benefit of today's skilful surgery, which enabled players like Procter and Willis to continue as fast bowlers minus their kneecaps. Denis had a series of operations which hampered his movements during the later part of his career, and finally caused him to give up altogether in 1958. Undoubtedly one of the greatest players of all time – and one of the nicest.

Alec Bedser

The 'Big Fella' was the first great English player to emerge after the Second World War. And what an entrance he made on to the stage of Test cricket – 22 wickets in his first two Tests against India in 1946. Unlike Hutton and Compton, who started their Test careers before the war, Alec only played two games for

Surrey in 1939, both against the Universities. He and his twin brother, Eric, were on the ground staff and spent most of their time bowling to members in the nets. As Alec showed such promise as a fast-medium bowler Eric decided to concentrate on becoming an off-spinner. The twins were born in Reading in 1918, Eric arriving just a few minutes before Alec. As boys they were brought up in Woking, where the old Surrey player Alan Peach taught them their early cricket. They used to walk two miles to school every day, where they even sang in the choir! Alec has always maintained that this daily walk gave his legs the strength which enabled him to take 1,924 wickets at 20.41 during his career (1939–60).

He remained remarkably fit, and except for his shingles on Len Hutton's Australian tour in 1954–5, I cannot remember him missing a Test because of any of the modern ailments which seem to afflict bowlers today – bad backs, sore shins, pulled rib muscles and so on. Alec has always opposed the modern thirty-minute warm-up exercises which now take place before the start of play every day. Based on the number of *back* injuries suffered by fast bowlers nowadays, it seems that he is right. I should love to have seen him or Fred Trueman balancing on one leg, as the other was placed on the shoulder of the physiotherapist! Good for the hamstrings, they say. The only way to keep fit as a bowler is to bowl, says Alec. I think he has a point.

He and Eric are identical twins and look remarkably alike. I learned to identify them fairly early on – Alec has the broader face – but they don't make it easy. They dress alike, wearing the same suit, shirt and tie. Even when they are apart they select the same tie, though whether it is instinct or whether they ring each other each morning I'm not sure. But when they *are* at home they are said to pick up in the morning the first sock or shirt which comes to hand, no matter who wore them the day before.

When they are together they carry on a joint conversation with you, each one picking up where 'the brother' leaves off. Alec had an excellent benefit (for those days) of £12,866. They wisely invested it in an office furniture business which, because of their hard work, integrity and large circle of friends and admirers, prospered. They were able to sell it and remained as consultants to the takeover firm.

Alec has never taken a holiday as such. He has used all the

spare time due to him to go on tours (in 1962–3 as assistant manager in Australia, and in 1974–5 and 1979–80 as manager) or to attend Test matches in this country (as selector from 1962 to 1981, and chairman for the last thirteen years of that period). He, like other players of his generation, has found it difficult to comprehend the large sums of money the modern Test player can earn, but in spite of the contrast in financial awards, cricket has brought Alec many useful contacts and a well-deserved OBE. [*He was knighted for his services to cricket in 1996.*] In return, he has put a great deal back into cricket, as selector, committee-man and, finally, president of Surrey.

As a man, Alec has high principles. Honesty, loyalty, hard work and good manners and behaviour come high on his list. He has never been an optimist, and even when things are going well he will find something to grumble at – a typical English trait. To him, 'things are not what they were in my day', but it is all said with a gentle smile on his broad face and underneath you realise there is a 'softy', something I am sure that the young England players whom he selected or managed came to recognise.

Finally, what about Alec the player? He was certainly one of the best fast-medium bowlers there has ever been – very much in the Maurice Tate mould. Both of them liked their wicket-keepers to stand up to them and give them something to bowl at. They both seemed to do the impossible – that is, to gain pace off the pitch. An optical illusion, no doubt, but Godfrey Evans would have confirmed the speed with which the ball came into his gloves.

Alec had the perfect swivel bowling action, and with his impeccable length and direction he was, strangely, mainly an *in*-swing bowler. I say strangely because with his perfect action and his delivery so close to the stumps one would have expected him to be an *out*-swinger, but to compensate he learned to bowl a devastating leg-cutter – drawing his enormous hand across the seam of the ball to produce what was in essence a fast leg-break. His feat of 236 Test wickets becomes all the more remarkable when one considers that for much of the time from 1946 to 1954 he alone bore the brunt of England's attack without support at the other end. Though no greyhound in the field, those large hands of his pouched 289 catches, and like many bowlers he was always happy to talk about his batting –

especially his night-watchman's 79 at Headingley against Australia in 1948.

To sum Alec up, he is a lovable person and a good friend who values honesty and loyalty. As a player he gave everything to his county and country. Since he retired he has put a tremendous amount back into cricket – far more than he ever took out. But cricket has been his life and that is certainly one thing about which he wouldn't grumble!

Arthur Morris

Arthur was one of the nicest, most popular, and most modest of all Test cricketers. I cannot remember ever hearing a word said against him. And in addition he was one of Australia's greatest batsman, averaging 46.48 in 46 Tests with an aggregate of 3,553 runs, and scoring 12 hundreds. In Sheffield Shield matches, his average for New South Wales was 65.

He toured England in 1948 and 1953 and became known as 'Bedser's Bunny'. Alec dismissed him as many as eighteen times, but in return Arthur also scored a good many runs off him. He scored 122 and 124 not out against England at Adelaide in 1947 (Denis Compton capped this with 147 and 103 not out in the same Test). Arthur followed this on Don Bradman's tour of England in 1948 with an outstanding series, scoring 696 runs with an average of 87. His consistency was amazing with scores of 31, 9, 105, 62, 51, 54*, 6, 182, 196. It was his partnership with Don Bradman of 301 in 217 minutes which enabled Australia to win a remarkable victory in the fourth Test at Headingley. They scored 404 for 3 in the fourth innings of the match to win by seven wickets.

Arthur made his top Test score of 206 against Freddie Brown's team in 1951, but he didn't do so well in England in 1953, despite starting off the series with scores of 60, 67, 30 and 89. However, he reminded Len Hutton and his team that he could still bat a bit by scoring 153 against them in the first Test at Brisbane in 1954.

I have deliberately given all these figures because I feel that Arthur's ability has never been fully appreciated. I rarely hear him mentioned when cricketers discuss great batsmen of the past. Perhaps he lived too much in the shadow of Don Bradman. He was a left-handed opener and was both elegant and stylish, with excellent footwork. He used his feet like a boxer to dance down the pitch, and as a result played slow bowling as well if not better than the quicks.

To be fair, I suppose he was lucky that in the first seven years of Test cricket after the war, he did not have to play against any really fast bowlers, until Statham, Trueman and Tyson reached their peak pace in 1953–4. Frank Tyson in Australia in 1955 was acknowledged to be the fastest bowler any of the current players had seen, and he did capture Arthur's wicket three times in that series.

Arthur was a fine fielder anywhere, with a good arm, and in the middle 1950s was probably the most televised bowler in Test cricket. He used to bowl slow left-arm chinamen, and Lindsay Hassett put him on to bowl that famous last over at the Oval Test of 1953.

England needed five runs to win to regain the Ashes for the first time in nineteen years. Bill Edrich scored a single off the third ball. Denis Compton then tried to sweep him down to the gas-holders for the four runs necessary for victory. The crowd were ringing the ground ready to dash on to cheer England's victory. As Denis swept they charged from all directions, but they had reckoned without 'The Claw' – alias Alan Davidson. He was fielding at backward square leg, stuck out his enormous left hand and stopped the ball. So there was a delay as the crowd had to make their way back behind the boundary line. Then Arthur fed Denis's sweep with another chinaman outside the leg stump. This time the ball sped past Alan towards the square-leg boundary. Once again the crowd swept on to the ground and surrounded the players as they made a dash for the pavilion.

Arthur's analysis was 0.5–0–5–0, and because of the tension and excitement of that last over every television shop in the country seemed to use the film of it for demonstration purposes. You only had to look in the shop windows to see Arthur bowling on about half a dozen sets. He was always immensely proud of that, and also of the two Test wickets he actually took that year, one against South Africa at Adelaide and the other against England in the third Test at Old Trafford. At a dinner at Claridges given in Arthur's honour, J. J. Warr acknowledged in his speech that Arthur had taken twice as many Test wickets as he had!

At the same dinner Arthur told of how he and his old friend

and captain Lindsay Hassett played in a charity match some time after they had both retired. It was the traditional Prime Minister's match against a touring team. Arthur went in first and made a few runs. When he was back in the pavilion he met Hassett coming out, who asked if he could borrow Arthur's bat. He played very well with it, and after he was out was surrounded by a cheering crowd of small boys. In a speech at the dinner that night the Prime Minister congratulated Hassett on his innings. 'And,' he went on, 'I'd like to say how typical it was of Lindsay's generosity to give his bat away to one of the small boys in the crowd.' Believe it or not, Arthur and Lindsay remained friends!

For more than twenty years Arthur was an active member of the Sydney Cricket Ground Trust. He devoted most of his time to trying to put something back into the game he loved to play. It was all entirely voluntary and mostly went unrecognised and unsung – but, being the nice person he was, he preferred it that way.

13 Ray Lindwall, Keith Miller, Godfrey Evans

Ray Lindwall

WHENEVER I AM ASKED TO pick a world eleven from all the Test cricketers whom I have seen, I always pick Ray Lindwall as my number one fast bowler. As to who partners him at the other end, I have to be very careful if Fred Trueman is listening. I just daren't leave him out!

Linders was to me the perfect model for any aspiring fast bowler to follow. His run-up was not too long; it was relaxed and he gathered speed as he approached the wicket. His sideways delivery was copybook, and when he wanted to be he was as fast as anyone, but one of his strengths was his well-disguised variations in pace – the *really* fast ball being kept in reserve and used sparingly. The batsman would be on tenterhooks, never knowing when it would come. He was essentially an out-swing bowler, but after playing league cricket in Lancashire he began to bowl the in-swinger as well. Like so many Test fast bowlers who have played in the leagues, he soon discovered that he would not get many wickets from slip catches – his pace was too much for amateur slip fielders. So he had to learn to hit the stumps! What made him such a class bowler was that he swung the ball so *late*.

Cricket historians always say what a hostile pair Lindwall and Miller were, and of course they bowled bouncers like any other fast bowler, but they did not do so in the abundance we see today. It was interesting to find on talking to the likes of Len Hutton and Denis Compton that, although they rated Lindwall as the better bowler, they always preferred to face him rather than Miller.

I was lucky enough to keep wicket to Lindwall in a Sunday charity match at Didsbury during an Old Trafford Test in either 1961 or 1964 – I forget which. He was over here as a journalist writing for an Australian paper. I was standing a long way back, although of course he was getting on a bit then, and anyway would not bowl flat out in a charity game. Len Hutton was standing alongside me at slip and I suggested to him that we asked Linders to bowl just one ball as fast as he could. I asked him to do so before the start of his next over, and also warned the batsman to keep well out of the way. Linders then bowled one wide of the off-stump and it came through into my gloves chest-high, and nearly knocked me over backwards – and that was when he was over forty. But it proved to me how fast he must have been.

Linders was strong and beautifully built, five feet ten inches tall with big shoulders. He was a superb fielder anywhere, and a good enough batsman to average over 20 with the bat and to score a hundred in the third Test at Melbourne in 1947.

Like many fast bowlers, he liked his glass of beer. I am always very careful to have some cans in the fridge if I have any Australian friends coming, as I know how cold they like it, but I committed a terrible crime at a supper party we gave during the MCC Bicentary match in 1987. We had used up the cans which had been in the fridge, so when Linders asked for some more beer I opened a tin which, although not warm was not, I thought, cold enough. So when I had poured it out, I put some ice into it. You should have seen his face! I might have just hit him for six, and I realised what he must have looked like to a batsman as he ran up to bowl. He soon forgave me, but I now realise that ice *in* an Australian's beer is sacrilege and I shall never do it again.

He had a slow Australian drawl with rather a husky voice, and he was one of the summarisers for ABC, during Ted Dexter's MCC tour in 1962–3. He had a good sense of humour and was good fun in the box. He told a good story, and at the Lord's Taverners' dinner for Bill Edrich and Denis Compton in 1986 he told this one about two friends of his who stayed for three days in Bangkok on their way back to Australia.

On the last day the wife told her husband to go and amuse himself while she went shopping. She asked him to pick her up in a couple of hours. The husband thought that he would visit one of Bangkok's famous massage parlours. He was given the address of one by the hall porter and duly rang the bell. An attractive Thai girl opened the door and he asked whether he could have one of their massages. She said certainly, and that it would cost him a thousand dollars. 'Oh,' he said, 'I can't afford anything like that. Two hundred would be the most I could pay.' She apologised and said that she was sorry but that was their price and she couldn't change it.

So he went off and visited one of the museums to while away the time before he collected his wife. This he finally did and was walking with her down the street, when he saw the Thai girl from the massage parlour walking towards them. 'There you are,' she said. 'See what you get for two hundred dollars!'

Trevor Bailey was an old adversary of Linders, but only on the field, where they had many a battle. Off it they were great friends, and this was proved at Sydney in the fifth Test in 1955. Bailey had made 72 and Len Hutton was about to declare. Bailey knew that Lindwall needed one more wicket to reach his hundredth against England, so he allowed himself to be bowled by Lindwall – the only time, I am sure, that he ever gave his wicket away. Cricket can be a tough game, however, especially when England play Australia. Four years later at Melbourne Bailey opened both English innings with Peter Richardson. He bagged a pair – each time falling to Lindwall! Such is gratitude.

Two final facts about Linders, perhaps not generally known by English cricket followers at least. He captained Australia once against India at Bombay in 1956 and remarkably, for one of the greatest fast bowlers of all time, he later ran a successful florist's shop with his wife Peggy in Brisbane.

Keith Miller

People often come up to me and ask: 'Where are the characters in cricket these days?' They then proceed to name a number of 'characters' from the past, and one name which always seems to crop up is Keith Miller. I must say he comes high up on my list.

First of all his appearance: tall, athletic, rugged good looks, imposing carriage and walk, all adding up to a dynamic god-like figure. You couldn't fail to notice Keith. I believe that even in these days of helmets he would have been easily recognis-able. His character matched his appearance – he lived life to the full and played cricket because he enjoyed it. He was competitive, as anyone who had to face his bowling would agree, but not to the extent that winning was the only thing that mattered. He had the gift of friendship. Even after bowling a particularly vicious bouncer, he would quite likely ask the batsman at the end of the over if he had heard the winner of the three-thirty. He had more friends round the world than anyone I can think of, and he kept in touch. On my seventy-fifth birthday the telephone rang and there was Keith wishing me many happy returns. He had rung Sir Leonard Hutton the day before for the same purpose. Other friends would suddenly get a call from Australia just to see how they were.

Somehow he communicated this innate friendliness to the crowds, and how he played up to them. Before running up to bowl he would paw the ground like a horse, tossing his head so that his mane of hair fell over his forehead. If the batsman hit him for six or played an outstanding stroke, Keith would applaud him. In 1956 at Lord's, when Australia won easily and he had taken five wickets in each innings, he somehow managed to seize the ball at the end of the match, and as he strode triumphantly from the field he threw it into the crowd, just like a winning golfer does on the last green.

Off the field he enjoyed the bright lights and the company of the female sex. He didn't believe in going to bed too early – even during a Test match – and you might find him at the Royal Albert Hall listening to a concert of classical music, one of his great loves. The other of course was racing, and most years you would see his handsome figure at Ascot in his grey top hat and tails, attracting more glances from the girls than other more reputed lady-killers. He would sometimes slip away from a match to a nearby course just to watch a horse he had backed. When over here he would make a regular morning call to his great friend Scobie Breasley, the Australian jockey with the bobbing head.

As befits his character, he gave gallant service to the RAAF during the war, and was over in England for the victory Tests of 1945. He captured the hearts of the spectators at Lord's with a brilliant display of batting in an innings of 185. Rex Alston always remembered it well, as Keith seemed determined to break the glass of the old BBC commentary box, which in those days was above the England dressing room.

He was undoubtedly a great all-rounder, and on his record a better bowler than a bat. He was a powerful driver and a good cutter and hooker, but he often appeared unhappy against spin on a turning pitch. He would get into an awful mess, and often nearly did the splits as he stretched out down the pitch. He was a brilliant fielder, especially in the slips, where behind a casual façade he made difficult catches look easy.

It is as a bowler that he was most feared, however. Lindwall may have been better, but it is surprising how many batsmen of that era have said they would sooner have faced him than Keith. They never knew what he was going to bowl, and with his height and good action he would dig the ball in, resulting in explosive bouncers. He varied his run-up, sometimes turning round when halfway back and bowling off a short run. I have seen him drop the ball during his run-up, pick it up in his stride and bowl it without stopping. He could bowl a variety of balls, as I learned to my cost when keeping wicket to him once in a charity match at Cranleigh. In one over he bowled six different balls, including a full pitch, a bouncer, a googly, a leg-break, and an off-break. The other I think was just straight on a good length.

I said that to him winning was not the first priority and that he didn't care for statistics and averages. He was a complete contrast in character to his Test captain in 1946 and 1948, and often disagreed with the tactics which Bradman used. In 1948 against Essex, the Australians scored 721 runs in one day, W. A. Brown and Bradman putting on 219 in ninety minutes for the second wicket. When Brown was out Miller strode out to join Bradman. He had had enough of this slaughter of a county attack, and proceeded – I suspect deliberately – to be bowled first ball by Trevor Bailey.

He was a natural cricketer who had little coaching and did most things by instinct. I remember that we were once making a programme about cricket coaching and the producers had booked Keith to explain the various ways of bowling in-swing, out-swing, etc. I asked him in rehearsal to show me the various grips, and he honestly didn't know! He just bowled naturally.

Many Australians say he was the best captain they ever played under, when he led the New South Wales side. He led from the front and played for a result, and was insistent that everyone enjoyed their cricket. Perhaps he was a trifle too devil-may-care to make an ideal Test captain. He was once leading out the NSW team on to the field at Newcastle. He strode majestically twenty yards in front of them, tossing his head as he walked with that long stride of his. Jimmy Burke ran up behind him and tugged at his sweater. 'Nugget, Nugget,' he said, 'we've got twelve men on the field.' Keith didn't look round or stop in his stride. He just gave that peculiar little cough that so often proceeded his speech and said: 'Well, tell one of them to bugger off then,' and went on walking. I think that says a lot about Keith's character.

There is also a story of his days in the RAAF. He had left their station 'somewhere in England' to go down to the local town for a haircut. When he had had his haircut, he saw one of his officers in the street. 'Ah, Miller,' said the officer, who was carrying a bag of golf clubs, 'are you going back to the station?' 'Yes, sir,' said Miller. 'Good. I wonder if you would mind taking my golf clubs back with you.' So Keith slung them across his shoulder and walked back to the station, where he saw his commanding officer. 'Ah, Miller,' he said, 'been playing golf, eh!' 'No, sir,' replied Keith, 'getting my hair cut.' And he was given seven days in detention for insubordination!

Godfrey Evans

For many years, every morning of a Test match before play started, a bustling figure with enormous grey mutton-chop whiskers would appear in our commentary box. It was 'Godders' with the latest Ladbroke betting odds for the day's cricket. He was their consultant expert, who assessed for them the condition and state of the game. He was always chirpy, smiling and full of quips. I don't ever remember him being put out by anything, certainly never down in the dumps. He was the eternal optimist.

This cheerfulness, supported by his tireless energy, was one of the qualities which made him such a great player for England. Even on the hottest days abroad he never flagged. In between overs he bustled from one end to the other, perky little steps, arms swinging – a busy man in a hurry. He would encourage flagging spirits with a reminder that the gin and tonics were waiting in the dressing room, ice tinkling against the glasses. He would rush from behind the stumps to make a poor return into a full pitch. He would ostentatiously applaud a good ball or a fine piece of fielding. He was a showman whom the crowds loved, and a wonderful support for his captain. He was also a great chatter-up of batsmen, something they didn't always appreciate.

His rise to fame was rapid. As an eighteen-year-old he

appeared in a few matches for Kent before the war in 1939. With Les Ames still having trouble with his back, Godfrey became the regular Kent wicket-keeper in 1946, and played for England against India in the third Test at the Oval – the first time I saw him. My first impression was his tremendous energy and flamboyant brilliance as he stood close up to the stumps.

He lost his England place in the first Test at Brisbane on Wally Hammond's tour of 1946–7. Paul Gibb played instead, but Godfrey kept wicket in the four remaining Tests. He then kept wicket for England almost continuously until his ninety-first and final Test against India at Lord's in 1959, when he took his (then) record of dismissals to 219. Appropriately, his last victim was a stumping, because in my opinion he was the greatest 'stumper' of all Test wicket-keepers. During the period from 1946 to 1959 he was occasionally not selected because of injury – Brennan, Spooner, Andrew McIntyre and Swetman replacing him – but in George Mann's tour of South Africa in 1948–9 Billy Griffiths played in the fourth and fifth Tests, taking Godfrey's place on merit.

As a wicket-keeper Godfrey was the man for the big occasion. Like many Test players he was at his best when playing for his country, but perhaps lost some of the incentive when keeping for Kent. He was the most spectacular wicket-keeper I have ever seen, and also the most brilliant. He did have his occasional off-days, however, the most disastrous being the last day of the 1948 Test against Australia at Headingley, when as a result of many missed chances at slip or behind the wicket Australia made 404 for 3 to win. But normally he was an inspiration to his side. He crouched close to the stumps, balancing on his toes. He stood up to fast-medium bowlers like Alec Bedser, who insisted on him doing so 'because I like something to bowl at'. Alec was basically an inswinger, and this meant that Godfrey often had to take the ball on the leg-side, which he did superbly. I was not there, but am told that in 1950–1 in Australia, when both he and Alec were in their prime, his taking of the swinging new ball on the fast, bouncy Australian pitches was miraculous. So much so, on his appeal of, 'How's that?' when he brought off a fast leg-side stumping in an up-country match all the square-leg umpire could say was, 'Bloody marvellous!'

Of course he had to stand back to the quick bowlers like Tyson, Trueman and Statham, and he hurled himself acrobatically in all directions to take seemingly impossible catches. Perhaps his greatest was when he caught the left-handed Neil Harvey off Tyson wide down the leg-side in the third Test at Melbourne in 1955. People who were playing in the match have told me that they had never seen anything like it. In the pre-war days of Oldfield, Duckworth and Ames, the wicket-keepers seldom flung themselves at the ball, and I suppose that Godfrey was one of the first of the great wicket-keepers to hurl themselves like goal-keepers. The crowds love it, and undoubtedly catches are taken which would never have been attempted in the old days.

As a batsman he always enjoyed himself, and with his twinkling feet (he was once a boxer) he ran very fast between the wickets and stole some outrageous singles. He loved to hit the ball, and scored 98 not out before lunch against India at Lord's in 1952. Two years earlier against the West Indies at Old Trafford he made the first of his two Test hundreds, and it only took him 2 hours 20 minutes. In contrast, in the fourth Test at Adelaide in 1947, he took 97 minutes to score his *first* run in a back-to-the-wall partnership with Denis Compton. But no matter what he scored, the cricket always came to life when Godders was batting.

Off the field Godders was always the life and soul of every party. His outrageous 'Carmen Miranda' won the fancy-dress prize on all the boat trips to and from Australia. In 1958–9, with Trevor Bailey, Frank Tyson and Raman Subba Row, he founded the 'Bowers Club', of which I had the honour to be elected a member. It was a male-only drinking club, and we would meet once a week and carry out various rituals invented and conducted by Godders, accompanied by the odd glass of wine.

He was always a gambler at heart, so he was especially happy in his consultancy job for Ladbrokes. Not all of his ventures were successful, however. Most of his benefit money went into chickens, but they all got the croup! He was in the marcasite business, and used to bring samples of his wares to the dressing room, but I believe his partner 'disappeared'. There was also the little matter of some land development on the Essex coast: unfortunately, someone forgot to obtain planning permission! At one time he was mine host in a pub on the A3 just outside Petersfield. You had to be a bit wary of calling in to see him, as he would greet you warmly and announce to the assembled drinkers that the drinks were on you! He was also the genial host at the Sportsman's Club, greeting all and sundry as if he had known them all his life. In spite of – or perhaps because of – all his varied activities, I doubt he ever became a millionaire, but he brought fun and laughter to all his countless friends and to every stranger he met.

For years after he had retired from cricket Godders still turned out in charity matches with his mutton-chop whiskers and the glasses which he later wore. He would crouch close up to the stumps and bring off miraculous stumpings, often down the leg-side, which was his speciality. He would keep for about an hour and then go off, having shown to an admiring younger generation what *real* wicket-keeping looks like.

14 Jim Laker, Neil Harvey, Trevor Bailey

Jim Laker

I KNEW JIM FOR A long time, first as a player, then later as a commentator, but it wasn't until the last few years of his life that I got to know him as a real friend. For two years we travelled together round England with a cricket show called *That's Cricket*. It consisted of a number of films and a panel of three people such as Jim, Freddie Trueman, Tom Graveney, Ray Illingworth and Trevor Bailey, chaired by myself. It had a simple format and played to big audiences. We did about twenty-five shows and filled places like the new Entertainment Centre in Nottingham (twice), the Fairfield Hall in Croydon (twice), and the Palace Theatre in Manchester.

It was the brainchild of music impresario Raymond Gubbay, who has put on so many concerts at the Barbican. In 1984 he had the Barbican booked for a concert one evening just after Christmas, so he thought, why not use it in the afternoon and have a show which would attract cricket enthusiasts of all ages? And so for three Christmases running we packed the Barbican, and it was a joy to see the wonderful mix of ages in the audience, with a large number of young boys home for the Christmas holidays.

Which brings me back to Jim. I had always known that he had a dry sense of humour, not always apparent in his television commentaries. He was always a slow, deliberate mover – calm and unhurried. It was the same when he spoke, either as a successful after-dinner speaker or when taking part in our show – his delivery was always slow and deliberate. He had a fund of cricket stories and told them beautifully, with a chuckle in his voice. His timing of the punch-line was perfect. He soon became the one regular member of our panel and got tremendous belly laughs wherever we went but, as anyone who ever heard him on television will know, he also had an outstanding cricket brain and great knowledge of the game, based on his own experiences in big cricket. So in addition to the 'funnies' he was a vital member of the panel in the serious discussions which we had about cricket in the programme.

I have unashamedly 'inherited' one of his best stories, and I am sure that he wouldn't mind. It was when he went to India with a Commonwealth team captained by Richie Benaud. The Australian left-arm bowler George Tribe was in the side and he had the Indian batsmen in a lot of trouble with his chinaman (the left-arm bowler's off-break). Time and time again he would force the batsman back on to his stumps and then rap him on the pad with one of his off-breaks. Each time he appealed, the Indian umpire would say: 'Very close, Mr Tribe – but too high. Another inch lower and I would have had to give him out.' Or: 'Sorry, Mr Tribe, but your big spin turned too much,' and so on.

After about six of these appeals Tribe trapped another batsman slap in front of the stumps. 'How about that one then?' he shouted. 'I nearly had to raise my finger, Mr Tribe, but I must give the batsman benefit of the doubt.' At this Tribe lost his temper, turned round and took the umpire by the throat, and, pointing him towards the batsman, said: 'Have another look.'

The terrified umpire did take another careful look and after a short pause raised his finger and said: 'You're right, Mr Tribe, he is out!'

Jim of course will always be remembered for his unbelievable analysis of 19 for 90 – in the 1956 Test against Australia at Old Trafford – one record I cannot believe will ever be broken, let alone equalled. It was the more remarkable because, although the pitch did later take spin, England, batting first, made a total of 459. Jim's Surrey colleague Tony Lock then bowled *69 overs* in the match and took *1 for 106*, whereas Jim only bowled *68 overs* for his 19 wickets. Goodness knows what would have happened to Jim these days in similar circumstances – his ten colleagues would have leaped on him, hugged him and kissed him. In 1956, after his final successful appeal for lbw, he just swung round, took his sweater from the umpire, and with head down walked with measured tread back towards the pavilion. There was the odd clap on the back from his team, but basically they were as shattered as he was by sheer disbelief at what had happened. They formed an avenue for Jim to lead them back into the pavilion, where ten minutes or so later I rushed across to get him to come to our television scaffolding to do an interview.

I always remember the scene in the English dressing room. There was shouting and jubilation and the popping of champagne corks, but Jim himself was sitting quietly alone in a corner, sipping something which looked strangely like orangeade. He came and did his interview, still in a daze, and unable to explain why he had taken so many wickets and Lock only one. I think he did go so far as to say he wouldn't mind taking the pitch around with him for the rest of his career, but he was too modest to admit that it was his superb bowling and their lack of technique in playing spin which really caused the downfall of the Australian batsmen.

There was no M6 in those days and, still in a state of shock, he drove slowly down the A34 on the five-hour drive to London, where, believe it or not, he had to play in a match the next day for Surrey at the Oval. And guess who it was against? The Australians, of course, in the second match of the tour against Surrey. In their first match in May, Jim had taken 10 for 88 and 2 for 42. In this second one he was a comparative failure with 4 for 44 and 1 for 17. This meant that at the end of the summer Jim's total number of wickets against the Australians was 63.

To return to Jim's drive home: he stopped at a pub in Lichfield for a snack and quite unrecognised, sat quietly in a corner and watched the television recording of his amazing feat. No one even offered him a drink. It's just as well he *wasn't* recognised, since he was driving.

His success against Australia must have delighted him since in 1948 they had collared him, and in 1953 he only played in three of the Tests and took just nine wickets. In fact he did not gain a regular place in the England team until 1956. One final analysis cannot be left out when looking at his records. It's 14–12–2–8 in the Bradford Test Trial in 1950 – an amazing piece of bowling on a drying pitch on a ground just five miles from his birthplace (Frizinghall).

In the field Jim was no greyhound but usually fielded at gully, where he was a safe catcher. With a top Test score of 63 he was a useful number nine and at Headingley in 1953 made 48 in a match-saving partnership of 57 with Trevor Bailey, who batted for 262 minutes for just 38 runs. They were together on the last morning with Jim scoring nearly all the runs. It was a beautifully sunny day and they were desperately playing for time. With two minutes to go before lunch Bailey summoned Laker to a mid-wicket conference. He looked up at the blue sky and dazzling sun and said to Jim who was due to play at the last over: 'Go to Frank Chester at square leg and appeal against the light.' Jim was amazed but Bailey urged him to do so, reminding him that they were then allowed one appeal per session against the light.

So, reluctantly, Jim went up to Frank Chester, who asked him what he wanted. 'I'm appealing against the light,' said Jim. Frank stared at him in disbelief but Jim said: 'We are allowed to do so by the present Test regulations, and it means that you must go and consult Frank Lee, the other umpire.' The seconds were ticking by and Frank reluctantly made his way over to the bowler's end. By that time it was almost half past one on the clock, and Lindsay Hassett the Australian captain stormed off the field in disgust. It was not a sporting ploy, but it saved England having to face another over before lunch.

Jim left Surrey in 1959 and went at Bailey's invitation to play for Essex as an amateur. At about this time a ghosted autobiography called *Over to Me* got Jim into hot water with both Surrey and Lord's, mainly because of some criticisms he made of Peter May. However, all was later forgiven and he was welcomed back to the Oval, where he did much useful work on committees and was always willing to help the young players on the staff with advice and coaching.

In 1970 I left BBC Television as one of their cricket commentators after twenty-four years, and from then until his sad death in April 1986, Jim and Richie Benaud were the main television commentators. Jim was a match for Richie. He learned to time his short, pithy comments to match the action and never spoke unless it was necessary. He was an excellent reader of the game, a kind critic and had a sound knowledge of tactics, something he probably learned from Stuart Surridge, whom he used to say was the best captain he ever played under. Surridge had a gift for leadership and, whereas he would get Tony Lock to do his best by a spot of swearing and an aggressive approach, he always treated Jim gently – a sound piece of psychology.

I must just finish with one other story which Jim used to tell so well on our cricket show, *That's Cricket*. He would remind the audience that in the 1984 series against the West Indies Pat Pocock was recalled to the England side for the fourth Test at

Old Trafford. There he bowled over forty-five overs and took four for 121, so justifying his selection, though he did make a pair when batting. At the Oval he didn't get a bowl in the West Indies' first inning, which closed at 190 towards the end of the first day thanks to Botham taking five wickets.

Pocock, always called Percy, was told by David Gower to pad up and prepare to go in as night-watchman if either Fowler or Broad got out early. He was naturally very apprehensive at the thought of facing the likes of Marshall, Holding and Garner in somewhat uncertain light. As it turned out, Broad was soon bowled by Garner for 4, and there was panic in the English dressing room as they couldn't find Percy.

After a brief search they found him in the washroom below the dressing room, gargling and cleaning his teeth. 'Hurry up, Percy,' they shouted. 'You're in as night-watchman. What on earth are you doing?' 'Oh,' said Percy, as he went up the stairs to collect his bat and helmet, 'I was just rinsing and cleaning out my mouth, in case Bernie Thomas [the physiotherapist] has to give me the kiss of life!' I wish you could have heard Jim tell that story.

Neil Harvey

He was easy to pick out on the field. Only five feet six inches tall, he moved very fast with small steps, and was a perky, cocky figure in the nicest possible way. Because of his height he always gave the appearance of being very close to the ground, and this helped him to be one of the best ever fielders in Test cricket. He prowled about in the covers, covering a tremendous amount of ground. He was as quick as lightning and his returns to the wicket-keeper came whizzing in over the top of the stumps. In later years he became equally good as a slip fielder. Incidentally, although a left-handed batsman, he threw with his right.

He ranks with Bradman, Greg Chappell and Allan Border as one of the most successful Australian Test batsmen. He started his Test career earlier than any of them, playing in his first Test when only nineteen years of age – the youngest of *any* Australian. He was successful straight away. He made a century in his *first* club match, and a century in his *first* game for Victoria. He scored 153 in his *second* Test against India in 1947, and then a year later at Headingley made a hundred in his *first* Test match against England. For the next fifteen years he was one of the mainstays of Australia's batting, normally going in at number three, occasionally at number four. He played 79 tests and made 6,149 runs at an average of 48.41.

I give these statistics, but I doubt if Neil himself knew their details. Averages meant nothing to him. He was one of that all too rare breed of Test cricketers who only enjoyed batting when he was playing strokes – and he had plenty of those. I suppose his greatest asset was his nimble footwork. He loved to dance down the pitch to the spinners, and occasionally to the quicker bowlers too. His defensive technique was faultless, and enabled him to play better than his colleagues on a turning pitch. He had all the left-hander's strokes through the off-side, and if he had a weakness it was because he was always prepared to have a go against anything outside the off-stump. He realised that he could have left many of the balls alone, but that to him would have been *boring*.

He had what at that time was an unorthodox way of dealing with short balls pitched on his stumps. He would step back to give himself room, and crash the ball through the covers. Nowadays of course in one-day cricket everyone tries to 'give themselves room', resulting in many who do so being clean-bowled. One other feature of his batting was his speed between the wickets. He was one of the best runners I have seen.

His biggest disappointment was when he took a pair in Jim Laker's match at Old Trafford in 1956. He may have blamed the pitch for his dismissal in the first innings, when he was bowled by a turner from Laker. But he had no excuse in the second innings. Colin Cowdrey caught him at mid-on off that rare Laker ball – a full pitch!

He made four tours to England in 1948, 1953, 1956 and 1961. Not many other Australians have done this, though Bertie Oldfield, Don Bradman, Greg Chappell, Rodney Marsh and Dennis Lillee come to mind as some who did. In 1961 Neil was vice-captain to Richie Benaud, and a very happy partnership they made. Richie had shoulder trouble after the first Test, so Neil was captain in the second at Lord's, which Australia won by five wickets. There's a nice story told about him and Alan Davidson. Alan had the reputation of being a bit of a hypochon-driac, and was always leaving the field with some 'injury' or other. He used to spend most of his waking hours on the massage table. In England's first innings he had hobbled off after taking one wicket, and when the Australians returned to the dressing room at lunch there he was lying on the table, groaning about some damage to his ankle.

Australia's bowling, robbed of Benaud, was not too strong and relied heavily on Davo to support McKenzie, Misson and Mackay. Davo and Neil got on well together – they both played for New South Wales. So Richie thought he would try to per-suade Davo to return to the field after lunch. He pleaded away at Davo without much success until he thought of a subtle ploy. 'This is Neil's first Test as captain. Won't you support him? He needs you badly out there.' Davo thought for a moment and then just as the team were leaving to go out to field, suddenly leaped off the table. 'For the little fellow,' he said, 'I would do anything. For him anything I'd do,' and with that he went back on to the field and promptly took four more wickets in a devastating piece of fast left-arm bowling. He took five for 43 and England were all out for 206 – May, Barrington, Lock and Trueman all falling to the rejuvenated Davo. This was the only time that Neil captained Australia and he was always proud of never having led Australia to defeat!

One interesting thing people may not have known about Neil. In later years – as befitted his position as a selector – he looked very imposing in his horn-rimmed spectacles, but he didn't just wear them for effect. He needed them. I discovered this in 1961 when I took Richie and Neil to see *The Sound of Music* at the Palace Theatre during the Lord's Test. As we took our seats in the dress circle, the lights dimmed and I saw Neil put his hand in his pocket and put on a pair of spectacles. I had never seen him in them before, so afterwards I asked him about them. He then confessed that he had always been short-sighted and couldn't even read the number on an approaching bus. I must say I was amazed – to think that such a superb batsman could not see clearly. How many runs might he have made if his eyesight had been normal? Even so, in that last tour in 1961 he made Test scores of 114, 73, 53, 35, and in the following year against Ted Dexter's team he made scores of 39, 57, 64, 154. Not bad for a batsman with a white stick.

Trevor Bailey

I suppose the best exponent of the forward defensive stroke in my time was Trevor Bailey, and ironically he lives in a road called The Drive! In most people's minds he will always be the dour defender, enjoying far more the minutes or even hours spent at the crease rather than the number of runs he scored. In a sense this is a false picture. In his early days he was a free stroke-maker, and for Essex throughout his career he was always happy to attack, but somehow in Tests the mantle of saviour and rescuer of his side fell on his shoulders. It became expected of him, and goodness knows there were plenty of occasions when England needed to be rescued.

So it became a habit with him, and once set in a groove he found it difficult to change his style. He revelled in a crisis and was a great baiter of the opposition. He would wait for a fast bowler to start his run and then step away from his wicket pretending he had a fly in his eye. You had to have guts to do that sort of thing to someone like Keith Miller, but 'The Boil' had plenty of them. And he never batted in a helmet, and seldom in a cap – just curly black hair to protect his head.

He enjoyed causing aggravation and frustration to his opponents – especially Australians! A good example of this was his 71 in four-and-a-quarter hours at Lord's in 1953 when on the last day he and Willie Watson's partnership for the fifth wicket of 163 saved England from certain defeat. A later occasion was at Brisbane in 1958 when for Peter May's side in the first Test he scored 48 in 7 hours 38 minutes! But at Brisbane in 1954 he had actually hit a six clean out of the ground off Ian Johnson. This proved two things: firstly, that he *could* hit the ball when he wanted to and, secondly, that an incentive can work wonders. A local businessman had offered £100 to the first batsman to hit a six in the match. The Boil had got to hear of this and decided to have a go. £100 went a long way in those days and it provided a spectacular party for the England team at Lennon's Hotel.

Trevor was basically a middle-order batsman, but in fact enjoyed going in first and on the 1958 tour opened the innings in four Tests. Years later in the commentary box, a gleam of appreciation would come into his eyes if he saw a batsman play a correct defensive stroke – head still, eyes on the line of the ball, bat slightly angled down, making contact with the ball just in front of the left foot. More than any other batsman The Boil used to 'smell' the ball.

He was a genuine all-rounder, and was one of the few Test players who could get into the side *either* as a batsman *or* as a bowler, supported by his magnificent fielding and catching close to the wicket. He did the double 8 times, scored a thousand runs 17 times and took 100 wickets 9 times. In 1959 he even made 2,011 runs and took 100 wickets, admittedly with a little help from a successful Scarborough Festival.

I first saw him bowl at Lord's in 1945 when, as a strapping young man in the Royal Marines, he played for the Royal Navy against the Army. He and his side-kick A. W. H. Mallett – also from Dulwich – both took three wickets. He was then fast and lively with a beautiful high action. As he developed he settled for accurate fast-medium with swing and movement off the pitch, and because of his action could extract bounce from the pitch. He took 132 Test wickets and for five years was the main support for Alec Bedser and Brian Statham. Undoubtedly his best bowling performance was on a shiny shirt-front pitch at Sabina Park, Kingston in 1954. He opened the bowling with Trueman and took 7 for 34 in 16 overs, which, coupled with Len Hutton's 205, enabled England to win by nine wickets and so square the series 2–2.

I mentioned earlier his fine close fielding, and against Australia in 1956 at Lord's I saw him make one of the best catches I have ever seen. Trueman was bowling at his fastest from the Nursery End to Neil Harvey the left-hander. A ball pitched on Neil's leg-stump and he hit it really hard round the corner. The Boil was at backward short leg and flung himself at full length to his right, making a brilliant one-handed catch inches off the ground.

Essex should be eternally grateful for their local Westcliffe boy. In addition to his all-round performances for the county he did sterling work as captain (1961–6) and secretary (1954–67). In those days Essex had their travelling circus of mobile score-board, and lorries carrying chairs, tents and so on. They played on at least six different grounds, and you can imagine the organisation required to prepare each ground for a first-class match. I have seen The Boil selling tickets at the gate, dealing with members in the secretary's tent, going out to toss and on occasions helping to mop up flooded marquees. But somehow he coped with it all, and in between his various duties – he would then go out and do his bit on the field. Luckily he has always had a great sense of humour – sometimes slightly wicked – and so he took everything in his stride.

Besides cricket he has had a versatile career. He got a soccer blue for Cambridge, played for Leytonstone and won an FA Amateur Cup medal. He used to be a fanatical cinema-goer and on tours or in the evenings of county matches would slip off to the local flea-pit. He was a tremendous party-goer and enjoyed his food and drink.

Australia 1958–9 was my first tour and The Boil made me welcome and helped me a lot. It was all new to me, but he was an old campaigner and knew all the ropes. I remember that when the MCC were playing Victoria he was not selected, so he took me up to the outback, where we visited a snake farm. We were both visibly shocked because the snakes were fed with live mice!

Anyway, it was lucky for him that he was not playing because there was a heatwave, with the dry hot wind from the Northern Territories making the Melbourne ground like a cauldron. It was difficult to breathe and all the cars, railings and seats became red-hot to touch. Out in the middle it was unbearable. The players had ice-cooled scarves round their necks, drinks were tucked away behind the stumps or hidden under caps and, uniquely, I should say, Colin Cowdrey, who was captain instead of Peter May, gave Trueman, Loader and Tyson one-over spells. Poor John Mortimore had to bowl twenty overs and as a result was sick on the pitch. He had been flown out as a reinforcement with Ted Dexter.

This led to the lovely story of the two old members reading their papers in a St James's Street Club. 'I see MCC have asked for reinforcements and they are sending out Dexter and *Mortimore*,' said one of them. 'What's that you say?' said the other. 'How many did you say they were sending – forty more?'

Since he stopped playing, The Boil has had a number of interests – public relations, importing German wines and countless other mysterious businesses, all of which, knowing The Boil, have been highly successful. He has been cricket and football correspondent for the *Financial Times*, and has shown his deep knowledge of both games with his critical descriptions of play.

He is now best known, however, for his long association with *Test match Special* on BBC Radio. He is the doyen of the commentary box, as he made his first broadcast in 1965 when I was still with television. He is a splendid person to have in the box, one hundred per cent reliable and professional, and able to fill in at a moment's notice and keep talking during any crisis.

He has other uses too. People are very kind and send us up the odd bottle to the commentary box. The Boil is a great silent remover of corks, so that listeners don't hear a loud pop in the background. You can always tell when he is in the box because several times a day he produces a high-pitched sneeze, which is usually repeated six times.

To sum The Boil up: he was a great and genuine Test all-rounder, who could have been an excellent England captain with his knowledge of tactics and techniques, but he broke his contract with the MCC by writing a book about Len Hutton's West Indian tour and he was never forgiven. He is a splendid companion and colleague both in and out of the box, though he is rather like a homing pigeon. After each day's play of a London Test he goes back to his wife Greta, and their home in The Drive. During other Tests he always goes home at weekends. He certainly enjoys his life.

15 The Four W's, Tom Graveney, Peter May, Brian Statham

The four W's

YES, I KNOW IT'S NORMALLY the three W's, but I am cheating slightly. I am adding Wes to Worrell, Walcott and Weekes. My excuse is that everyone calls him Wes, so that the Hall becomes superfluous. He is also such a great personality and was such a magnificent fast bowler that he merits joining the ranks of the three musketeers. Together they form a perfect contrast in character and skills, and during their playing time were the driving force which took the West Indies to the top of the International League. There are and were many other fine players who contributed to the successes of the West Indies – I have already included Sobers, Lloyd and Richards – but space prevents me from naming them all. It would make a book in itself.

Frank Worrell

Of my four, Sir Frank Worrell during his short life had more influence on West Indies cricket than possibly any other West Indian. He was the first black man to captain them, and welded together the various islands with all their differences into a team. He was dignified, calm, friendly and had that indefinable attribute of charisma. He was captain in 15 Tests, winning 9, losing 3, drawing 2 and tying 1, and his behaviour both on and off the field was always impeccable. He could have played in more Tests had he not decided to study economics first at Manchester University, and later in Jamaica, where he went to live and became a senator in their Parliament. He was, like the other three, born in Barbados but for some reason was unhappy there.

The highlights of his captaincy were undoubtedly the famous Brisbane tie in 1960, and the dramatic last-over finish at Lord's in 1963 which ended in a draw. On both occasions it was his calm leadership which controlled the natural exuberance of the West Indian players. The 1960–1 Australian tour ended with an unprecedented tribute to him and his team. They paraded through the streets of Melbourne in a motorcade cheered by an estimated 500,000 people lining the route. His own personal accolade came in 1964 when he was knighted by the Queen for his services to the game. He retired after the 1963 tour of England and sadly died of leukaemia at the early age of forty-two. Again, uniquely for a cricketer, a memorial service was held for him in Westminster Abbey. It was a tribute and recognition, not just of his captaincy and prowess as a cricketer, but of his outstanding qualities as a man.

The emphasis on his captaincy and character tends to overshadow his skills as a player. He was a graceful batsman with plenty of strokes, good footwork and immense powers of concentration. He played in 51 Tests, scoring 3,860 runs with the remarkably high average of 49.48 and scored 9 hundreds. He enjoyed playing a long innings, as scores of 261 and 197 not out against England will indicate. He was also a useful left-arm bowler, sometimes slow but more often fast-medium, and took 69 Test wickets, though they were fairly expensive at 38.72 apiece. I shall always treasure the memory of keeping wicket to him in a charity match in Kent. I remember standing up to him, so he must have been bowling his slows. Sadly I cannot remember whether I caught or stumped anyone off him, but the odds are that I didn't!

Clyde Walcott

Clyde Walcott was a complete contrast to the feline grace of Worrell. He was six feet two inches tall, burly, immensely strong and one of the hardest hitters the game has ever known. There was never much competition to field at mid-off or mid-on when he was batting. He drove with great power off both the front and back foot and, as if this was not enough, was a fierce square cutter and hooker. In 44 Tests he scored 3,798 runs at the high average of 56.68, twelfth best of all Test cricketers. Like Worrell he enjoyed going on after reaching a hundred. He scored fifteen hundreds in Tests, including 220 and 168 not out against England. Perhaps his best ever achievement was in the West Indies against Australia in 1955. He was at the pinnacle of his career and in five Tests scored 827 runs at 82.70, including five hundreds, and twice scored two hundreds in one match – a Test record. This was a tremendous feat against bowlers like Lindwall, Miller, W. A. Johnston and Benaud. He must also hold another unusual record. In a Test against India at Bridgetown in 1953 he had scored 98 when he was given out (lbw) by his uncle (J. H. Walcott)!

He was a versatile cricketer. In spite of his height and bulk he was a more than competent wicket-keeper, especially to the slows, but I cannot quite remember seeing him flinging himself about as Dujon did in later years. He eventually gave it up after slipping a disc and having his nose broken. At a pinch he could also bowl, medium-paced in-duckers or off-cutters – whatever they were, he did take 11 Test wickets. He continued his versatility after he retired from Test cricket in 1960 and went to live in Guyana. He became a cricket organiser and coach, commentator, manager of the West Indies side to England in 1976, and president of the West Indies board. Finally he too received a knighthood – a just reward for a big friendly man.

Everton Weekes

Everton DeCourcey Weekes had the broadest grin in cricket, and was the most prolific scorer of the three W's. He played in 48 Tests and scored 4,455 runs with an average of 58.61, putting him seventh in the list of Test averages, 0.06 behind Ken Barrington but above Hammond, Sobers and Hobbs. He was smaller than Walcott but seemingly equally powerful, with every known stroke in the game. Words like 'plunder', 'murderous', 'savage' and 'thrash' are constantly used by writers describing some of his innings, and he could be quite merciless in the way he tore into even the strongest attacks. He had two special assets: nimble footwork and guts.

People who played against him in the Test at Lord's in 1957 say that his 90 in the second innings was one of the best and bravest innings they have ever seen. Trueman, Bailey and Statham were exploiting the famous ridge at the Nursery End, and the ball rose sharply every time they hit it. Weekes suffered a cracked bone in a finger of his right hand. In spite of this – and he was obviously in great pain – he attacked the bowling for two-and-three-quarter hours and hit as many as sixteen fours in a superb innings – a tremendous display of guts. I am sure that Godfrey Evans was sorry to have to appeal when he finally caught him off Trevor Bailey.

Everton's most prolific spell of batting came in 1948–9. He scored 141 against England at Kingston in the fourth and final Test of Gubby Allen's tour in March. The following November the West Indies toured India and in the first three Tests he scored 128, 194, 162 and 101. In the fourth Test at Madras he was run out for 90! I suspect that just for once there was no grin on his face! He might have gone on to score many more Test runs but he was forced to retire early because of a bad thigh injury. After retirement his chief claim to fame was as a world-class bridge player – appropriately enough, since he was born in Bridgetown – and he became the third of the three W's to be knighted.

Wes Hall

Lastly, the intruder W. Wes Hall. One of the fastest ever Test bowlers, with probably the longest run-up to the wicket. I remember being in the commentary box at Sabina Park and Wes starting his run from just below us. If we had had longer arms we could very nearly have patted him on the head. He was tall (six feet two inches) and gangling with long arms and legs. In spite of his long run he had tremendous stamina and could bowl for long spells. In 1963 at Lord's in England's second innings on the last day he bowled for nearly three-and-a-half hours unchanged. This of course meant a very slow over-rate, which made England's task much harder.

If you were a spectator it was a joy to watch him as he ran up, gaining pace and lengthening his stride as he approached the stumps. The batsmen, I am sure, held a different view, as they waited for the ball to be hurled at them at something like 90 mph. He could move the ball in the air but it was primarily his pace which won him most of his 192 Test wickets at 26.38 apiece. He had a lovely action as he delivered the ball, left arm high in the air, right arm stretched right back, rather as if he was about to throw a javelin. He followed through a long way down the pitch, often ending up a few yards from the batsman. He could – and did – bowl a fearsome bouncer, but though batsmen feared and hated him *on* the field, he was one of the most popular cricketers *off* it.

He became a smiling gentle giant, witty, friendly and a superb mimic. He seldom stopped talking and he is reported to have told a reporter when he first became a senator in Barbados: 'If you think my run-up was long, wait till you hear my speeches!' He progressed from senator to minister in charge of tourism and sport, and selected a most suitable assistant – Gary Sobers. Wes worked tremendously hard to supply tourists with more facilities than just the sun and the beaches.

It was a coincidence that on the occasions of both the Brisbane tie and the 1963 draw at Lord's he was the bowler to bowl the last over. In Brisbane Australia needed six runs off an eight-ball over to win with three wickets still to fall. At Lord's England needed eight runs to win with two wickets to fall. Wes, under the calming influence of Frank Worrell, kept his head on both occasions, and made certain that he did not bowl a no-ball.

Like most bowlers, he fancied himself as a batsman and there was fierce competition between himself and Charlie Griffith as to who went in above the other. In fact, at the Brisbane tie Wes made his top Test score of 50, and on Colin Cowdrey's tour in 1968 he saved West Indies from defeat in the first Test at Port-of-Spain. He put on 68 for the ninth wicket with Gary Sobers, and batted throughout the final session. As a batsman he had, and played, all the strokes – many of them brilliantly spectacular. The only trouble was that on most occasions he failed to make contact with the ball!

He will always remain one of the greatest characters of cricket, and I treasure the memory of him running up to bowl with the gold crucifix hanging from his neck, glistening in the sun. Like so many West Indians he was always passionately fond of horse racing, and had shares in racehorses in Barbados. What I didn't know until recently was that it had been his ambition as a boy to become a jockey. With his six-foot two-inch frame and well-built body I bet the horses are glad that he didn't.

Tom Graveney

I was lucky enough to see Cyril Walters play. He was the most graceful of batsmen and I would gladly have settled for him, until I saw the elegance and grace of Tom Graveney. Old cricketers have also written and spoken of the two Palairet Brothers, L. C. H. and R. C. N., who played for Somerset in the 1890s. They were both famous for their graceful style, but anyone who saw Tom Graveney will have seen at least their equal. From the moment he glided out to the wicket, tugging at the protruding peak of his cap, he looked all that a cricketer should be. Immaculately turned out in spotless white, he had a certain quality which attracted attention. Once at the crease, every movement was of graceful elegance, not just with his attacking strokes but also in defence. Even when he was not scoring runs, he was never boring.

Basically a front-foot player, he drove beautifully through the off-side and also amassed many runs by steering the ball through empty spaces between square leg and mid-on. He stroked the ball rather than hit it and was a remarkably consistent scorer. His career spanned the years from 1948 to 1972, and during that time he scored more runs than any post-war first-class cricketer – with one exception, Geoff Boycott. Geoff passed him in his final season in 1986, scoring 48,426 runs against Tom's 47,793. Tom also made 122 hundreds, scored 2,000 runs seven times, and 1,000 twenty times. That makes him sound like a run-making machine, but he was not just that. He was a batsman who compelled you to watch and enjoy the manner of his batting.

Whereas the cricket public loved him, he was not always so popular with the selectors when it came to playing for England. His Test appearances came in fits and starts. When he was not chosen the reason given was that he was not a grafter. True enough, his elegant stroke-play meant that he sometimes took a risk and got out, and so compared unfavourably with the dour, unattractive defensive techniques employed by some of the top Test scorers. But even so, in 79 Tests he scored 4,882 runs at an average of 44.38 – a useful man to have in your side!

Funnily enough, he scored far more runs against the West Indies than against Australia, off whose attack he only made one hundred – in the fifth Test at Sydney in 1955, when the rubber had been won. Compare that with his amazing form against the West Indies. In the 1957 series in England he made 258 and 164 against them. Then there was his sensational return when he was recalled at the age of forty to play in the second Test at Lord's. He made 96 and 30 not out, followed by 109, 32, 8, 19 and 165 run out! Two years later at Port of Spain he played a beautiful innings of 118 in the first Test of Colin Cowdrey's tour. So his front-foot style proved highly successful against fast bowlers, as well as against spinners like Sobers and Gibbs.

His career did not run entirely smoothly. Like so many good cricketers he was born in the north-east at Riding Mill, Northumberland, but he went to Bristol Grammar School and played for Gloucestershire from 1948 to 1960, captaining them in 1959 and 1960. There was then a little 'local difficulty' when an amateur, Tom Pugh, was appointed captain in his place.

After a year's break for qualification in 1961, he went to Worcestershire, where he was also captain for three years. It was during his time there that he became an even more accomplished batsman, and his final ten years were the most successful of his career.

As if his Test career had not been interrupted by enough strange selectional decisions, it was to end in an even stranger way in 1969. He played in the first Test against the West Indies at Old Trafford and played his usual stylish innings, this time 75. He had, however, promised an organiser of one of his benefit matches to play in a match at Luton during the Sunday of the Old Trafford Test. There was some misunderstanding between him and Alec Bedser, chairman of the selectors. Tom thought he had made it plain that if he were selected to play in the Test, he would have to honour his promise to play at Luton. Anyway, as a result he was dropped and never played for England again.

When he retired in 1970 he played a few more first-class matches in Queensland, where he was player-coach for two years. He then ran a highly successful pub near Cheltenham racecourse. After he gave that up he became as stylish in his television or radio summaries as he ever was with his batting.

There are two facts about Tom which are not always known by cricketer followers. First, he captained England once – in the fourth Test against Australia at Headingley in 1968 as a result of an injury to Colin Cowdrey. He did not win the match, which was drawn, but he enjoyed the experience. And by coincidence the Australian captain was Barry Jarman, also captaining for the first and only time because of an injury to *his* captain, Bill Lawry.

The other fact not generally known is that in the 1955 Test against South Africa at Old Trafford he actually kept wicket for England. He modestly says that he made 0 and 1 in the match and dropped quite a few catches at slip, so when Godfrey Evans broke his right-hand little finger, Tom was 'chosen' to deputise for him. There were no volunteers for the job, and for a very good reason. Frank Tyson – just back from his triumphant tour of Australia with Len Hutton (he took 28 wickets in the series) – was bowling at his fastest, and everyone at the time said that for two years or so he was the fastest bowler anyone had ever seen. Tom stood halfway back to the boundary and prepared apprehensively to take the first express. It was down the legside. Tom stretched out to try to take it, and the ball broke *his* little finger. It still looks the worse for wear.

Peter May

When I became a television commentator in 1946 I was introduced to the world of first-class cricket. I had been an avid follower from a distance for over twenty-five years, but now I was to meet and work with the first-class players themselves. After six years of war without the county championship there was plenty to talk about, but in most conversations a new name kept on cropping up. There was talk about a new Hutton or Compton, still only seventeen years old but said by George Geary to be the best young batsman he had ever seen. The boy was Peter May, who was still at Charterhouse, where George was the highly respected and much loved coach. Peter had got into the first eleven there when only fourteen years old, and, what's more, headed the batting averages at the end of the summer. Three years later he made a brilliant 146 at Lord's, playing for the Public Schools against the Combined Services.

In 1948 he began his National Service in the Royal Navy as Writer May and made his first-class début for the Combined Services. By 1950 he was up at Cambridge, where he gained a blue for the next three years. In the same year, after the university match, he began the first of his fourteen seasons with Surrey. One interesting fact which often traps contestants in sports quizzes: 'Peter May was captain of Cambridge. In what year did he captain them in the University match at Lord's?' The answer is that he never did. He was not captain at cricket but at soccer.

He played in his first Test match in 1951 at Headingley against South Africa, and inevitably he scored a hundred (138). Alas, I was not there to see it. At that time there was no Holme Moss transmitter, so BBC Television was still unable to cover matches at Old Trafford or Headingley. Peter wasn't so successful in his first encounters with the Australians in 1953. When Surrey played them at the Oval Peter was deliberately subjected to some short fast bowling from Lindwall, Davidson and Archer. They were determined to eliminate this up-and-coming star, and succeeded. He made 0 and 1, and when selected for the first Test he only made 9. He was then dropped until the final Ashes-winning Test at the Oval, where he played two vital innings of 39 and 37.

It was tough going, but from then on he played in the next 54 Tests until the first of his back operations in July 1959. His highest Test score – and perhaps his most significant innings – was his 285 not out against the West Indies in England's second innings in the first Test at Edgbaston in 1957. His stand of 411 with Cowdrey not only saved the match for England but finally released England from the grip of Ramadhin, who, after bowling 98 overs in the innings and taking 2 for 179, was never again a real threat to England.

How good a batsman was Peter, and did he live up to his early reputation as a future Hutton or Compton? I believe that he is still the outstanding English batsman who started playing *after* the war. There are obviously a few contenders for this title – people like Cowdrey, Graveney and Boycott – but somehow Peter just topped them all. He was technically perfect in both defence and attack. He played very straight and was equally good on the back or front foot. He had every stroke, but his speciality was the perfect on-drive, not the easiest stroke to play, as inevitably the batsman has to play slightly across the line of the ball. He was a stronger and more forceful batsman than Cowdrey, without perhaps the latter's delicate timing. He may not have been as graceful as Graveney, but certainly matched Boycott for temperament, determination and love of making runs.

Not only in his technique, but also in his bearing and appearance, he was an ideal example for young players to follow. He was always immaculately turned out – shirt, flannels, pads and boots all spotlessly white. He usually batted without a cap, and all through his career had a boyish look. He was a very safe catcher and fielder, though for a soccer blue he was not noticeably fast over the ground.

He captained England forty-one times and Surrey from 1957 to 1962, and Richie Benaud reckons that he was the best England captain he played against. He absorbed a lot of his cricket knowledge from Len Hutton and played the game as hard as Len had out in the middle, but off the field he appeared shy, modest and sensitive. Although friendly and co-operative, he was not an easy person to interview. He gave little away and parried questions about tactics or what had happened on the field, usually saying that the boys had tried hard and done their best. He also held the strange belief that it was not necessary for him to tell a Test batsman what to do. He said that anyone selected should know how to react to the state of the game, and did not have to be told to score more quickly or to go on the defensive.

It was a sad day for England when he retired from Test cricket in 1961. He had been captain for six years between 1955 and 1961, and had been forced to leave the West Indies tour in 1960 due to trouble in the lower part of his back. He had previously had an operation which went wrong, and batted in great pain for the first three Tests. It meant that he missed the 1960 Test series against South Africa, but he returned in 1961 against Australia, playing in the last four Tests, three of them as captain. And that was it. He had a promising career in the City with a large insurance firm, and over the years he had become tired of criticism from the press. Strangely, they were often critical of him, especially on the 1958–9 tour of Australia, when England lost four of the Tests, although their team had been heralded as the most powerful ever to leave England.

They were, however, handicapped by a succession of injuries to vital players, and the appearance of two new Australian fast bowlers, Meckiff and Rorke. The former's action was suspect, to say the least, and in the end he was no-balled out of Test cricket. Rorke had an enormous drag and would deliver the ball from something like eighteen yards from the batsman. Cowdrey once said that he didn't dare to play forward, in case he hit him. So from a playing point of view the tour was an unhappy one for May, but even worse for him was the way the press attacked him for having his fiancée with him for part of the tour. She was Harold Gilligan's daughter, Virginia, whom Peter subsequently married. As I've said, he was sensitive and he never really forgave the press.

After becoming a highly successful businessman, Peter put a lot back into cricket, both with Surrey and as chairman of the selectors from 1982 to 1988. Once again he had to put up with a lot of flak over Test selections. Obviously the selectors *did* make mistakes, but if one is honest one has to admit that there was not all that much talent from which to select. Peter gave as good as he got to his critics, and although not able to watch as much cricket as he should, he seemed to enjoy the challenge.

When Peter did get any spare time he devoted it to driving a horse box to the various events in which his four 'horsey' daughters took part, but I think he would rather have faced Lindwall or Miller at their best than have got on a horse himself!

Brian Statham

When asked to give the perfect example of what a cricket professional should be, I always choose Brian Statham – or George as he was known to his friends. There are and have been many others who have come near his standard, but he is always top of my list.

He was quiet, modest, loyal, completely free from temperament and a great trier who never gave up. It all sounds too good to be true, but it is. And you can add to all that a lovely dry wit, delivered with a slow smile and a slow Lancashire drawl.

Physically he was wiry, lean, loose-limbed and apparently double-jointed. He had a smooth run-up and a fine action, with his arm so high that it brushed his right ear. He was really fast and he obtained his 252 Test wickets by his accuracy with length and line. He invariably bowled *at* the stumps, on the principle that if the batsman missed the ball, then he was certain to bowl him. He didn't swing the ball in the air but moved it either way off the pitch, and in his Test career proved a magnificent foil to Trueman and Tyson. I suppose that in a sense he was always the junior partner, frustrating the batsmen from the other end. What's more, if there was an uphill slope and a headwind he would be the one chosen to run up it and bowl into it.

Arthur Gilligan told me a story which he swore was true. In a Test match at Perth, Statham had a long spell bowling into the 'Freemantle Doctor' – a stiff breeze which blows up in the middle of the day off the nearby Swan river. At close of play a lady came up to Arthur Gilligan and said: 'Mr Gilligan, would you please give these tablets to Brian Statham.' 'Yes, of course I will. But why?' replied Arthur. 'Oh,' she said, 'I heard you say in your commentary that Statham was suffering from the wind.'

Statham was nicknamed 'the greyhound' or 'whippet' because of his speed in the field. He usually fielded down at long leg or third man, and swooped on the ball and threw with a strong arm into the gloves of the wicket-keeper. He was a left-handed bat and could keep his end up in a crisis. He usually batted at number eleven for England, but occasionally – to his delight – was promoted to number ten or even nine. And once – though please don't spread it around in Yorkshire – he went in *above* Freddie Trueman in the Lord's Test against South Africa in 1955.

I hope I haven't made 'George' sound too perfect, but in addition to what I have already said he was a wonderful tourer, always giving of his best both on and off the field. If journeys or hotels were bad or disorganised – and they often are on tour – he took it all calmly without moaning. And on the field if he missed the stumps by inches, or had an appeal turned down, there were no histrionics. He just got on with the job of trying to get batsmen out.

Just one last thing. He is the only bowler I know who after a long hot day in the field would take off his boots and socks and then talk to his feet – apologising for the way he had treated them!

16 Richie Benaud, Fred Trueman, The Two Little Masters

Richie Benaud

WHO IS THE NATTIEST DRESSED cricket commentator? Who has the neatest coiffure? Who captained Australia in six series, winning five, and drawing one? Who took more Test wickets than any other Australian spinner? Who was the first Test cricketer to make 2,000 runs and take 200 Test wickets? I am sure your buzzers went after the first question, without need of further clues. Yes of course, it's Richie Benaud.

I first met Richie during the 1953 Australian tour of England, when, to be honest, he was not a great success. He played in three Tests, took two wickets for 174, and made 15 runs in five innings, but he finished the tour with a flourish and a warning of things to come. Against T. N. Pearce's eleven at Scarborough he made 135 in 110 minutes, hitting eleven sixes and nine fours, his first hundred in England. He was always a fine driver of the ball, and as his career developed he became a complete stroke-player, which made him into a genuine Test all-rounder.

It was as a leg-spin bowler that he really made his mark, however. He had a fine high action which, especially on overseas pitches in Australia, South Africa and the West Indies, enabled him to get bounce into his deliveries. He was a great one for practising and spent hours in the nets perfecting his mixture of leg-breaks, googlies, top-spinners and flippers. He was not afraid to bowl the latter, which he picked up from Bruce Dooland, and took quite a number of his 248 Test wickets with it. He described it to me as a ball held in the tips of the first and third fingers of the right hand. It is squeezed or flipped out of the hand from underneath the wrist – rather like flipping a cherry stone. The object is to bowl it just on or outside the off-stump. It hurries from the pitch, usually straight but sometimes from off to leg. It is a surprise ball which often traps a batsman who has played back.

Richie was not a big spinner of the ball, but he was always accurate and with his flight, line and bounce was difficult to score off. English pitches did not suit him, but in spite of a bad shoulder he did win the fourth Test for Australia at Old Trafford in 1961 by bowling his leg-breaks round the wicket into the rough outside the leg-stump. His analysis is worth noting – superb figures for a slow bowler: 32–11–70–6.

The fact that he was a brilliant close fielder, especially in the gully, made him the complete all-rounder, but it was as a captain that he probably did most for Australia. He was certainly the best post-war captain whom I saw. He had everything a captain needs. He was a natural leader who inspired his teams to play above themselves. He was a motivator and he animated and encouraged them both on and off the field, where he placed great importance on a happy dressing room. On the field I'm afraid he was really the starter of the hugging and kissing which goes on so much today. I asked him about it once and he said he was prepared to do anything if it helped to take wickets. Tony Lock carried on the habit when he came to captain Leicestershire – so much so that Maurice Hallam, normally an excellent fielder, once dropped two catches running down at long leg. When asked why he hadn't caught them, he is said to have replied: 'What, and be kissed by Tony Lock. Not bloody likely!'

Richie was an amazingly good reader of a game, and was quick to spot and memorise an opponent's weakness. He tried to be a positive captain and would attack whenever he could, but he was not prepared to 'play ball' unless the other side responded. A perfect example of this was the fifth Test at Sydney in 1963 against Ted Dexter's side. The series was level, and a thoroughly dull game followed England's desperately slow first innings of 321.

Off the field Richie was the best PRO of any captain I have seen. At the end of each day, however hot and tired, he would meet the press, television and radio, and answer questions about the day's play. He took as much trouble to learn to commentate as he did to learn to bowl. When still captain of Australia he joined TMS for radio commentary on the South African Tests in England in 1960. He soon picked up the tricks of the trade and joined BBC Television when he retired from Test cricket in February 1964.

People often ask me why we have to have an Australian on BBC. The answer is simply that he is the best. He has tremendous knowledge of the tactics and techniques of the game, is quick-witted and knows when to talk or not to talk. He is also a very good summariser at the end of the day's play. He is fluent, knowledgeable, unflappable and remembers all the details of the play. What more can a producer ask for?

In his spare time – which is very scarce – Richie is a dedicated golfer and thinks nothing, during a Test match, of getting up at five o'clock to play a game of golf before going off for a day's commentary. He is also a great connoisseur of food and wine, and at the end of a season he and his wife Daphers sometimes go off for a gastronomic holiday in France. It may seem as if I have eulogised Richie too much, but he is an exceptional person, combining, as he does, his knowledge and experience of Test cricket with the ability to put it over on television.

Fred Trueman

As I have said before, people often say to me: 'Where are the characters in first-class cricket today?' and they usually add: 'As there used to be, with people like Freddie Trueman.' He certainly was – and still is – a remarkable character. Larger than life, belligerent, with a quick temper usually matched with a shaft of Rabelaisian wit. Intensely patriotic and strongly to the right in his politics and opinions.

He tells a story as well as anyone I have ever heard. They are usually blue and laced with expletives, but given the right audience they are very funny, and when he retired from first-class cricket he did a round of the clubs as a stand-up comic. He has become one of the most 'in demand' of all after-dinner speakers. With his cigar and excellent timing he can keep going for well over an hour. He gets over the difficulty of speaking to a mixed audience by saying: 'If any of you ladies want to know what a stag night is then listen to me' – and then proceeds to give his normal act! He enjoys telling stories and one-liners and usually has a fresh one when he arrives at the commentary box each morning – like the time he asked me if I knew about the flasher who had decided to retire. When I obediently said no, Fred said: 'Well, he's decided to stick it out for another year.'

He was a great entertainer and played to the crowds with his ferocious gestures and expressions. He was tough and physically strong and kept going far longer than the modern fast bowlers. He not only gave his all for England, but also in ordinary county games for Yorkshire, and he regularly took 100 wickets a year. I cannot remember him losing his Test place through injury or strains. He acquired the reputation of being temperamental and difficult to handle, and the press always pictured him as a 'naughty boy', who drank large quantities of beer and made unacceptable remarks to officials or dignitaries on tour. Certainly, one or two captains preferred not to take him on tour, and he has often said that had he gone on the tours to Australia in 1954–5, and South Africa in 1956–7 and 1964–5, he might well have taken 400 Test wickets. In fact he was not a beer drinker, and on tour I always found him a bit of a loner. As with Winston Churchill many apocryphal stories are told about him – such as when he was meant to have said to a West Indian official at a dinner, 'Pass the salt, Gunga Din' – but here is one which I believe to be true.

When he came in to bat at number ten in a Test against the West Indies in 1954, Jeff Stollmeyer crowded him with four short legs, a silly point, close gully, and two slips. All the fielders were surrounding the stumps, with Fred glowering in the middle of them. 'If you bring any of these b---s in any closer, I'll appeal against the flippin' light,' he said to Jeff.

Another story concerns the present Bishop of Liverpool, David Sheppard. Back in the 1950s, before he became a clergyman, Sheppard was an outstanding captain of Cambridge and had already played in four Tests for England.

Evidently the Roman Catholics challenged the Church of England to a needle cricket match at Lord's. The Archbishop was very keen to win and ordered David Sheppard's ordination to be hurried through so that he would be qualified to play. This was duly done and David played at Lord's. The Archbishop rang up during the luncheon interval to find out the latest score. 'Oh, your Grace,' said the canon in charge of cricket, 'we are not doing very well. We won the toss and batted and at lunch are 55 for 5.'

'Oh dear,' said the Archbishop, 'that's bad. What happened to the Rev. David Sheppard?'

'He had back luck, your Grace. He had to retire hurt at 0. He was knocked out by a bouncer which hit him on the head. It was bowled by a fast bowler the Roman Catholics had called Father Trueman!'

Fred was certainly one of the great Test bowlers of all time, and not just because he was the first one to take 300 Test wickets. He did this in the fifth Test at the Oval in 1964 against Australia. He knew he had taken 299, and when Ted Dexter appeared to be hesitating as to whom to put on to bowl Fred seized the ball and measured out his run. I was lucky to be commentating on television at the time and saw Colin Cowdrey catch Neil Hawke – an old friend of Fred's – at first slip. There were emotional scenes of congratulations and I remember that Colin actually hugged Fred – though I don't think he went so far as to kiss him.

He was genuinely fast and for years was much feared on the county circuit and also by some batsmen in Test cricket, especially by the Indians in his Test début against them in 1952. Later he learned from Ray Lindwall the importance of varying his deliveries in pace, and not bowling every ball flat out. He had a long curving run, with his ample bottom acting as a thrust to his slightly bowed legs. He bowled from very close to the stumps with a classical swivel body action, left arm high and his eyes looking over his left shoulder. As a result his main ball, which got him so many of his wickets, was the out-swinger, which swung away late.

In Tests he could and did bowl bouncers, but used them sensibly as a warning and deterrent to the batsmen. He has said that he never wilfully tried to hit a batsman, only to frighten him. I believe him, but he would not deny that *on* the field he hated batsmen, and if he had been hit or snicked for a four, he would walk back to his mark muttering probably unmentionable words to himself. Sir Robert Menzies once speculated in a speech exactly what it was that Fred did say, and came to the conclusion that he must be reciting Greek Iambics!

As a batsman Fred enjoyed having a crack, and with his great strength and a mighty swing hit the ball for many a six, usually in the region of mid-wicket and long-on. When necessary he had a perfectly sound defence and could play a responsible innings which enabled him to make three first-class hundreds.

He was a fine fielder at short leg, especially leg-slip, where with his cap at a jaunty angle, he picked up many spectacular catches. He also had a good arm from the deep, and varied it sometimes by throwing left-handed.

He tells a delightful story of his last match for the Combined Services, for whom he played when doing his national service in the RAF. The match took place the day after the final Test at the Oval in 1953, where in his first Test against Australia his four wickets helped England to regain the Ashes after nineteen years.

When the Combined Services took the field, as an England bowler he naturally expected to be put on first with the new ball. But the naval lieutenant-commander who captained his side thought differently, and threw the ball to a rather portly army captain. Fred was surprised and, muttering to himself, automatically went to leg-slip where he had been fielding for England in the recent Test. 'What are you doing there, Trueman?' asked the lieutenant-commander. 'Go down to long leg. Major Parnaby always fields at leg-slip and has done so for many years.'

So a disgusted Trueman went off to long leg swearing loudly, this time not to himself. He was slightly cheered up when the very first ball went straight through Major Parnaby's hands at leg-slip, and Fred made little effort to save it going for four. At the end of the over he got a rocket from the lieutenant-commander for his behaviour. 'You'll never play again for the Combined Services, Trueman.'

'You're too dead right I won't,' replied Fred. 'I come out of the RAF tomorrow!'

Since he retired Fred has been a much valued member of our *Test match Special* commentary team. His earthy wit enlivens the dullest day and his forthright comments on modern cricket evoke varying reactions. Some people agree with him heartily that things are not what they were. Others think he goes on a bit.

On one occasion he was saying what a unique game cricket was, because everything was done sideways. 'Remember,' he said to the listeners, 'it's a sideways-on game. Everything should be done sideways – the batsman's stance, the bowler's action, the fielder's throwing and so on.' A few days later he received a letter which went something like this:

Dear Mr Trueman,

I heard what you said about cricket being a sideways game. I tried it without success the other day. In the first over I was hit twice on my left temple, twice on the left cheek of my bottom, and the other two balls each went for four byes. You see, I am a wicket-keeper! I don't think your theory works!

He and I are very different people, but we have always got on famously and pull each other's legs whenever we can. It's been a happy time in the box, even with Fred's pipe and cigars. What a character, and what a great bowler!

The Two 'Little Masters'

No book such as this would be complete without a tribute to the two greatest batsmen from India and Pakistan. They were both small (Hanif five feet four and Gavaskar five feet four and three-quarters). They both enjoyed playing long innings and accumulating runs. Their techniques were remarkably similar and a model for any schoolboy. They both had the virtues of dedication, patience and tremendous powers of concentration. They were both extremely courteous, friendly and polite, and it was a real pleasure to have them both up in the commentary box during the summer of 1987.

Hanif Mohammad

Hanif Mohammad was one of four brothers, all of whom played Test cricket for Pakistan. They were Wazir, Hanif, Mushtaq and Sadiq, born in that order. Now to add to them there is Hanif's son, Shoaib. When Hanif played in his last Test at Karachi against New Zealand in 1969, it was his brother Sadiq's first Test. This meant that three brothers played for their country in a Test for the first and only time since the Graces W. G., E. M. and G. F. played for England at the Oval in the first Test in this country against Australia in 1880.

Hanif has black curly hair and always seemed to bat bare-headed. He *could* play all the strokes but seldom did, preferring to soldier on and let the runs come with well-placed pushes.

For such a prolific scorer he had rather disappointing Test figures. In 55 Tests he scored 3,915 runs with an average of 43.98. He scored 12 centuries, including the fourth highest individual score in Tests – 337, which he made against the West Indies in Barbados in 1958. It is the longest ever Test innings and the longest in first-class cricket – 16 hours 10 minutes. It's interesting to note that Len Hutton's 364 took only 13 hours 17 minutes, and Gary Sober's 365 not out a mere 10 hours 14 minutes. This 365 not out was curiously made only just over a month later than Hanif's 337 – in the third Test at Kingston. It says something for the excellence of the West Indian pitches at that time.

Hanif was told an amusing story about his innings. A West Indian supporter watched the first part of it perched perilously on the branch of a tree. He stuck it out for most of the day as Hanif continued relentlessly to add run after run. In the end, either from the heat or sheer boredom the spectator went to sleep, and fell with a resounding crash to the ground, knocking himself out. He was rushed to hospital, where he remained unconscious for some time. When he eventually came round, the hospital nurse told him that he had been 'out' for two hours. Quick as a flash he said: 'I only hope that Hanif has been too!'

It was Hanif and his brother Mushtaq who originally introduced the reverse sweep, as used by Ian Botham, Mike Gatting and John Emburey among others. It is a fun stroke and should never be used on an important occasion. When it is used the ball must be pitched outside the off-stump, otherwise the batsman exposes his wicket to the bowler, but if it *does* pitch outside the off-stump why not cut it or drive it, depending on its length? The reason given for using it is to take advantage of there being only two or three fielders on the off-side.

I once saw it used in a club match, and it caused quite a furore. The Eton Ramblers were playing the RAF Halton just after the war. Colonel A. C. Wilkinson was batting for the Ramblers. He was a fine batsman who had played for the Army, and a very brave man who had been awarded the GC for clearing a minefield single-handed. He also had an impish sense of humour and a quick temper. He soon got bored batting against the RAF and found run-getting too easy. So he thought he would experiment, and proceeded to play a succession of reverse sweeps against their leg-spinner. This infuriated the RAF captain, who was an Air Vice-Marshal. He thought it was an insult to his bowler and that Colonel Wilkinson was mocking him. There was an awful row between the two of them, so that at the end of the game everyone left in a huff without the usual after-the-match niceties.

A few months later Colonel Wilkinson went to the Golf Ball at Grosvenor House. There were various sideshows, including a small putting green. As he passed this the Colonel saw a large figure stooping to pick his ball out of the hole. He quickly recognised his old adversary, the Air Vice-Marshal. So without any hesitation he went up and gave the A V-M a terrific kick up the backside. 'There you are,' said the Colonel. 'So far as I am concerned the incident is now closed!'

But I have digressed again as usual. One strange thing about Hanif's career was his comparative failure in Test matches in England. He came on three tours, in 1954, 1962 and 1967, and only made one hundred – 187 not out at Lord's in 1967. In the other twenty-two Test innings which he played in England, he only scored 429 runs at an average of 19.50.

In January 1959 he scored 499 at Karachi against Bahawalpur. It took him only 640 minutes – not bad going – and incredibly he was run out off the last ball of the day trying to get his 500th run. It remained the highest score in first-class cricket until Brian Lara's record-breaking 501 at Edgbaston in 1994.

Sunil Gavaskar

Inevitably, when writing about these two 'Little Masters', figures and records keep cropping up. The technique which produced all these runs seems to take second place. As I said, their styles were not dissimilar and were both based on the basic rules for batting: sideways on, head down and keep absolutely still. They both got to the pitch of the ball and watched it right on to the bat. They were both equally good against speed or spin.

Sunil Gavaskar – or 'Sunny' as he became – exemplified all these virtues. His small compact figure was usually topped by a white floppy hat, underneath which he had his own home-made helmet. His Test record is remarkable – 125 Tests, 10,122 runs, second only to Allan Border, and more hundreds (34) than anyone else. Only his average of 51.12 is surprisingly low, and it is exceeded by as many as twenty-two other players.

Unlike Hanif he kept more of his big scores for Test matches, and seemed not to worry too much about the other first-class matches in which he played.

It is not difficult to pick out the best innings which I saw him play. It was one of the great fight-backs in all Test cricket, and took place in the fourth Test at the Oval in 1979. England made 305, and India 202. In their second innings England made 334 for 8 declared, leaving India with 438 to get to win. Gavaskar and Chauhan opened for India and by the start of the fifth morning they had progressed to 75 for 0, still needing 363 to win at just over a run a minute. Gavaskar was superb, ably backed up by Chauhan. They never seemed to hurry but the score crept slowly upwards and by tea had reached 304 for 1, Botham catching Chauhan in the slips off Willis for a splendid 80.

With Vengsakar as partner Gavaskar increased the pace and masterminded the whole thing beautifully. As they went for the runs wickets began to fall and Gavaskar was finally caught by Gower at mid-on off Botham for 221, which included 21 fours and had lasted just over eight hours. It deserved to win the match for India, but with England using the regrettable delaying tactics which are now so regularly used in Tests, India still needed 15 to win off the last over. They only got six of them, so it was a draw, but none of us would have grudged them what would have been – and so nearly was – a sensational victory.

Another innings of his that I will always treasure was his magnificent 188 in the MCC Bicentenary match against the Rest of the World. He had to face an opening attack consisting of Malcolm Marshall and Richard Hadlee, supported by Clive Rice, John Emburey and his fellow Indian Ravish Shastri. He dealt with them all in great style and it was a joy to watch the battle between bat and ball. Although not a Test, it was such a unique occasion before a packed crowd that everyone was trying to the full. During the match Gavaskar announced his retirement from Test cricket, and one wondered why. His batting was such perfection, and he showed the enthralled spectators every stroke in the book. A great innings, on a great occasion and a fitting curtain to his brilliant career. When he came up to be interviewed after his innings, we tried to persuade him to continue Test cricket but he was quite adamant.

Gavaskar had two strange lapses during his career. He put

up an extraordinary performance at Lord's in 1975, in the first Prudential World Cup match against England. England had made 334 for 4 off their 60 overs, which admittedly left India with the mammoth task of scoring at a rate of about 5.6 runs per over. Not impossible, but not easy against the England attack of John Snow, Peter Lever, Geoff Arnold and Tony Greig. Anyhow, Gavaskar decided it wasn't on and proceeded to make 36 not out in 60 overs before a 20,000 crowd. Neither they – nor his team – were pleased, especially when he is said to have told them that it was a good opportunity to have some batting practice!

His other equally unaccountable lapse was at Melbourne in 1981 in the third Test against Australia. He had had a bad run of scores in the previous two Tests – 0, 10, 23, 5. He then made only 10 in the first innings of the third, but he found his form at last in the second innings and had scored a good 70 when he was given lbw to Lillee. Whether he had hit it or not I don't know, but he was so angry and upset at the decision that he persuaded his partner, Chauhan, to walk back to the pavilion with him. The game came to a stop, but Chauhan was ordered by his manager to return to the field and all was well. Apologies followed, but it was a strange incident and not typical of 'Sunny'.

Both the 'Little Masters' captained their countries from time to time, and it did not seem to affect their form with the bat, but it is not as captains that they will be remembered. They will stay in my mind as two stylishly correct batsmen who had outstanding powers of concentration and patience and an insatiable desire to make runs – as many of them as possible.

17 Colin Cowdrey, Gary Sobers, Ken Barrington, Ray Illingworth

Colin Cowdrey

ON 30 JULY 1946, I went to Lord's to sit in the sun and watch some schoolboy cricket. The previous day in the Clifton v Tonbridge match a thirteen-year-old playing for Tonbridge had made 75 out of 156 and then had taken three wickets with teasing leg-breaks. Michael Cowdrey, the papers called him and he was said to be the youngest player ever to play at Lord's. I thought I would have a look at this infant prodigy. I was rewarded by seeing him make 44 in his second innings and then win the match for Tonbridge by taking 5 for 59 with his highly tossed leg-breaks; three times he enticed the batsmen down the pitch and was rewarded by three stumpings. He was small but already had a slightly rotund figure.

I enquired about him and was told that his father – a great cricket enthusiast – lived and worked in India and had deliberately given his son the initials MCC. It didn't need an expert to predict a promising future for the young boy, and for once the promise was fulfilled – though not so far as the leg-spin went. Like so many small boys who bowl leg-breaks, as he grew taller they seemed to lose their teasing flight, but his batting got better and better. Three years playing for Oxford University were followed by his selection for Len Hutton's MCC tour of Australia in 1954 at the age of twenty-one. Sadly, his father died before Colin played his first Test, but he did know that Colin had been chosen for the tour and that the MCC gimmick had borne fruit.

From then on Colin was an essential and seemingly inevitable member of the England team: 114 Tests with 7,624 runs, 22 hundreds and 120 catches, captain 27 times, 6 tours of Australia, vice-captain 4 times. An incredible record, and yet somehow it might have been even better.

As a batsman, though heavily built, he was remarkably light of foot with an exceptional eye – two assets which made him such a fine racquets player. He always played straight and had every stroke in the game – and stroke is the right word. He never seemed to hit the ball, but by superb timing seemed to 'waft' it away to the boundary. The late-cut, the off-, straight- and on-drive, and his own particular sweep were strokes I remember best. His sweep was more of a paddle, with the bat vertical rather than horizontal, and played very fine.

His defence was as solid as a rock, and he developed – perhaps overdeveloped – a skilful use of his pads as a second line of defence. The best example of this was his 154 in a record partnership of 411 with Peter May in the first Test against the West Indies in 1957. It is still the highest fourth-wicket partnership in all Test cricket, and successfully put paid to the mystery spin of Ramadhin. By sound judgement of where his off-stump was, Colin used his pads not just as a second line of defence but also a first line. It proved effective, but wasn't pleasant to watch.

He not only played spin well but was even better against fast bowling. He showed his class by always seeming to have plenty of time to play the ball, and never had to hurry. He often opened for England and played some of his biggest innings when going in first. But he was equally happy and effective batting lower in the order.

I am not the only one to think that, great player as he undoubtedly was, he could perhaps have been the greatest. So what was the flaw which stopped him reaching even greater heights? Strange to say, it was a lack of confidence in his own ability. He would often start off an innings brilliantly and then suddenly for no apparent reason shut up shop and get into all sorts of difficulties. In spite of his tremendous successes he would every now and again begin experimenting with a new grip on his bat or a new stance for his feet. Perhaps too he lacked the final killer instinct. But no matter – he was a great batsman in every sense of the word.

He was in the highest class as a slip fielder, that class including Hammond, Miller, Simpson, Sharpe, G. Chappell and Botham. Of course the quickness of his eye helped, but he believed in practice and you could always see him taking part in the catching sessions round a slip machine. It was the same with his batting. He had a net and a bowling machine in his garden. This not only gave him practice but helped him to coach his sons, two of whom – Christopher and Graham – followed him into the Kent side, with Chris having also played in six Tests. Colin's wife, Penny, was also a useful bowler and I once convulsed the commentary team by saying that 'her swingers were practically unplayable' (she had taken five wickets when playing against Graham's junior school).

This lack of confidence and a killer instinct perhaps prevented Colin from being a great captain, though he was a sound enough tactician and a natural leader of men. On a tour he ran a happy ship and always included the media in this. He was a good communicator and his public relations were superb. Nothing was too much trouble, and he paid innumerable visits to schools and hospitals, as well as striking the right note at all the social functions. If a problem cropped up on or off the field, however, he was strangely indecisive.

A perfect example of this was the fourth Test in Trinidad in 1968. Sobers had sportingly declared to set England to score 215 in 165 minutes. At tea England had lost Edrich and were behind the clock, but Boycott and Cowdrey were batting well and, with so many wickets in hand, it seemed definitely worth while for England to take risks and go for victory. Colin had to be persuaded that it was possible, his inclination being to play safe. As it was, he and Boycott attacked the bowling and England won with three minutes to spare. But it had taken quite a lot of persuasion by Ken Barrington, in particular, to convince Colin that he was capable of playing in the way he finally did.

As a character he was kind, caring and sensitive, and was a great one for saying 'thank you'. At the end of a tour, everyone would get a little note thanking them for their support. He didn't always have the best of luck, and Sunday, 25 May 1969 was a black day for him. He broke his achilles tendon during a John Player match at the Mote Ground at Maidstone. I swear I could hear the crack as I sat on the boundary. It meant the end of his captaincy of England just as he had built up his team after the successful West Indies tour, and the more dramatic one in Pakistan. He was naturally disappointed, especially as it had always been his ambition to captain England in Australia. Out of his six tours he was vice-captain four times – 'always the bridesmaid . . .' – but he had his compensation with his successful captaincy of Kent for fourteen years.

He was a great cricketer, a very nice person and achieved perhaps his final ambition when he was elected president of the MCC in their bicentenary year. Again he was struck down by bad luck. There were a few 'local difficulties' at Lord's, resulting in a special general meeting, but by this time Colin had suffered from heart trouble and needed an operation, from which he recovered slowly. He was unable to attend the meeting nor attend the wonderful bicentenary match in August.

As usual, he showed great courage throughout his troublesome presidency and it is something which he always showed on the cricket field. I remember him well coming down the steps at Lord's in that marvellous Test against the West Indies in 1963. He had had his left forearm broken by Wes Hall, but with two balls left and six runs needed for victory he came out to join David Allen, his wrist in plaster, and the prospect of facing a ball from Wes Hall. If he had had to do so he had decided to bat as a left-hander, with his right hand holding the bat.

Another occasion was at Kingston, Jamaica, during the famous tear-gas riot. I can see him now walking towards the stand from where the crowd was hurling bottles. With his hands held up he advanced into the shower of bottles to try to pacify the angry crowd. He didn't succeed, but he proved what a worthy captain of England he was.

Gary Sobers

Was Gary Sobers the greatest all-rounder the game has ever known? Or was W. G. Grace? Well, to have seen W. G. play first-class cricket you would now have to be about one hundred years of age, as he played his last match in 1908. So there could possibly be some people still alive who were lucky enough to have seen *both* play, and they alone can speak with any authority. But the large majority of us, who never saw W. G., will I am sure select Gary from all the other possible candidates like Hirst, Rhodes, Woolley, Hammond, Botham, Imran Khan, Kapil Dev, Miller, Benaud, Davidson and Hadlee.

It is difficult to think of a more complete cricketer. As a batsman – like all the greats – he had a sound defensive technique, but in attack with a high backlift and perfect timing the power of his strokes had to be seen to be believed. His sizzling drives and crashing hooks were hammered to the boundary, leaving the fielders helpless to stop them. The best example of this was his 254 for a world eleven against Australia in Melbourne in 1972 – an innings which Don Bradman said was the best one he had ever seen in Australia. I was lucky enough to see it too, and shall never forget the speed with which his shots reached the longest boundaries in the world. It was fantastic, with scorching drives, cuts and hooks. Towards the end he went completely berserk and played many unorthodox strokes with his feet nowhere near the ball. The crowd went mad and even the Australian fielders were applauding some of his strokes.

He played fast bowlers and spinners equally well, and like all the greatest players saw the ball early. There were no helmets in his day, and I cannot ever remember seeing him bat in a cap. He also never wore a thigh pad and was able to cut so well because he used a light bat – about 2 lb. 4 oz. Against the spinners he worked it out that if he went down the pitch to hit them, it gave them an extra means of getting him out – stumped. In fact he claims that he was only stumped once in his career, though there was another occasion when a stumping chance was missed by the wicket-keeper. Gary played all spinners from the crease – if the ball was well pitched up he could still drive it. If it was short he had plenty of time to play it off the back foot.

With his amazing Test record it is remarkable that he batted so often at number six, and I suppose if he had regularly gone in higher up he would have made even more runs. He was naturally an attacking player, but he could discipline himself and by defensive batting got West Indies out of quite a few crises. He played his first Test for the West Indies at the age of seventeen in 1954, and was then regarded as a promising orthodox slow left-arm bowler who could bat a bit. He had to wait four years for his first Test hundred and then (as Bobby Simpson did at Old Trafford in 1964) he obliged with a triple century – his 365 not out, which passed Hutton's 364 and remained the highest individual Test score until Brian Lara's record-breaking 375 in Antigua in 1994. A comparison with Hutton's innings is interesting. Len was just twenty-two years old, batted for 13 hours 17 minutes and hit 35 fours. Gary was still only twenty-one, batted for 10 hours 14 minutes and hit 38 fours. They were both of course knighted by the Queen in 1975,

Len at Buckingham Palace and Gary on the Garrison Savannah in Barbados, less than a mile from where he was brought up.

One man will always remember Gary more than anyone else – Malcolm Nash of Glamorgan. He it was who bowled the over at Swansea in 1968 in which Gary hit six successive sixes – a record 36 off the over. (This was equalled by R. J. Shastri for Bombay against Baroda at Bombay in 1984–5.) The one consolation for Malcolm was that at least he has his name in the record pages of *Wisden*. Actually he has got it in twice because Frank Hayes hit 34 off one over from him at Swansea in 1977. Gary's feat set him on a different plane to other greats like Bradman, Hobbs, Hutton and even W. G. I cannot imagine them ever doing it.

Gary's great advantage over the other contenders for being the greatest all-rounder ever was that he was a three-part bowler. There was the slow left-arm orthodox with which he started, but which he gradually used less and less once he had learned to bowl the chinaman and googly. His best wicket-taker, however, was his fast left-arm-over-the-wicket style, and when I say fast, I mean it. He was deceptive, with a lazy loping run and a perfect sideways action, but when he wanted to he could bowl as fast as anyone. Like Alan Davidson he would run the ball away across the right-handed batsman, and then bowl the deadly – and often unsuspected – ball which swung in late at the batsman and earned Gary a good few lbw's. I suppose of all the bowlers I have enjoyed watching running up to the wicket, Gary and Michael Holding were the two most pleasing. They seemed to glide over the ground.

Gary was naturally a beautiful mover – rather like a cat. He slunk over the ground, giving slightly at the knees, and was light of foot and exceptionally quick in movement and reaction. This is what made him such a magnificent fielder, especially in his later years when he used to gobble up catches at very short leg-slip off Lance Gibbs. But wherever he fielded he caught the eye by the grace of his movements.

He succeeded Frank Worrell as captain of the West Indies for thirty-nine Tests. He perhaps enjoyed cricket too much to make an ideal captain. That sounds cynical but means that he liked a good game of cricket and was prepared to attack and take risks to obtain it. The best example of this was in the fourth Test match at Port of Spain against Colin Cowdrey's side in 1968. He declared, giving England the sporting chance of scoring 215 runs in 165 minutes, which they succeeded in doing with three minutes to spare. No modern captain would ever be so generous, and the wrath of the whole Caribbean fell upon him. From being a national hero he became a scapegoat. It was understandable because this one victory gave England the series, but Gary had enjoyed his game of cricket and took it all smiling. He gave the best possible reply to his critics. In the next Test he made 152 and 95 not out, and took three wickets in each innings.

I mention his smile because it was never absent for long, and as a person he was modest, had great charm and a delightful sense of humour. He lived a happy family life in Barbados as a young man, and was a good soccer player as a boy. He had two passions besides cricket: horse racing and golf. He had many opportunities to indulge in the former when he played for Nottingham from 1968 to 1974. I only wish that it had been more profitable for him. He would have made a fine professional golfer, and when his knee began to trouble him thought seriously of abandoning cricket for a belated golfing career. He played whenever possible and he could beat the best. He was a true all-rounder in every sense of the word, and I find it difficult to believe that there will ever be a better.

Ken Barrington

One of the most popular and best-loved Test cricketers I ever met was Ken Barrington – or Barrers to me. He had a craggy face, a large hooked nose, an engaging grin and an impish sense of humour. He also had a tendency to malapropisms, for example: 'A lion never changes his spots.'

He was also a splendid mimic of movement. He would put on a large black beard, a small cap on his head, skeleton pads on his legs and a towel tucked underneath his shirt to give him a belly. And lo and behold – there was W. G. Grace to the life. You may have seen a film clip of the GOM, batting in a net, with his left foot cocked up in the air, and his jerky strokes speeded up by the old film camera. Barrers copied this to perfection. I once saw him in a Test match in Cape Town in 1965, where the game had reached a stalemate. To liven things up he proceeded to give a lifelike impression of Jim Laker bowling. The joke was that he bowled so well that his analysis read: 3.1–1–4–3.

He was born in the county town of Reading, where his father was a soldier in the Berkshire regiment. As a result he had a love of the army all his life, and not for nothing did the players call him the Colonel. He gave a marvellous impression of a marching military band by drumming his fingers on a tin tray.

He was an avuncular figure on a tour, counsellor and coach and always ready with sympathy and advice for those in any sort of trouble, either on or off the field. There was always laughter around when he was about, both at his malapropisms and his genuinely funny remarks.

He was very emotional and could become desperately unhappy at unkind criticism by the media. I remember the first Test against New Zealand at Edgbaston in 1965. He made 137 out of England's 435, but it took him 7 hours 17 minutes and, when approaching his hundred, he stayed on 85 for over an hour. Then to make matters worse, as soon as he had completed his hundred, he promptly began to hit out and hit three or four boundaries. He was slated in the press, and on television and radio, and on the surface it did look like a selfish innings. I gave him a lift back to London and he was very upset and downhearted – even more so ten days later when he was dropped from the next Test as punishment. But you couldn't keep him down for long and his chirpy humour soon came back. And so did he. He was reselected for the final Test and made 163!

It was his emotional reaction to the pressures of modern Test cricket that so sadly brought about his sudden and premature death in Barbados in 1981. He was assistant manager to Alan Smith on Ian Botham's ill-fated tour. All the dramas and crises proved too much for him. He was bowling his leg-breaks in the nets one afternoon, and died in his hotel that night after a heart attack. So England lost a lovable person whose loyalty, determination and fighting spirit had served his country so well.

He started his first-class life as a hard-hitting batsman, and when selected for the first two Tests against South Africa in 1955 he made 0, 34 and 18 before being dropped. He went back to Surrey and had a good think. He realised that in five-day Tests survival was all-important, and he worked out a method which made him one of the most difficult batsmen in Test cricket to get out. He changed his stance and stood almost square-on to the bowler. He cut out all dangerous strokes, and when he was recalled to Test cricket in 1959 he became England's Rock of Gibraltar.

He was a great man in a crisis, of which he had many to face. If he felt any pressure, he never showed it. He strode confidently to the wicket with a determined measured tread, and chin stuck out. Wally Grout once described him as 'trailing a Union Jack behind him'.

In contrast to his rather grim Test style, I twice saw him reach a Test hundred with a six, once in Adelaide in 1963, and again at Melbourne in 1966. Both shots were high pulls over long-on and it's worth noting that his 115 at Melbourne took only 2 hours 29 minutes, uncommonly fast for Test cricket.

In the field he was a safe and sure catcher anywhere, including the slips. He was also a very accurate thrower, ballooning the ball high in the air to drop with a plop right into the wicket-keeper's gloves. He was also a much underrated and underbowled leg-break bowler. He got plenty of bounce and break, and learned to bowl the flipper from Richie Benaud. I saw him take 7 for 40 against Griqueland West in South Africa in 1965. During that tour I kept wicket to him in a charity match near Cape Town. The batsman went down the pitch to a leg-break. He missed it. So did I. It bounced and hit me on my right tit. You should have seen Barrers' face! He never let me forget it. Whenever we met, no matter where it was, his first greeting was always: 'Hello Johnners, how's the right tit?'

I must end by paying a tribute to him as a Test batsman. His figures say it all: 131 innings (15 not out), 6,806 runs, highest score 256, average *58.67*. Only Herbert Sutcliffe (60.73) and Eddie Paynter (59.23) of England batsmen had better averages, though Hammond (58.45), Hobbs (56.94), Hutton (56.67) and Compton (50.06) were all breathing down his neck.

Ray Illingworth

I have always called him Illy, but Yorkshire folk give him his full Christian name of Raymond. He is one of the longest serving cricketers in the modern game, playing from 1951 until 1983. I can only think of Fred Titmus (1949–83) who can beat that. Not even the old-timers like Wilfred Rhodes (32 years),

Jack Hobbs (29 years), Frank Woolley (32 years), Phil Mead (31 years) and George Gunn (30 years) can do more than equal him – but remember that their careers contained four blank seasons during the Great War. I concede that W. G. Grace played for 29 years for Gloucestershire and then for another four for London County, but for first-class county matches I think Illy is the winner. He was fifty-one when he finally retired.

He always kept himself remarkably fit and on the field appeared to be completely relaxed and never overexerted himself. He preferred to field in the gully, where he was a very safe catcher. He had a short run-up, running lightly on his toes. He bowled fairly flat off-spin, with a well-disguised floater. His main assets were his length and direction, he bowled very few bad balls, and could be relied on to drop the ball on a sixpence from the word go. He was not a great spinner of the ball, but his accuracy and reading of a batsman's weaknesses brought him 122 Test wickets. He was an effective but rather ordinary-looking batsman, though captaincy of England seemed to inspire him to greater heights and he played a variety of match-saving or match-winning innings for his country.

On the surface, then, a technically efficient all-rounder, but from the moment he became captain of Leicester in 1969 he became a different man – and player. He blossomed in a job which he did exceedingly well both for Leicestershire (one County Championship, two Benson and Hedges Cups and two John Player League Cups) and for England (12 wins, 14 draws, 5 losses). He was a shrewd tactician, full of cricket knowledge handed down by past Yorkshire players. As I've said, he read a batsman's weakness as well as anybody I know, and this was reflected in his field placings. He was a players' captain. They liked him because they knew exactly where they were with him – he spoke his mind, was strictly honest, and would stand no nonsense. He wanted to win and expected everyone to try as hard as he did. They also knew that he would always support them in any brush with administrators and fight for their cause. He appears as a paragon of virtue, and in most senses he was, but he regarded his main job as winning a series and it is *on* the field that matches are won. Off it he lacked some of the social graces and tended to play a low-key role in PR. He was, however, helpful and truthful with the media and was one of the easiest captains I ever had to interview. He gave straight answers, and never waffled.

His playing life was divided into three. For seventeen years he played for Yorkshire, but in the end quarrelled with the committee (not the first – nor last – Yorkshireman to do so!) because they refused to give him a three-year contract. Mike Turner of Leicestershire snapped him up and, as captain for ten years, he transformed them as a team.

As he approached fifty years of age his playing career seemed to be ending. After much thought and discussion he accepted Yorkshire's invitation to return as manager to try to restore their fortunes. He didn't have a very happy time there, in what had become a civil war between the pro- and anti-Boycott factions. In the mid-summer of 1982 he took over the captaincy himself from Chris Old and in the following year achieved an ironical result. Yorkshire, the bastion of traditional cricket, were bottom of the County Championship table but won the forty-over frolic of the John Player League. This was achieved largely by Illy relying on the spin bowling of himself and Phil Carrick – his final gesture to prove that spinners can and should play a successful part in limited-over cricket.

Illy is a highly organised person. Like a true Yorkshireman he has made and saved his pennies to give him a secure future. After his retirement he became a regular in the television commentary box, where his dry wit and quick reading of the game proved invaluable. It was nice to have him around us in the commentary area, although he did rather tend to invade the radio box round about tea-time. Like us he has a penchant for chocolate cake – and it's amazing how he would sniff out the arrival of a new one.

He'll admit, I think, that on the whole he's been lucky, and in spite of one or two setbacks things have worked out well for him. The highlight of his career would for him undoubtedly have been the 1970–1 Ashes-winning tour of Australia. He – like Hutton – went there with just one purpose and he achieved it in a highly professional manner. It must have been a sweet moment for him when he was carried triumphantly off the field at Sydney by his team.

He had shown his determination and toughness in that final Test when he led his team off the field in protest against the manhandling of John Snow by an angry spectator, and the shower of bottles and tins which were hurled on to the field. I defended his action at the time as I happened to be comment-ating, and was supported by two old Australian captains, Richie

Benaud and Bill Lawry, but many of the English press disagreed. Illy's action made the crowd realise that they would be robbed of any more cricket if they went on throwing things, so, after an announcement, the playing area was quickly cleaned up and play restarted in under a quarter of an hour. Of course, theoretically it was wrong to take his team off without the permission of the umpires, but it needed courage to do so and it worked.

One other feature of his captaincy was that he was prone to underbowl himself. Cynics – and they may have something – used to say that he didn't much fancy bowling on any pitch which didn't give a spinner some help.

As I've said, on the whole he's a lucky person, as proved in 1971. After the Ashes victory we wrote a pretty awful song to a delightful old music-hall tune. When we got back to England we recorded it at the Decca studios. Vic Lewis – that most enthusiastic of cricketers and collector of cricket-club ties – organised a wonderful accompanying orchestra drawn from all the top session musicians in London who were cricket supporters. The end product, called *The Ashes Song*, sounded smashing to us, though the public didn't think so. We hoped it would top the charts but in fact our total royalties were £53.86. There was no point in dividing this up, so we decided to have a draw at the Test Trial in Hove in 1973. Who better to make the draw than the England captain? And whose name did he pull out of the hat? Yes, you've guessed it. Raymond Illingworth, none other.

18 Five Aussie Keepers, Graeme Pollock, Geoff Boycott

Five Aussie Keepers

Bertie Oldfield

T HE FIRST AUSTRALIAN WICKET-KEEPER I actually saw was J. L. Ellis, who was the reserve wicket-keeper to Bertie Oldfield on the 1926 Australian tour of England. He wasn't needed for any of the Tests and in fact never played in a Test. I only remember him because he kept wicket against Gloucestershire at Cheltenham in 1926, which was the first time I ever saw the Australians play. I can see him now standing miles back to the fast bowling of Gregory, and remember that when he went to take one ball wide down the leg-side his left glove came off.

I then saw Bertie Oldfield at Lord's in 1930, a neat dapper little man, rather sparrowlike in his movements. He was a beautiful wicket-keeper to watch, quiet and immensely efficient as he stood right up behind the wicket with his large black gloves, which he kept rubbing together rather like Uriah Heep.

He was stylish in everything he did and had a perfectly balanced crouch – just up on his toes, hands pointing down in front of him. There is a wonderful photograph which shows him in this position with Wally Hammond just finishing one of his classic cover drives – and Bertie is still crouching down. What a lesson to young wicket-keepers. When standing back he was, like so many other keepers of the time, seldom if ever seen flinging himself about. Somehow he always seemed to get across to the wide balls.

In 1948 he joined our television commentary team in the two London Tests, and with his high squeaky voice was a model of good-mannered criticism.

I visited him in his sports shop in Sydney in the 1960s and

there he was, birdlike and immaculate in white flannels. He sold me – at a *slightly* reduced rate, a pair of his wicket-keeping gloves, and I used these until I gave up playing. At the same time I met and talked to the gnomelike figure of Clarrie Grimmett at Adelaide. I asked him about Bertie, who of course got so many of his 130 Test victims off the bowling of Grimmett. He only played in 54 Tests, but even so his total of 52 stumpings beats everyone else, the second best being 46 for Godfrey Evans for 91 Tests. Bertie actually caught 9 and stumped 28 off Clarrie. I was singing Bertie's praises, with which Clarrie agreed but added with a mischievous smile: 'But he missed a lot off me too.' Bowlers are not the most grateful of people!

Don Tallon

The next great wicket-keeper was Don Tallon, nicknamed Deafy because he was! He toured England in 1948 and 1953, and undoubtedly should have been chosen for the 1938 tour. Why he and Grimmett were not selected is still a bit of a mystery, especially as Grimmett had had a most successful season in the Sheffield Shield. Ben Barnett came instead of Tallon, and F. A. Ward instead of Grimmett. Ward played in only the first Test, where his bowling analysis was 30–2–142–0. Barnett fared much better. He was a good wicket-keeper, not quite in the super class. Remarkably, in the four Tests played he got no victims at all in three of them, but made three catches and two stumpings in the fourth Test. He always remembered the final Test at the Oval when Len Hutton made the record-breaking 364. Poor Ben is said to have missed stumping Len when he had scored 34 – just imagine what he was thinking as Len piled up the runs. He was a charming man and settled in England after the war. He played for Buckinghamshire, and also in a lot of festival cricket, and turned out regularly for the Lord's Taverners.

Don Tallon was tall for a wicket-keeper, with long arms, and was a brilliant performer. I once asked Lindsay Hassett in the 1970s who was the best wicket-keeper he had seen – and remember that Lindsay played for Australia before and after the war, so had the opportunity to either play with or see all the Test wicket-keepers from the mid-1930s until he gave up summarising for ABC in 1986. He unhesitatingly plumped for Don Tallon, and it's a judgement I feel one must accept in spite of Evans, Knott, Taylor, Grout, Marsh and so on. Surprisingly, Tallon only played in the first Test at Trent Bridge on Lindsay's 1953 tour.

As I've said, he was a bit deaf. When, one evening during the match, Australia were struggling against the superb bowling of Alec Bedser (he took 14 for 99 in the match), Lindsay said to Tallon as he went out to bat: 'Give the light a go, Deafy' – meaning appeal against the light. Tallon thought he had said 'give it a go', and proceeded to attack the bowling and make a lightning 15 before being caught off Tattersall when going for another big hit!

Gil Langley

For the remaining four Tests Gil Langley took over from Tallon. He was heavily built and rather podgy, and was the first of the modern keepers to stand back to medium-pace bowling. At the time it seemed a travesty of wicket-keeping to see him standing back to someone as slow as Slasher Mackay, but he wasn't just a stopper. He was most effective, dropped very little, and possibly made catches which he would not have held if he had been standing up. As proof of how effective he was, in only 26 Tests he bagged 98 victims and tops every Test wicket-keeper past or present for the best average number per Test – 3.769. He had a very short Test career – 1951 to 1957 – and when he retired he became a Labour politician in South Australia, finishing as the Speaker of the Parliament there. I can't offhand think of any other Test cricketer with such a distinguished political career.

Wally Grout

After Gil Langley came the great Wally Grout, who so sadly died from a heart attack in 1968 when only aged forty-one. His fifty-one Tests were also crammed into the short time of nine years, and he was already thirty when he played his first Test. He was the epitome of what many people imagine an Australian to be. He was tough, gravel-voiced, hard-swearing, and he enjoyed racing and betting. He had the will to win and played

Test cricket the hard way, but he was always the complete sportsman.

In the first Test between England and Australia at Trent Bridge in 1964, John Edrich reported himself unfit on the morning of the match. Fred Titmus was chosen to open the innings with Geoff Boycott, playing in his very first Test. They put on 38 for the first wicket but not without an augury of 'things to come'. Boycott called for one of his famous quick singles, and Titmus loyally responded to what looked like an impossible call, but he collided with the Australian opening bowler, Corling, and fell to the ground. The ball was thrown to Wally Grout who, seeing what had happened, sportingly refused to break the wicket. I wonder if this would happen today.

Wally will best be remembered for his partnership with Alan Davidson, off whom he caught 43 with Alan bowling his fast-left-arm-over-the-wicket and swinging the balls away from the batsmen. But he was also a brilliant taker of spin and was responsible for many of Benaud's and Kline's wickets. I know that Richie places him very high in his list of Test wicket-keepers.

As I've said, Wally had a rich command of expletives, and it amused me when at the end of a dreary drawn Test match at Sydney in 1963, he publicly complained that Ted Dexter had sworn at him. The biter bit!

Rodney Marsh

My final Aussie keeper is Rodney Marsh, with the incredible total of 355 Test dismissals in 96 Tests, second only to his successor in the Australian team, Ian Healy, with a record-breaking 395 dismissals in 119 Tests. I saw Marsh in his first Test at Brisbane against Ray Illingworth's MCC side. He was sturdily built, with a figure not unlike that of Gil Langley, but although there was a suspicion of overweight he was remarkably fit and had tremendous energy, flinging himself here, there and everywhere. At that time his enthusiasm outweighed his skill and he did not always take the ball cleanly. In fact he earned the name of iron gloves; this was rather unfair to a young twenty-three-year-old and it not only annoyed him, but acted as a spur for him to prove himself.

This of course he did and he was a regular member of Ian

Chappell's successful side, becoming the vital apex of the Lillee–Thomson–Marsh triangle. I don't know how many catches he missed off this formidable pair of fast bowlers, but he certainly managed to catch 116 off them (Lillee 88 and Thomson 28). He also kept well when standing up to spinners like Mallett, Gleeson, O'Keeffe and Bright. So after his unfortunate beginning he can point to the records and rightly claim to have been one of the most successful of all Test wicket-keepers.

On the field he was part of Ian Chappell's 'sledging' team, and it was lucky that in those days there was no microphone built into the stumps, as some of the language would have put the transmitters off the air! But although he played hard, he was always fair. You may remember his gesture in the Australian Centenary Test at Melbourne in 1977. Randall had been given out caught by him in answer to a universal appeal from the Australian side, but Marsh indicated to the umpire, Brooks, that the ball had not carried and Randall was allowed to continue his great innings of 174.

Marsh was fun to meet off the field, and I had an enjoyable evening sitting next to him at the English Centenary Dinner in London in 1980. I remember he left the table at one point to go and check on the final racing results. He was a keen betting man, and at Headingley in 1981 gladly accepted the 500–1 odds against England winning. They of course did so, and Marsh and Lillee won some money, if not the Test.

He was probably at his best during Mike Denness's tour in 1974–5. Lillee and Thomson were then at their peak, and were a terrifying combination for the batsmen to face. I saw Marsh having a net on the No. 2 ground at Sydney (now alas no more). I asked him how his hands were standing up to the pace of the dreaded pair, and he showed them to me; they looked sore and bruised. He said he protected them by putting plaster round the joints of his fingers. Quite a few wicket-keepers do this, but it is an awful bore having to bind all the tape round the fingers every time you go out to field. I told him that his fingers reminded me of an old radio comedy series back in England – *Much Binding in the Marsh*. He looked at me blankly. He had never heard of the show! But always after that I used to call him Much Binders. He didn't seem to mind.

Graeme Pollock

Graeme Pollock was one of those unlucky South African cricketers who after 1970 were prevented by politics from playing
any more Test matches. By 1970 he was already one of the
outstanding batsmen in the world and was still only aged
twenty-six. What he might have achieved is anybody's guess,
but he would surely have rivalled all the other 'greats' in terms
of the number of Test runs and hundreds he made.

He was an infant prodigy, encouraged and coached by his
father, who was a newspaper editor who played for Orange
Free State. Graeme was also helped by his elder brother, Peter,
three years his senior. Peter became a fearsome fast bowler
who took 116 Test wickets for South Africa. In fact I made one
of my many unfortunate remarks about him. He came over to
play for the Rest of the World side at the Scarborough Festival
in 1968. He was on his honeymoon and brought his bride with
him. We were televising the game with Denis Compton as
summariser and myself as commentator. Peter ran up to bowl,
slipped and twisted his ankle. He hobbled off and it was soon
announced that he had a badly swollen ankle. 'What bad luck,'
I said to the viewers, 'especially as he is on his honeymoon
with his pretty young wife. But he'll probably be all right in the
morning if he sticks it up as soon as he gets back to the hotel.'
A perfectly innocent remark, but made to appear otherwise by
the uncontrolled laughter of Denis.

Back to Graeme. He scored his first Currie Cup hundred at
the age of sixteen, and made his Test début at Brisbane against
Australia three years later. At the age of nineteen he made over
1,000 runs on the tour for an average of 53.27, and scored the
first two of his seven Test hundreds in the third and fourth
Tests.

I was lucky enough to see three of his hundreds. The first
was at Port Elizabeth against England on Mike Smith's tour of
1964–5. It was a superb innings and he became the only Test
player other than George Headley to score three Test hundreds
before the age of twenty-one. The second one I saw was even
better. He made 125 at Trent Bridge the following summer in
the second Test against England, off only 145 balls with 21
fours. South Africa had been struggling against the medium-
pace seamers of Tom Cartwright, who took 6 for 94. They were
80 for 5 when Graeme was joined by his captain, Peter Van Der

Merwe. They put on 98 runs together, of which Van Der Merwe's share was 10!

Graeme's innings was one of the best I have seen in Test cricket. The conditions were humid and there was dampness in the pitch – typical English conditions – but right from the start he dominated the bowlers, who besides Cartwright included John Snow and Freddie Titmus. I shall never forget the timing of his off-drives through extra cover, and the power of his back strokes and cuts off anything short. This was the first time many people in England had seen him in top form, and it was good that those not at Trent Bridge could see him on television.

People were soon talking of a second Frank Woolley. I only saw Frank in his later days: tall, willowy, stiff-backed, but my impression of him was that he was more effortless than Graeme. The ball went off his bat far and often high, but he appeared to stroke it, rather than power-drive like Graeme.

But there was better still to come – at Durban in 1970 in the second Test against Australia. Graeme made 274, his seventh and last Test hundred and the highest Test score for South Africa. He and Barry Richards slaughtered the Australian attack, vying with each other to see who could score the most fours. They put on 103 in an hour after lunch. I was commentating on radio with Charles Fortune and Alan McGilvray, and it was one of the most thrilling commentary periods I have ever had. Graeme finished with a 5 and 43 fours and the crowd at Kingsmead rightly went mad.

Graeme was fair-haired, over six feet tall, strongly built and had a slow shambling gait. I believe that basically he was lazy – at least he never seemed to hurry himself, whether batting or fielding. This was deceptive because, like all the great batsmen, he saw the ball early and had that much more time to play his stroke. He used a very heavy bat for those days, just under 3 lb., which today of course is common enough. His technique was a perfect blend of power and timing, and not even Sobers could rival his crashing drives through the covers. Like Hammond he had a reputation for being primarily an off-side player, and not so strong on the leg-side. In fact, on that 1970 tour by Australia in South Africa, Graham McKenzie and Alan Connolly both tried to concentrate on his leg-stump. Precious good it did them, though perhaps on occasions it slowed him down a bit. His scores of 49, 50, 274, 52, 87, 1, 4 help to show what a fine all round stroke-player he was.

Although not a fast mover in the field, Graeme was a safe catcher at slip, and he also liked to bowl the occasional leg-break. But they were only *occasional*, as his captains did not quite have the same high opinion of them as he did! How difficult it is for a batsman to persuade anyone that he can bowl. On the other hand, bowlers through necessity have every opportunity to show if they can bat. Whether they bat at number ten or number eleven, there is always the odd crisis when they can prove their mettle.

Graeme was also one of those people who succeed in any sport at which they try their hand. Even so, at one time he did have a spot of eye trouble and actually tried to play in glasses, but he soon discarded them and finished his career in South Africa in a blaze of glory. What a pity it is that so few cricket-lovers in England were able to see this blond giant play on the cricket grounds of England. They can justly say 'we was robbed'. It was also sad that the MCC did not invite him as one of their many overseas guests to attend the bicentenary match at Lord's. Thanks to a sponsor in South Africa he did finally come, and we were glad to welcome and interview him in the commentary box. But I think the MCC did their members – and the general public – a disservice by denying them the chance to welcome one of the greatest left-hand batsmen of all time.

Geoff Boycott

I cannot honestly say that I *know* Geoff Boycott, though he has always been most friendly to me. I call him Boycers and he and my Yorkshire-born wife get on like a house on fire. I covered four MCC tours which he was on, but never really got close to him as a friend. He is a complex character – an enigma – and seems to have a dual personality. I am often asked what he is really like. I always refer the questioner to England or Yorkshire players who have *played* with him. They can give a truer picture.

There is so much to admire in him and in what he has achieved. He was born and brought up in the mining village of Fitzwilliam and became a clerk in the Ministry of Pensions. He was pale-faced, wore glasses and looked an unlikely cricketer.

He had been encouraged and supported by an uncle and the rest of the family, and when still a small boy showed a grim determination to become a great cricketer. Whilst other boys played and went to the cinema, he would practise – a word that was to become synonymous with him throughout his career.

In 1962, at the age of twenty-two, he played his first match for Yorkshire and in his second county game was responsible for the first of the many run-outs for which he became famous. The following year he made a hundred in his first Roses match against Lancashire. In 1964 he played for England against Australia and scored the first of his twenty-two Test hundreds. It was an incredibly swift rise up the ladder.

It is a story of complete dedication, determination, self-discipline and single-mindedness. As the story of his life unfolds, it is sad to say that perhaps it is more accurate to substitute the word selfishness for single-mindedness. I have always felt that he could have been the perfect golf professional, where all these attributes are essential. He could have played for himself and would have relished the hours of practice necessary to reach the top.

From the start he had this love of batting. Nothing else mattered. He read, questioned, watched and copied to achieve a defensive technique which would prevent bowlers from getting him out. In this he was so successful that he became one of the greatest *defensive* batsmen of all time. Any schoolboy could copy him. Everything was right – sideways on, straight bat, head still, nose 'smelling' the ball. You'll notice that I have qualified my praise by using the word 'defensive'. I have never considered him as a great batsman, pure and simple. He was an insatiable accumulator of runs, but rarely tried to get on top of bowlers by *attacking* them. The only time I ever saw him take an attack apart was in the Gillette Cup Final of 1965 when he made a brilliant 146 against Surrey.

I once asked him why he so seldom tried to 'master' a bowler. He replied quite honestly that he was the best batsman on the side, be it Yorkshire or England. It was therefore essential for him to remain at the crease for as long as possible. Let the others take the risks and make strokes, whilst he slowly accumulated runs at the other end.

It was the same with his famous run-outs. Why was it always the other chap who was run out and not him? Again came the answer that he was the best, and that it was in the interests of his side for the other batsman to make the sacrifice. He has in fact been heard to call out to a young Yorkshire batsman with both of them stranded in mid-wicket: 'Sacrifice, sacrifice.'

There was a famous run-out during the Adelaide Test on Ray Illingworth's tour in 1971. Geoff called for a run on the off-side but the fielder hit the stumps at the bowler's end and he was given run out. He flung his bat down on the ground and stood with his hands on his hips, before being 'steered' towards the pavilion by Greg Chappell. Again I asked him about this and strangely he admitted to me that he *was* out, but he went on to say that he was only out by a few inches, and that the margin was so small that any umpire should have given the batsman the benefit of the doubt.

None of this made him popular with his fellow players, and was one of the reasons for so many young Yorkshiremen becoming discouraged and failing to live up to their early promise. But strangely enough the Yorkshire public seemed to be mesmerised by his runs. The more he scored, the more they worshipped him, and he always had a tremendous following wherever he went. Little did they realise that the *more* runs he made, the *less* likely were Yorkshire to win. He took so long about it.

A perfect example was in 1971 – his first year as captain of Yorkshire. He had a wonderful season – for Yorkshire alone he scored 2,197 runs with 11 hundreds and an average of 109.85. And yet Yorkshire had what *Wisden* described as 'the worst season in their history'. They finished thirteenth in the County Championship, and had the longest sequence of seventeen matches without a victory which the county had ever known. They scored a lot of runs, but far too slowly, and only picked up 47 batting bonus points compared with 82 scored by Kent. Only three sides scored fewer than 47.

Against all this you have to set all the good things in Geoff's career as a batsman. His dedication has never been rivalled – he put in hours and hours of practice. On tours on the rest day of a Test others would play golf or go on the beach, but Geoff would be down at the ground batting against any young boys willing to bowl at the Master – and there were always plenty of them. To have bowled Boycott was the highest accolade.

Not naturally athletic, he kept himself wonderfully fit. He went to bed early, only drank the occasional glass of white wine, and never exposed himself to the heat of the sun. No lying around a pool for him. And on the field he looked a wraithlike figure: sleeves down, shirt collar turned up and sometimes a neckerchief round the neck. And always a cap. He may have worn a white floppy hat on occasions but I don't remember them. He was always neatly turned out, with immaculately white trousers, pads and boots.

It's not surprising that he became such a vast accumulator of runs. In five-day Test matches – especially abroad – he did a wonderful job opening for England. He seemed to revel in the good light and faster pitches. The latter seemed to help his favourite scoring stroke, which he executed so well – a square drive off the back foot on the off-side, either side of cover. And of course he has some incredible figures. He averaged over 60 in eleven English seasons, and between 50 and 60 on six more. Twice – in 1971 and 1979 – he averaged over 100. And he just managed to pip Tom Graveney on the post as the most prolific scorer of post-war batsmen. He scored 48,426 against Tom's 47,793.

Geoff has a deep knowledge of the game and its tactics, and has always studied the strengths and weaknesses of other players. He enjoyed being captain and one ambition, which he never achieved, was to be made captain of England. He did captain them in four Tests on the tour to Pakistan and New Zealand in 1977–8, but only as a stand-in for the injured Brearley. It would be untrue to say that he was a popular captain and he also suffered the indignity of leading England to their first ever defeat by New Zealand.

It was the same when he captained Yorkshire from 1971 to 1978. His tactics were sound enough, but it was not a happy period in Yorkshire cricket. There was no real team spirit, and they won no trophy in any of the four competitions in that time. A cricket captain has to be like the old cavalry officer who always saw the men and horses fed before he had his own meal. A cricket captain has to think of the other ten members of his side before himself. It became obvious that such a single-minded person as Geoff could never be a leader of men.

As a southerner – albeit married to a Yorkshire woman – I refuse to get embroiled in all the internal quarrels in which Geoff was involved. Suffice to say that controversy seemed to follow him wherever he played, ending with the sad finish to his Test career when he came home early from India after achieving his (then) record 8,114 Test runs.

He so often crucified himself. He played in no Test cricket between 1974 and 1977. It was a self-imposed exile because of his disappointment over Mike Denness being given the England captaincy instead of him. When one thinks of the number of Test runs he denied himself over this period, one must appreciate how strongly he felt. Needless to say, being Geoff, when he *did* return against Australia at Trent Bridge in 1977 he made a hundred. And just to show that he had lost none of his reputation for bad calling, he ran out local hero Derek Randall!

He was I think unfairly criticised by Tony Greig, who accused him of lacking the courage to face the dreaded pace attack of Lillee and Thomson in Australia in 1974. His colleagues also felt that he had let them down and left them to face the barrage of bumpers, but I don't agree with Tony. Geoff has always had guts and I have never seen him flinch nor back away when facing a fast bowler. Discomforted he may have been, but he was always technically correct right behind the line of the ball.

He made himself into a good fielder and perfected his throw so that on the seventy-five-yard English boundaries at least, the ball would land plop into the wicket-keeper's hands right over the stumps. He was also quite a useful medium-pace in-swing bowler. He always bowled in a cap – like Ronald Colman in the film of *Raffles*. Once, in a big match at Lord's, he even reversed his cap with the peak over the back of his neck, like motor-cyclists used to do. He did it just to amuse the crowd and it is worth repeating what a happy rapport he used to have with crowds all over England.

Nowadays, as one would expect, Geoff writes and talks very sensibly about cricket. However, two headlines from his pieces in the *Daily Mail* about England's tour of New Zealand in 1988 did make me chuckle. It just goes to show how much easier it is to play in the commentary box rather than out in the middle. They read: 'Time we speeded it up' and 'Go-slow spoils perfect day'. He is an excellent summariser on either television or radio, and I suspect that he will now try to devote himself to this in his retirement.

Let's hope too that he now has time to make friends. Surely the fight is over, and controversies a thing of the past. It is sad that, because of his devotion to his own career, he left behind so few real friends in the cricket world. His future is assured after two highly successful benefits and his autobiography, for which he attended more signing sessions than even Sir Edward

Heath did for his! Good luck, then, to Boycers. I wish him well as I finish with this apocryphal story.

Geoff reported to St Peter at the Pearly Gates, who asked who he was. St Peter looked at a list which he had, and then said: 'I'm sorry. There's no Geoff Boycott on the list. If you are not on it, you can't come into heaven. So please go away.'

Geoff walked off very disgruntled, but after five minutes' thought went back to St Peter and said: 'Look, I don't think you realise who I am. Geoffrey Boycott of Yorkshire and England. 8,114 Test runs, 22 Test hundreds, 48,426 first-class runs. One of the greatest batsmen of all time. Please let me in.'

St Peter got very annoyed. 'I repeat, if you are not on the list, you cannot come in. For the last time, please go away.'

So Geoff reluctantly left and as he did so a small old man with a long grey beard came up to St Peter and, when asked his name, said: 'Geoffrey Boycott.'

'Oh do come in, Mr Boycott,' said St Peter, 'we are delighted to see you. Please come straight into heaven.'

An old cricketer who was standing by said to St Peter: 'What's going on? You turn away the *real* Geoff Boycott, and admit this old man with the long grey beard who pretends he is Boycott but obviously isn't!'

'Oh,' said St Peter, 'we have to humour him. He's God and he keeps on thinking he's Geoffrey Boycott!'

19 Mike Procter, Derek Underwood, Clive Lloyd, Alan Knott

Mike Procter

NOT MANY PEOPLE HAVE COUNTIES named after them. Worcestershire was of course known for many years as Fostershire because of the seven Foster brothers – B. S., G. N., H. K., M. K., N. J. A., R. E. and W. L. – all of whom played for the county. So did H. K.'s son C. K. But the same honour was accorded Mike Procter during his sixteen years with Gloucestershire. Especially during his successful captaincy from 1977 to 1981, the county became known as Proctershire, so great was his influence and popularity. He was tall, fair, chubby-faced and strong as an ox. He bowled very fast off a prodigiously long run. He charged in at a terrific rate, hair flopping, ground shaking. He must have been an awe-inspiring sight to a batsman. He delivered the ball 'off the wrong foot' square on to the batsman, with a whirlwind arm action. As a result he bowled mainly in-swingers, but occasionally resorted to fast off-breaks.

He only played in seven Tests, all against Australia in South Africa. In three Tests in 1967 he took 15 wickets and in 1970, 26 wickets in four Tests, making a total of 41 wickets – an average of a fraction under 6 wickets a Test – 5.85. This compares with Syd Barnes's average of 7.00 and just beats Clarrie Grimmett's 5.81. Otherwise Proccers beats all the other Test bowlers for rate of strike. Of course it's not really fair to compare his figures with bowlers who have taken 300, 200 or even 100 more wickets than him, but it does give some sort of clue as to what he might have achieved had he played in more Tests. It is difficult truly to assess his speed, but when fully fit he must have been as fast as any of his contemporaries.

He came over to England with his friend, Barry Richards, in 1965. Both intended to qualify for Gloucestershire and they both played in one match – against the visiting South African side. They didn't do too badly either. They were top scorers in a total of 279, Richards 59, Procter 69, and put on 116 for the fifth wicket in just over ninety minutes. *Wisden* reported that Proctor (sic) was the dominant partner. They finished that season as dressing-room attendants at the Oval during the fifth Test against South Africa – a useful way of absorbing Test match atmosphere.

They both came back to England in 1968, Richards to play for Hampshire, and Procter for Gloucestershire, and from then on until he had to retire in 1981 due to bad knees Proccers was the mainstay of Gloucestershire. Besides his bowling he was a magnificent field anywhere, and as a batsman pure and simple would have been worth his place in any Test side. He was a magnificent stroke-player who scored at a very fast rate. Because of the amount of bowling he had to do, he didn't achieve as much as Richards with the bat, but I reckon there was little between them in actual technique. What a difference in temperament, however. Richards, the casual rather bored player who needed crowds and incentive to bring out his best, and Proccers, who just loved to play cricket. He was a great trier and never gave up, and he gave everything he had towards helping Gloucestershire. And they loved him for it.

What's more, he brought success to W. G.'s old county. In 1976 and 1977 they finished third in the County Championship, only just behind the leaders. In his first year of captaincy Gloucestershire won the Benson and Hedges Final at Lord's. He was an inspiring captain and cared for his players, who would have followed him anywhere. A perfect example was in the Benson and Hedges Final. A young player called David Partridge had not made much impression in the match. He didn't get an innings and so far as I remember dropped a catch, and was looking rather out of things fielding under the grandstand balcony. When it became apparent that Gloucester-shire were going to win, Proccers called him up to have a bowl. His three overs were expensive, and cost 22 runs, though he did take the valuable wicket of Alan Knott, but the point was that Proccers wanted him to have a share in the victory. A most thoughtful piece of captaincy.

Proccers performed some splendid feats. He scored 1,000 runs in a season nine times, and took 100 wickets twice. He did the hat-trick four times in county matches – in 1979 in two successive matches against Leicestershire and Yorkshire. What's more, in the Leicestershire match he also made a hundred before lunch! And there's more to come! In his hat-trick against Yorkshire at Cheltenham all his three victims were lbw – something he also achieved in his 1972 hat-trick against Sussex, bowling round the wicket at a tremendous pace.

As if all the above was not enough, he once scored six hundreds in consecutive innings for Rhodesia. So all in all a remarkable player who because of his skills, guts and keenness would always be *my* all-rounder in any world eleven – just so long as Gary Sobers was unfit to play!

Derek Underwood

I have always called him Unders, but then I never had to play against him. Those who did, call him Deadly. A very apt name, as anyone who saw him wheeling away for twenty-five years will testify. I was lucky enough to see him as a seventeen-year-old in his first sensational season for Kent, when he became the youngest bowler ever to take 100 wickets in a season – 101 actually, and he took exactly the same number in 1964. But his third season was a comparative failure – he only took 89!

I always enjoyed watching him bowl in those early days. Fair-haired, fresh-faced and already with those large flat feet. His parents followed him around wherever he played, and I could always be certain of a good cup of tea and a bun during the tea interval, when I would join them at their car. They were intensely proud of him, and supported and encouraged him in everything he did. He was a unique bowler. There has never been one quite like him. He was near-medium pace and usually cut the ball rather than spin it. His main weapons were his perfect length and line, his flight and variations in pace. He also had a well-disguised 'arm' ball, bowled a little faster, and from which Alan Knott made many leg-side stumpings.

His accuracy frustrated even the best batsmen. They could never collar him, and it was extremely difficult to hit him over the top. He always liked to start with a maiden over, after which he would get in a groove and was quite happy to bowl all day. He just loved bowling. 'If you don't bowl you cannot take wickets,' he once said. As you can imagine, every captain enjoyed having him in their side. It meant that you could block one end, and experiment at the other.

On a rain-affected pitch he was practically unplayable, as in addition to turn he got bounce out of the pitch as well. Strangely, he was not quite so devastating on a dry pitch which was cracking up and losing its top surface. But he will go down as one of the greatest slow bowlers – only Wilfred Rhodes and George Lohmann were younger when they reached their 1,000 wickets. Unders did it in his seventh season at the age of twenty-five. His 297 Test wickets could well have been at least a hundred more had he not decided to sign for Kerry Packer and later go on the 'rebel' tour to South Africa. Like most of the others who did the same, he did it for the sake of family security, and gave himself a strong financial base. It is difficult to criticise anyone who puts his family before his own career, but I personally felt very sad at his decisions. He and Alan Knott were both sadly missed by England, though after the famous Packer law case, they were allowed to play for Kent during the English summers.

He enjoyed batting and became the automatic night-watchman for both England and Kent. He had a good defensive technique but loved to play his favourite scoring stroke – over mid-wicket's head. Not strictly orthodox but often effective. In his capacity of night-watchman he always showed tremendous guts against the fast bowlers, in spite of getting a sickening blow on the mouth (before helmets) from a Charlie Griffith bouncer in his first Test at Trent Bridge in 1966. Possibly his happiest moment was when he scored his maiden century at Hastings in 1984 at the age of thirty-nine.

Unders decided to retire at the end of 1987 and he was sadly missed by Kent, and even by his opponents. He is such a nice, modest person, with a hearty laugh, and real enjoyment of life. A final example of his love of and dedication to cricket was the way he made himself into a good fielder. With his flat feet he was not naturally athletic, but he was a safe catcher and had a good arm which he used effectively from his usual position down at long leg. Let's hope that someone somewhere discovers another Unders, with both his skill and technique and his lovable reliable character.

Clive Lloyd

It would be difficult to find a more unlikely-looking athlete than Clive Hubert Lloyd. Spectacles, drooping head – often covered by a white floppy sun hat – a round-shouldered figure with a shambling, gangling gait. As he walked to the wicket he would prod the ground impatiently with his bat. And what a bat! It was the first of the real heavies, weighing at least 3 lb., possibly more. The handle was of double thickness, and once at Robertsbridge in Sussex, where the bats are made, I tried to get my hands round it and failed. I thought my hands were fairly big, but his are very large with long fingers.

He is six feet five inches tall and had immensely strong forearms which enabled him to wield his giant 'club'. He was one of the hardest and biggest hitters I have ever seen, and his favourite stroke was the lofted drive, when the ball seemed to 'sail' clean out of the ground. He was equally severe on any-thing short, hitting the ball off the back foot just wide of cover, or hooking it hard and high over the square-leg boundary. In contrast, he could defend as well as anyone if necessary, since his basic method was so correct.

Early in his career the England bowlers used to think he was a sucker to the ball just outside his off-stump, before he got his eye in, but in later years there was not much sign of this. His figures cannot portray the extent to which he could turn a match by his hitting, nor the number of times when, but for him, a high run-rate required for victory would never have been achieved. Even so, 7,515 runs – fourth only to Viv Richards (8,540), Gary Sobers (8,032) and Gordon Greenidge (7,558) – for the West Indies in Tests at an average of 46.67, and 31,232 first-class runs at an average of 49.26 do prove that he was one of the outstanding batsmen in post-war years.

These figures do not of course include his performances in limited-over cricket, where he excelled, both for the West Indies in their two Prudential World Cup Final wins in 1975 (102) and 1979 (13), but also for Lancashire in their run of victories in the Gillette Cup Final. They did the hat-trick – 1970, 1971 and 1972 – and won again in 1975; and Clive contributed scores of 29, 66, 126 and 73 not out.

Not many batsmen have been reported to the police for aggression – at least not on the field! But once in a match against Kent at Dartford I saw him pepper a row of adjoining houses with a string of giant sixes. An elderly lady was so terrified that she dialled 999 and called the police for help!

Clive never seems to have been handicapped by his glasses, which he has had to wear since, as a young boy, he was injured in breaking up a fight. He did try contact lenses for a short time in 1973, but soon gave them up. Like other great batsmen such as Sobers and Compton, however, he did have great trouble with his knees, though thanks to several operations he was able to continue batting as well as ever, right up to the end of his career. Indeed, in May 1988, in a charity match against the West Indies touring team led by Viv Richards, I saw him make a swift 37 not out against their bevy of fast bowlers, with several sixes soaring over the boundary in the typical Lloyd fashion.

The knees did affect his fielding, however, and he was forced in the end to spend most of the time in the slips. He had been a superb fielder in the covers – as good as Colin Bland, and there is no higher praise than that. He was like a giant cat prowling about and would pounce on the ball with tremendous speed, hurling the ball at the wicket like a rocket. But although he was a great loss in the covers, he caught many good catches at slip, and in all caught 89 for the West Indies, second only to Gary Sobers. To complete his all-round ability he occasionally bowled *right*-arm medium-pace, although of course he was a *left*-handed batsman.

Off the field Clive is a friendly person, gruff but with a good sense of humour, and is a surprisingly amusing after-dinner speaker. He became a British citizen in 1984 and settled happily in Cheshire, where he has done much charity and social work, mostly connected with finding work for the young unemployed. He and his wife also converted a house to become a rest-home for the elderly. He is a compassionate man who also likes to coach and encourage young cricketers.

He has a strong personality which, combined with his other qualities, made him a natural leader and a great captain of the West Indies. His record is remarkable. He was their captain in 74 Tests, of which the West Indies won 36 and drew 26, and at one time they went 26 successive Tests without defeat, including 11 successive wins in 1984. And of the eighteen series in which he was captain, only two were lost.

It's not just these results which made him such a successful captain, however. He had the ability – like Sir Frank Worrell – to weld together all the differences and rivalries of the West

Indian islands, and inspired loyalty from what became a happy and united side. From the commentary box it often looked as if his captaincy was a 'piece of cake'. He just stood in the slips and rang the changes on his four fast bowlers, with the very occasional spinner thrown in. Of course it wasn't really as simple as that, but it would have been fascinating to see him captain a weak side and then judge his tactics and judgement.

He had one hiccup during his years of captaincy. In 1978 he had a disagreement with his board of control over the Packer affair. He was a leading player in the World Series cricket and resigned as captain of the West Indies at Georgetown just before the Test against Australia in March 1978. Ali Kallicharran took over the captaincy for the remaining three matches and went to India as captain in six Tests a year later, but by the end of 1979 all was forgiven and Clive was back at the helm in Australia.

There was one side of Clive's captaincy with which I didn't agree. *On* the field he could be ruthless, quite unlike the friendly figure *off* it. He seemed to tolerate the frequent bowling of bouncers from his plethora of fast bowlers, which brought a nasty smell of intimidation into the game. People go to watch batsmen playing strokes, not ducking and weaving to avoid injury. A perfect example was the Close–Edrich partnership at Old Trafford in the third Test in 1976, when they were both battered all over the body by Roberts, Holding and Daniel and had to duck and weave their way through a most unpleasant evening. Neither the umpires nor Clive did anything about it, though Bill Alley did warn Holding towards the end. Clive has always maintained that it was up to the umpires to take the necessary action allowed by the laws. Technically of course he is right, but for the sake of cricket I still feel he should have stopped it. He later admitted that 'our fellows got carried away'!

I also disagreed with his tactics in employing a slow over-rate. Unfortunately, all other countries have also been guilty from time to time, but I don't excuse them either. Clive used it in order to give his fast bowlers with their long run-ups a longer rest between overs. He somewhat cynically defended himself by saying that if they had bowled more overs in a day, they would have won their Test matches a day or so earlier! He also made the point that the crowds didn't seem to mind, as there were always big attendances at all the West Indian Tests. One thing he couldn't deny, though. West Indies' usual slow over-rate made it virtually impossible for any opposing side to have sufficient time to build up a big enough score to beat them.

In spite of these personal criticisms of mine, however, there is no doubt that Clive will go down in history, not only as a great batsman and fielder, but also as a man and captain who had a tremendous influence for good in West Indies cricket. I doubt if many will ever captain their country more times, and I wish this recent British recruit a very happy and prosperous retirement.

Alan Knott

Knotty was responsible for me making one of my worst-ever puns – and that's saying something! At one time he used to play for Dartford, as did Derek Ufton, another Kent wicket-keeper. I was discussing which of them usually kept wicket for Dartford. 'Well,' I said, 'due to Knotty's commitments with Kent it was more Ufton than Knott!'

When he finally retired in 1985 – not owing to loss of form but to a dodgy ankle – cricket lost one of its great characters. He was not the usual run of Test cricketers. His health came before everything, so he didn't smoke, drank only the occasional glass of sherry or wine, and went to bed early. He was meticulous with his preparations before play, hence the fact that he was seldom ready in time and could usually be seen trotting out behind the others as they left the pavilion.

He wore a shirt several sizes too big so that it didn't restrict his movements. Underneath he always wore a flannel on the small of his back to soak up sweat. Like his shirt, his trousers were baggy, not tight round the bottom as they are today. His gloves had always been well-broken-in, so they looked old and scruffy, but they were comfortable. And he always had a handkerchief sticking out of his left pocket (Wally Hammond's dark blue one was always in his *right* pocket) to make it easier to blow his nose. He thought of everything, and during a match interval would have a complete change of clothing after a shower. This did not give him much time for lunch, but he was a sparse eater. Once on the field he indulged in those strange exercises which became famous on television – swinging his arms, bending his knees and touching his toes. He had a genuine fear of stiffening up.

As a wicket-keeper he was for years the best in the world, far more consistent, especially for Kent, than Godfrey Evans. He was as agile as a cat, and brought off some incredible catches standing back to the fast bowlers. Just as Godfrey had been so brilliant standing up to Alec Bedser, so was Knotty when he stood up to Derek Underwood, who at his pace on a turning wicket was very difficult to take.

My one 'quarrel' with Knotty was that he did not always stand up to medium-pace bowlers like d'Oliveira or Woolmer. He claimed that he was more certain to take catches standing back than up. For a wicket-keeper of his quality that seemed to me nonsense. I am a great believer in the pressure that a wicket-keeper exerts on a batsman, when standing close to the stumps. We used to argue about it, and this led to quite an amusing story. Knotty asked me if I would write something in his benefit brochure. I said I would be very happy to do so, but on one condition – that if Bob Woolmer came on to bowl in one of the Tests against the West Indies in 1976, Knotty would promise to stand up to him for at least one over. He promised to do so.

Sure enough, Woolmer came on to bowl at the Oval. To my delight I saw Knotty go up to the stumps, then look round at our commentary box and give the thumbs up. The left-handed Fredericks was the batsman and to my horror Woolmer's first ball was wide outside his leg-stump – not an easy ball for a wicket-keeper to take. I thought, oh my goodness, here come four byes. But needless to say, Knotty got across outside the leg-stump and made a brilliant take. He stood up for the next five balls, and then stood back for Woolmer's subsequent overs – but he had kept his word.

It was very difficult to say whether Knotty or Bob Taylor was the better keeper. Bob certainly stood up more and was far quieter and more unpretentious, compared to the more spectacular keeping of Knotty. I think it's fair to say that they were both equal and that they both qualify to be compared with the best Test keepers ever.

Knotty was, of course, by far the better bat. He could play either game – defensive or attacking. When defending he was strictly orthodox, playing with a dead straight bat, but when on the attack he was the greatest improviser I have ever seen, not forgetting John Emburey of the more recent players. He could cut and drive, and I saw him hit a six over extra cover in

Auckland in 1971, but his favourite stroke was the sweep, played off the most unlikely balls, even those outside the off-stump.

The most astonishing innings I saw him play was his 82 in the fourth Test at Sydney in 1975. Lillee and Thomson were at the height of their powers, and were a terrifying combination with their devastating pace and short-pitched bowling. When they *did* pitch the ball up he hit them through the empty spaces in the covers for four. If it was short outside the off-stump he would deliberately steer it over the top of slips' heads. In one hour after lunch he made 56, 33 of them in three overs against the second new ball. Lillee and Thomson were not too pleased, but how proud I was to have seen such a brave and brilliant innings. Remember, Knotty was a small man, but he was very quick on his feet and had tremendous guts. He didn't have that jutting-out chin for nothing!

His record of 269 dismissals in 95 Tests would have been even more remarkable had he not signed up with Kerry Packer, and later had not gone on the 'rebel' tour of South Africa, but loyal as he was to England his family always came first and he was determined to set up a firm financial base for them. I see him only too rarely these days, but when we do meet the wicked twinkle in his eye is still there, his mischievous smile and his impish sense of humour. And when you see those piercing brown eyes you can understand why he was such a great wicket-keeper.

20 Barry Richards, Greg Chappell, Dennis Lillee, Imran Khan

Barry Richards

I HAVE OFTEN BEEN ASKED the nearly impossible question to answer: 'Who is the best batsman you have ever seen?' It is difficult to answer because there are so many candidates, and they have played at different times against varying strengths of bowling. Who can attempt to choose between Bradman, Hammond, Compton, Sobers, Hutton, May, Cowdrey, Greg Chappell and Viv Richards, to name just a few? They were all great and each had his own special style. So I normally play safe and reply: 'I will tell you who was the most perfect batsman technically, whose every stroke was an exact copy out of the textbooks. There may have been batsmen who were his equal, but you cannot be better than perfection.' I then, usually to the surprise of the questioner, nominate Barry Richards. Note *Barry* not *Viv*.

He had, and played, every stroke off both the front and back foot. With a high back lift he played beautifully straight, and used his feet far more than the others I have mentioned, with the exception of Bradman, Hammond and Compton. He would even dance down the pitch to the fast bowlers, just like George Gunn used to do, except that George walked casually down the pitch, rather than dance.

Barry's technique was backed by his supreme confidence in his own ability, and an insolent contempt for all bowlers. Goodness knows how great his achievements would have been had he had the incentive of Test cricket, where he could match his skills against the world's best. Sadly, he became bored with county cricket – there was not sufficient challenge. I sometimes thought that he must have felt like a father playing against the boys in the parents' match. He was *that* good, and so much better than his contemporaries. It was all a sad waste of talent.

262

He once said that he dreaded having to go down to the ground every day at 9.30 am. I remonstrated with him about this, and pointed out how lucky he was compared with so many other people like miners, office or factory workers. I pointed out rather pompously that he had been given these great gifts and should do his best to make full use of them, but it all came down to the fact that he needed a challenge from his equals and, robbed of Test cricket, he very seldom got it.

In fact he only played in four Tests – against Australia in South Africa in 1970. He didn't do too badly either! 7 innings, 508 runs, and an average of 72.57. I was lucky enough to see all these innings, as Charles Fortune of SABC had kindly asked me along to be the 'neutral' commentator with Alan McGilvray and himself. Barry never once failed, and how's this for consistency: 29, 32, 140, 65, 35, 81, 126. That 140 alone was worth travelling all the way to South Africa. He reached his hundred in the first over after lunch off only 116 balls.

There then took place one of the most thrilling partnerships I have ever seen in Test cricket. He and Graeme Pollock put on 103 runs in an hour, completely pulverising the admittedly not too strong Australian attack of McKenzie, Connolly, Freeman and Gleeson. It was not like most big partnerships, where one batsman does most of the scoring whilst the other plays second fiddle. On this occasion Barry and Graeme matched each other with four after four. It was thrilling to watch and I felt privileged to be there to see such perfect stroke-play. It must have given Barry a bitter taste of what might have been, although at the time the South African tour to England in the summer was still due to take place.

Barry is tall with fair curly hair, and good-looking with an engaging smile. I always found him a friendly person, but he could undoubtedly be temperamental, brought on I am sure by his frustration. In the end he decided to prove his greatness by selling his skill to the highest bidder. He was perhaps the first top cricketer to realise his true commercial worth, and this may have made him appear greedy and grasping.

He played, of course, with great success and panache for Hampshire after one experimental match for Gloucestershire. He went there originally because of his great friend Mike Procter. As I have mentioned, they were both given a trial and played in just one match – against the visiting South African side in 1965.

Mike continued to play for Gloucestershire, but Barry did not make up his mind immediately what he really wanted to do. So it was not until 1968 that he began his ten years' career with Hampshire, and what a first season he had. He scored 2,395 runs, the next highest aggregate by any of the other Hampshire batsmen being 990 by Barry Reed. He scored over 1,000 runs for the county nine times before trying to sell his wares elsewhere, and played with great success for South Australia in 1970-1 when he made 356 runs against Western Australia – 325 of them coming on the first day.

He returned to England to play for the Rest of the World in the five 'Tests' against England in place of the cancelled South African tour. Strangely enough he didn't really take advantage of this opportunity to prove his great talent, only averaging 36.71 with 257 runs from his eight innings. After he left Hampshire he signed up with Kerry Packer and was one of the successes in the World Series cricket.

In addition to his batting he bowled off-breaks off a short run and gave the ball an enormous tweak, and with only 77 wickets in his career was much underbowled. He was a good catcher anywhere, especially in the slips.

I have seen him on my various trips to South Africa and interviewed him in our commentary box during the Lord's Bicentenary match in 1987. He was geniality itself and half admitted that he regretted not having enjoyed county cricket as much as he should have done. I felt that he was casting a longing eye out on the middle and would dearly have loved to have been batting out there against the likes of Marshall and Quadir. At the age of forty-two I reckon that he would still have shown them a thing or two and delighted the large crowd of cricket connoisseurs who came to the match.

Greg Chappell

I am sure that he will regret it until his dying day. It was a snap decision taken on the spur of the moment, which prompted an action totally contrary to the spirit of cricket. It happened at Melbourne on 1 February 1981, in the third of four Finals between Australia and New Zealand in the Benson and Hedges World Series Cup.

New Zealand had won the first match and Australia the

second, so it was an important game to win. Greg Chappell was captain of Australia who batted first and made 235 for 4 off their 50 overs – just about par for a winning score. There was a controversy when Chappell – on 52 – refused to walk when Snedden claimed to have made a low catch at deep mid-wicket. The New Zealand team appealed vehemently to the umpires, who both gave it not out because they said they hadn't been looking! They were evidently both watching for short runs.

There was therefore some slight ill-feeling between the two teams, especially as Chappell went on to make 90. Thanks to a fine 102 not out by Bruce Edgar, New Zealand were only just behind the clock when the last over came, and they still needed 15 to win with four wickets in hand. It was to be bowled by Trevor Chappell, the youngest of the three brothers. The other bowlers had all completed their allotted ten overs each. Richard Hadlee hit the first ball for four, and was lbw to the next: 11 runs needed, four balls and three wickets left. The new batsman, Ian Smith, hit a couple of twos before being bowled by the fifth ball. So in came Brian McKechnie with 7 runs needed to win, or 6 for a tie, off the last ball of the match.

It was then that Greg did the dirty trick. He ordered his brother Trevor to bowl this final ball underarm all along the ground – in cricket parlance a 'sneak' or a 'grub'. McKechnie was no great batsman and would have been pushed to hit a six off a slow half-volley on this huge Melbourne arena. Even had he done so, Australia would not have *lost*. It would have been a very worthy tie with McKechnie a justifiable hero, but it was not to be. The grub made such a task completely impossible, and McKechnie made no attempt to hit the ball in protest.

All hell broke loose and Greg's decision must still haunt him. In a telegram to the Australian Prime Minister, the New Zealand Prime Minister accused Australia of cowardice. The whole cricketing world on television, radio and in the press mercilessly criticised Greg's sportsmanship – or lack of it. He later publicly regretted what he had done, but of course his reputation as a sportsman suffered irreparably.

This was a pity because his action was not really characteristic of Greg. Admittedly, he had a strong will to win and played the game harder than most out in the middle, but except for the unpleasant habit of 'sledging' which he had learned from his brother Ian, when he was captain, he always played fairly. And later, when he took over from Ian, he appeared to become more relaxed and less aggressive. But he was undoubtedly a tough character; tall, dark and handsome, he sported a beard for much of his career and didn't smile too often. He could be petulant in his reactions. I remember seeing him once slap a streaker on his bare bottom with his bat.

As a cricketer he must be among the top five ever produced by Australia. He had a good pedigree. His mother was Vic Richardson's daughter and she used to bowl to her three sons in the garden. Brother Ian was the loud, confident extrovert, while Greg was more reserved. He divided his playing time between South Australia, where he was born (57 matches), and Queensland (51). He was a tower of strength to the latter and restored an interest in the state side and improved their standard of play.

As a batsman Ian was the more aggressive and enterprising, and more willing to take risks and take on the bowlers, but Greg was the more correct. He had an upright style, was stiff-backed with a high back lift, and played with the straightest of bats. To start with, his main stroke was the on-drive between mid-on and mid-wicket – he played it as well as Peter May, and that is saying a lot – but as time went on he developed a repertoire of strokes all round the wicket.

I was lucky to see his first Test innings at Perth in 1970 against Ray Illingworth's side. He made 108 and immediately showed his class by the way he played the pace attack of Snow, Lever and Shuttleworth on the fast Perth pitch. He seemed to have plenty of time to play his strokes, the majority being on-drives. Towards the end of his innings he cut loose and completely dominated the England bowlers – his last 60 runs coming in only 13 overs, or just under the hour. So he scored a hundred in his *first* Test innings, and fourteen years later he scored 182 against Pakistan at Sydney in his *last* Test innings – the only Test batsman ever to do this double.

During this innings he also became the first Australian to score 7,000 runs in Test matches. He passed Don Bradman's total of 6,996 runs, but has always modestly disclaimed any relevance in this. He points out that he had 151 innings against Bradman's 80. It was also his 24th Test hundred, a total only exceeded among Australian batsmen by Bradman (29), Border (27) and Steve Waugh (25).

Also in the Sydney match Greg caught his 122nd catch in Tests, passing Colin Cowdrey's previous record of 120. He was a fine fielder anywhere, but in later years fielded mostly in the slips, where he made so many of his catches. He always gave the impression that he was casual, and made no fuss nor showed any sign of elation when he took a catch, but he made many brilliant ones, plucking the ball out of the air in the manner of Hammond, Cowdrey or Sharpe.

As if all this was not enough, he was one of those invaluable change bowlers, who look innocent enough from the pavilion but are in the habit of picking up a vital wicket to break a stand. He was medium-pace and did a bit in the air and off the pitch, and undoubtedly learned much about the art of bowling during his two seasons with Somerset in 1968 and 1969. His experience of the more difficult English conditions also did much to help his batting.

Greg also created a (then) Australian record by captaining them in 48 Tests. He could have been captain in many more Tests and could have scored another 1,000 runs or so, had he not signed up with Kerry Packer, where he was a great success. I saw him play in three of the five matches in the World XI v Australia series in 1972, and he batted brilliantly, scoring 425 runs at an average of 106.25 in the three matches.

Oh, I have forgotten, there is yet another record which he broke and now shares. In 1974 against England in Perth, he became the first non-wicket-keeper to catch seven catches in a Test. This was later equalled by Yajurvindra Singh against England for India at Bangalore in 1977.

So that is Greg Chappell, a superb player rivalling the best in all Test cricket. He was always pleasant and friendly to me, and is a far nicer person than his unfortunate action with the sneak at Melbourne would suggest.

Dennis Lillee

All games have their controversial figures – cricket perhaps more than most. And Dennis Lillee certainly qualifies as one of them. Off the field he was intelligent, friendly and normally well mannered. I say normally, because he did once break protocol by thrusting a pencil and paper at the Queen for her autograph during one of those presentations in front of the pavilion. But as I say, he was friendly enough, and didn't seem to mind that, for obvious reasons, I used to call him Laguna.

What a change when he was on the field, however. With his longish black hair and moustache he was a ferocious and swarthy-looking person – rather like those gauchos in cowboy films. He was quick to lose his temper and often blasted the unfortunate batsman with savage verbal abuse. As a weapon he had a lethal bouncer which he didn't fail to unleash when he felt like it.

There were several ways of dealing with his temperament. You could keep quiet and disregard his abuse. You could – if you had the guts – taunt him, as Trevor Bailey would have done and Derek Randall did, especially in that great innings of his in the Centenary Test in Melbourne. Or – if you were good enough – you could challenge him and match your skill against his, as Ian Botham did on several occasions, but especially at Old Trafford in 1981. England were in trouble – 104 for 5 – when Botham came in at number seven. He played himself in for his first thirty runs, then Lillee was given the new ball and the fight was on. Botham proceeded to show Lillee who was the master. Lillee gave it all he got and bowled very fast from the Stretford End. He tried Botham with three vicious bouncers, which were all contemptuously flicked off his eyebrows by Botham, and went sailing over long leg for six. The battle was won, but perhaps only Botham could have won it in such a daring and devastating way.

Apart from his personality, what sort of bowler was Lillee? He was as fast as anyone else since the war, but like Lindwall learned to conserve his energies and keep his really fast ball up his sleeve. He had a flowing run-up to the wicket and a perfect action, with a high right arm and his chin tucked in behind his left arm as he peered down the pitch. He could swing the ball and move it off the pitch; he cleverly disguised his variations in pace and his yorker was as lethal as his bouncer. It's impossible to say whether he was better than Lindwall or not, but without doubt he was one of the greatest fast bowlers of all time.

I first saw him on Ray Illingworth's tour in the sixth Test at Adelaide, when he got off to a good start with 5 for 84 in the first innings in which he bowled in Test cricket. He was to take five wickets in a Test innings another twenty-two times, and ten wickets in a Test seven times. He impressed everyone at Adelaide, and the English batsmen realised what they would have to face for the next twelve years or so.

He always studied the art of bowling and took the trouble to learn about English conditions by playing in the Lancashire League in 1971. He was still only twenty-one years old, and his future looked assured when he took 31 wickets the following year on Australia's tour of England under Ian Chappell. But then tragedy struck. He suffered stress fractures of the lower spine and it looked as if his playing days were over – but he was saved by his character, determination, discipline and guts. For more than a year he had painful treatment and carried out demanding remedial exercises. He refused to give up, and it paid him handsomely. He came back to Test cricket against Mike Denness's team in Australia in 1974, and with Jeff Thomson devastated the England batsmen with some of the fastest, most ferocious and dangerous fast bowling I have ever seen. Lillee took 25 wickets in the series and would have taken more had he not bowled only six overs in the final Test, before he bruised his right foot.

He never looked back after that and took his Test total to 355 wickets, tenth in the list of all Test bowlers. He would – like Underwood and several others – have taken many more had he not been one of the first to sign for Kerry Packer after the Centenary Test of 1977. When 'peace' was declared two years later he returned to play in thirty-seven Tests, until a bad knee forced his retirement in 1983. But, being Lillee, he came back again, playing for Tasmania in 1987 and for Northamptonshire in 1988. To undertake a busy season in county cricket after all his injuries and at the age of thirty-eight was proof of his determination and courage.

He was a useful batsman when he felt the occasion called for it. His highest test score was 73 not out at Lord's in 1975, and it remained his highest score in all first-class cricket. He came in at number ten with the score at 133 for 8. He put on 66 with Edwards, and a further 69 with Mallett for the last wicket. He hit three huge sixes and eight fours and batted for two-and-a-quarter hours, which just shows what he could do. This was the match where a streaker ran on for the first time ever in a Test match. As he did the splits over the stumps at the pavilion end, Alan Knott, who was the non-striker at the Nursery End, said it was the first time he had ever seen *two* balls coming down the pitch towards him.

Lillee made four tours (1972, 1975, 1980 and 1981) of England and at the start of the 1981 tour he caught pneumonia and didn't play until the second Prudential match on 6 June. But he was fit by the time the Tests came along and took 39 wickets in the series. When he had his pneumonia he was treated by a lady doctor, 'Micky' Day, who looked after some of the staff at Lord's. She unwittingly encouraged Lillee to break the law, telling him that she would only declare him fit for play if he came in and changed his sweaty shirt after every bowling spell. So there was Lillee walking off – presumably with the permission of the umpires – and a substitute coming on to take his place. At that time the law stated that no fielder should leave the field to change his clothing or to have a rub-down. Nowadays they can do so, but no substitute is allowed on to take their place. So Dr Day caused a change in the laws.

I have earlier said that Lillee was short tempered and became an aggressive character once on the field of play. There were two famous instances when his temper got the better of him. Both, funnily enough, occurred in Perth – perhaps the famous 'Freemantle Doctor' affected his liver! Anyway, in 1979 against England he came in to bat with an aluminium bat which a firm was trying to market. Both the umpires and Mike Brearley objected, and there was a ten-minute delay while Greg Chappell tried to persuade Lillee to use an ordinary bat. He finally agreed but flung the aluminium bat forty yards or so away in anger. This unfortunate episode caused another change in the laws, which now state that 'the blade shall be made of *wood*'.

The other incident occurred at Perth in the first Test against Pakistan in 1981. Javed Miandad was captain of Pakistan, and he was not the most popular player in any cricketing country. He could be infuriating, and somehow got up Lillee's goat. Lillee deliberately tried to impede him when he was going for a run, and then aimed a kick at Javed's backside. Whether he actually connected I'm not sure, but Javed was so angry that he then tried to hit Lillee with his bat. With hundreds of thousands of young people watching on television, it was pathetic and unacceptable that two grown men playing for their countries should have behaved like this.

One final piece of unusual behaviour from Lillee was when, in the 1981 Test at Headingley, with Australia only needing 130 to win, the odds against England were 500–1 (these were assessed by Godfrey Evans, and proved rather expensive for Ladbrokes). As they watched England going out to field, Lillee and Marsh saw a friend going off to back England. Hearing the odds, they are said to have shouted: 'Put a fiver on for us.' I think it was more of a joke than anything else, with nothing sinister in it, especially as Lillee made 17 in a gallant stand of 35 for the ninth wicket to try to win the match for Australia.

After his retirement from Test cricket Lillee proved himself an astute businessman by putting money into the great Australian film success *Crocodile Dundee*. I am thankful that I never had to bat against him, but I am pleased that I saw him at his fastest and best, with his Australian crowds encouraging him as he bustled in on his long run-up to the wicket with shouts of, 'Lilleeeeee, Lilleeeeee.'

Imran Khan

As always seems to happen when I am travelling in a London taxi, the driver was talking cricket to me through his glass partition. With all the traffic noise it's not always easy to hear what they say, and it's necessary to shout back one's answers, but it is nice to know how many people *are* interested in cricket. What about Botham? Why don't we sack the selectors? The questions come thick and fast. 'I was in the City the other day,' said my driver, 'and there was a queue about two hundred yards long outside a bookshop. And do you know,' he added, 'they all seemed to be women.' I wasn't at all surprised when he informed me that, on making enquiries, he was told that Imran Khan was inside signing copies of his new book.

He was certainly the most glamorous player in modern cricket. He was a dashing figure with striking good looks and 'come up and see me some time' eyes. He had a soft beguiling voice and, at the time, was one of the most eligible bachelors alive. He came from a well-to-do family in Lahore with strong cricketing traditions: two previous Pakistan captains, Javed Burki and Majid Khan, were his cousins, and as an added bonus his uncle was chairman of the Lahore selectors! This may have helped with his selection to tour England in 1971 when still only eighteen years old. He was already a tearaway fast bowler and a useful batsman, but it didn't do him much good. In the first Test at Lord's he was run out for 5, and although he bowled twenty-eight overs for only 55 runs he didn't take a wicket, was dropped, and did not play in the remaining two Tests.

From then on, however, he became Pakistan's pin-up boy

and was revered and hero-worshipped by every cricket follower – and that meant most of the population. Proof of his popularity came in 1987 when he publicly announced that he would play no more Test cricket, but by public demand – and, it is said, some 'persuasion' from the president, General Zia – he decided to go as captain to the West Indies. The result was a thrilling series. Pakistan won the first Test by nine wickets, the second was honourably drawn, and the West Indies won the third in an exciting two-wicket victory. Tony Cozier, the West Indian commentator and writer, headlined his report 'Imran's Triumphant Return', and he went on to say that Pakistan were inspired by the personal example and leadership of their captain.

He has undoubtedly been an inspiration to Pakistan cricket, and perhaps because of his upbringing has always been a natural leader. He is highly intelligent, and as a result of his playing ability he was always able to lead by example. When he went up to Oxford for three years he was, unusually, elected captain in his *second* year, a tribute to his character. As Frank Worrell did for the West Indies, so was Imran able to weld the different personalities in Pakistan into a close-knit team with tremendous confidence in their ability to win.

As a player he was one of the great Test all-rounders. At one time he was possibly the fastest bowler in the world, but time – and the odd injury – tempered him into a bowler in the Lindwall–Hadlee mould. He could still bowl as fast as most, but used his speed less frequently. He was mainly an in-swinger, with a fine high action and an inexhaustible supply of energy. With a new ball he occasionally bowled an out-swinger, and could bowl a yorker and a bouncer as well as anybody. He had various injuries, including a broken left arm as a boy, and a stress fracture of his left shin which kept him out of Test cricket for three years. Even so in 88 Tests between 1971 and 1992 he took 362 Test wickets at the low average of 22.81, and five wickets in an innings 23 times. He learned a great deal of his bowling skills during his six seasons with Worcestershire from 1971 to 1976 before moving to Sussex, for whom he continued to play for the next decade. He enjoyed the night-life of London, where he lived, and he used to commute daily to Hove for his cricket.

His bowling rather overshadowed his batting. He usually batted at number seven and was a powerful hitter who could turn a game with his forcing strokes backed up by a sound defence. Perhaps he should have scored more than his 3,807 runs in Tests, but he put most of his energy into his bowling. Needless to say, with such a fine physique and athleticism he was a magnificent fielder anywhere.

Imran is very much his own man. He knows what he wants and usually gets it. He has had his occasional brush with the authorities – his option to play for Packer is an example – but his charm and good manners have helped to make his path easier. He is an intensely proud man who liked nothing better than to fight for Pakistan with all the energy, guts and skill that he could muster. He retired from cricket after leading Pakistan to a marvellous victory in the World Cup in Melbourne in 1992. He has done them proud, and they reward him with fervent hero-worship.

21 Bob Taylor, Richard Hadlee, Viv Richards, Mike Brearley

Bob Taylor

IT IS OFTEN SAID THAT wicket-keepers are born and not made. If that is true then Bob Taylor was certainly born to the job. He and Keith Andrew had the best pair of hands of any of the Test wicket-keepers whom I have seen. They were both quiet and undemonstrative, but wonderfully efficient, either standing back or up to the stumps. Others, like Marsh, Evans or Knott, were more spectacular, but Bob in his quiet way caught just as many of those impossible-looking diving catches. He was a perfect model for any young keeper to follow: left foot between middle- and off-stumps, crouching low with his eyes just above the bails, the fingers of his two hands pointing downwards as they gently touched the ground. He stayed down until the last possible moment, making absolutely sure of the line of the ball. Once up, he was incredibly quick to move either to the offside or, far more difficult, to the ball outside the leg-stump.

A wicket-keeper standing up is taking the ball blind outside the leg-stump. Here I am sure that instinct, as well as practice and experience, plays a large part. Again, when watching Bob, you could see a slight 'give' in the hands at the moment of taking the ball, a sure safeguard against bruising when keeping to fast bowlers.

You will notice Bob's record of 1,648 career dismissals, 121 more than his nearest rival John Murray. Bob will tell you that it's not the number of catches and stumpings you make that matters, however – it's the number of misses by which a wicket-keeper should be judged. Had the records been kept I bet that Bob's misses would have been fewer than anyone else's. One of his assets was his consistency, day in, day out, no matter whether playing for his country or county. He was such a perfectionist that he gave up his short captaincy of Derbyshire because he felt it was affecting his concentration behind the stumps.

He was the ideal professional and an exemplary tourist – uncomplaining, cheerful, loyal and helpful to the other players. He had to wait for eleven years before he played in his first Test; he was in the shadow of Alan Knott, acting as his understudy waiting to go on stage. I was lucky to be there when he achieved his ambition. It was in New Zealand at Christchurch during Ray Illingworth's 1971 tour. Illy asked Knotty to stand down to reward Bob for his patience and loyalty. He had the pleasure of keeping to Derek Underwood on a substandard pitch which took a lot of spin. Unders took 6 for 12 and Bob got his first three Test victims. Knotty took over for the next Test at Auckland and perhaps to prove a point made 101 and 96! Bob could never compare with Knotty as a batsman, though I did see him play several useful defensive innings in Test partnerships, especially his top Test score of 97 at Adelaide in 1979.

I shall always remember Bob on the field with his white sunhat turned up in front. Godfrey Evans was famous for the way he lifted the morale of a tired fielding side, but, in his quieter way, so did Bob. You could often see him running after a perspiring bowler at the end of an over, just to give him an encouraging pat on the back.

Off the field, as I've said, he was a perfect tourer. He was at his best at the many official functions which a team *has* to attend. He earned himself the nickname of 'Chat' for the way he chatted everyone up, but what was so nice about him was that he would always volunteer for those private parties to which the team did *not* have to go. You could bet on Bob being there – the perfect ambassador for his country.

Sadly, towards the end of his career he became slightly disillusioned with the behaviour and attitudes of his younger colleagues. He retired in 1984, but had a remarkable if brief comeback against New Zealand at Lord's in 1986. The England wicket-keeper Bruce French had been struck on the back of the helmet when batting against Richard Hadlee. He was unable to field, so Bill Athey took over behind the stumps. Someone then had a brilliant idea, to which the New Zealanders generously agreed. After his retirement Bob had become a very popular and efficient PRO for Cornhill, who, of course sponsored the

Tests. He had been entertaining some Cornhill guests to lunch in the Cricket School. After seeing that they were all looked after, he started to have a prawn cocktail himself, but he was soon interrupted by a request from the pavilion to take over as substitute behind the stumps.

He readily agreed because he has always kept himself fit and plays regularly in charity matches, so he collected his gloves from the back of his car, where he always keeps them 'just in case'. He had to borrow from various people a shirt, boots and trousers, and of course a box! He had a marvellous reception as he ran on to the field – the same grey-haired figure in his white sunhat. And needless to say, although out of first-class practice, he kept wicket immaculately – as he always did.

Richard Hadlee

There are many arguments for and against overseas players playing in the County Championship. Those *for* say that it enables spectators in England to see great players from all over the world regularly in action every summer, instead of every four years or so when their countries tour England. The county secretaries say that the acquisition of a top overseas player gives every county (except Yorkshire) a better chance of winning one of the four competitions. They also claim that it gives our young players the chance of playing with and learning from the overseas stars.

Those *against* say that our young players are denied opportunities in their county team. The overseas player so often gets preference in the batting order, or is given the new ball which would otherwise be taken by a home-bred player. They also point out that many who come here are not already stars. They come here to *learn* their cricket under English conditions and then use their improved skills and experience to beat England in Test matches. Personally I am in favour of the present restriction on overseas players, which means that each county is only allowed to register one player not qualified for England.

All this brings us to Richard Hadlee, who by playing over here from 1978 to 1987 benefited both his county and himself. In this period, under the captaincy of South African Clive Rice, Nottinghamshire became one of the top counties: they won two Championships and a NatWest Trophy, were finalists in the

Benson and Hedges, and came second twice in the Sunday League.

As for Hadlee himself, he came here as a fairly ordinary tearaway fast bowler who had taken 89 wickets at 31.58 apiece. By the time he retired from cricket in 1990 he had taken a (then) record-breaking 431 Test wickets at an average of 22.30.

The daily hard grind of county cricket forced Richard to adjust his methods. He cut down his run and learned to concentrate on swing and movement off the seam. He was nearly as fast as before and could still unleash a really fast ball which he used sparingly. Like Lindwall, Trueman, Lillee and Marshall, he simply relied on skill rather than speed.

He was a dedicated cricketer, and number four out of the five sons of Walter Hadlee, the old New Zealand captain. So he was brought up in a cricket atmosphere and was soon taught the finer points of the game. He always set himself targets, and with his sense of purpose and determination he usually achieved them. He was said to have a number of slogans, which he kept repeating to himself as the occasion demanded – a sort of self-hypnosis. And how well they worked for him, Nottinghamshire and New Zealand. He did the double in 1984 (the first since 1967) and topped the bowling averages in 1980, 1981, 1982, 1984 and 1987, but his slogans let him down slightly in 1987. I am sure he had planned to do the double in his last season for Notts. He just achieved his 1,000 runs, but only took 97 wickets. Even so, only two other bowlers did take 100, Neil Radford with 109 and Jonathan Agnew with 101. But they bowled 150 and 186 *more* overs respectively than Richard.

So what made him such a great bowler? He was tall (six feet one inch), lean and wiry with long arms and a whippish action – not unlike Brian Statham in build. He had a perfect sideways-on action and bowled from near the stumps. He swung the ball away from the batsman, and could then bring it back off the seam. His shortened run was about twelve yards, and he had a long raking stride. Because his arm came over so high he produced a lot of bounce, and he kept a good line and length with only the occasional short ball. Richard was a bowler whom any young player should copy to the last detail.

As a batsman he was a left-hander who used to go in at number eight or nine and then try to knock the cover off the ball, but he gradually improved his defence without sacrificing his ability to strike the ball a long way, often high in the air.

He improved so much that he became a genuine Test all-rounder. In 86 Tests he made 3,124 runs at an average of 27.16 and in his last county season he topped the Notts batting averages with 1,025 runs. (Needless to say, he also topped the bowling averages.) To complete his skills as an all-rounder Richard was a fine fielder anywhere, moving fast and with a good arm. What a chap to have on your side.

His batting reached a peak in the NatWest Final at Lord's in 1987 against Northants. He made 70 not out in 61 balls, hitting two giant sixes and four fours. At one time Notts needed 51 off only five overs, but thanks to Richard and Bruce French this was reduced to 8 runs needed off the last over, to be bowled by David Capel. French was run out for a splendid 35 off the first ball. The next Hadlee hit for a towering six into the 'free' seats at the Nursery End. The third ball he pulled to the Tavern Stand for four, and Notts had won a thrilling game, coming from behind when all had seemed lost.

Richard went out in a blaze of glory at the end of his time with Notts. Thanks to his fine all-round performance and the inspirational captaincy of South African Clive Rice, they won both the County Championship and the NatWest Trophy. They nearly did the hat-trick, finishing second in the Refuge Assurance League, only two points behind Worcestershire.

By the beginning of 1988 Richard had reached Ian Botham's record total of 373 Test wickets. This meant that he was equal with Botham at the start of the first Test against England at Christchurch on 12 February 1988. A big crowd came to see their local boy make good – like Denis Compton at Lord's, Richard used to sell score-cards at Christchurch. But it was not to be. His analysis was 18–3–50–0 before he injured a calf muscle trying to stop a hard drive from Robinson. He didn't bowl again in the series, and whereas he might have retired from Test cricket if he had passed Botham, he decided to tour India with New Zealand in November 1988. He broke the record in the first session of the First Test with his dismissal of Arun Lal.

Richard went on to become the first bowler to pass 400 Test wickets – this time against India at Christchurch – and he retired from cricket in 1990 after taking a wicket with his last ball of the game in the third Test against England at Edgbaston. He was knighted for his services to cricket later that year.

Both New Zealand and Nottinghamshire owe a debt of thanks

to Wally Hadlee for producing such a magnificent all-round cricketer, and such a thoroughly nice person as well.

Viv Richards

How great a batsman was Viv? The answer must be that he was one of the greatest ever, but from pure figures alone it is impossible to compare him with others like W. G. Grace, Jack Hobbs or Don Bradman. For example, the Don played in only 52 Tests over a twenty-year span from 1928 to 1948, which of course included the war years, and there was no Pakistan. There were also far fewer tours, and the Don himself never went to South Africa, New Zealand, the West Indies or India. On the other hand, over eighteen years from 1974 to 1991 Viv played in 121 Tests with 8,540 runs and an average of 50.23. The Don made 6,996 runs and averaged 99.94.

They had one thing in common, however. They were both head and shoulders above their contemporaries, and both imposed themselves on a game of cricket. They could win or turn a match by their outstanding individual performances. But in one respect Viv was an original. Most, if not all, of the great batsmen of the past have been orthodox with odd individual variations. A schoolboy watching their strokes could safely try to copy them, but in no way should a youngster try to follow or emulate Viv's method of batting.

He was immensely strong and used a very heavy bat. He had a wonderful eye and played mainly across the line of the ball towards the on-side. This did not mean that he could not cut, off-drive or even hit straight, but let's say that he favoured the area between the bowler and the square leg. He was an immensely powerful hooker, and thought nothing of pulling a ball from *outside* the off-stump over square leg for six. He was in fact a great hitter of sixes, which on the whole the likes of Bradman, Hutton, Compton, May, Chappell and Boycott were not. Gary Sobers, Clive Lloyd and Wally Hammond, on the other hand, did enjoy hitting the ball in the air.

Viv's other asset was his supreme confidence in himself. In fact he would probably have scored many more runs had he not been such an impatient starter, seldom trying to play himself in. He was an arrogant figure on the field, with a distinctive swaggering walk. He never wore a helmet and showed the utmost contempt for the fastest of bowlers. He was always the most vulnerable against spin – possibly because he had so little practice against it.

There is no doubt that if one were asked to pick the two outstanding destroyers of bowlers since the war one would unhesitatingly pick Ian Botham and Viv. They were both able to turn and win a match practically on their own, and both were inspired by the big occasion. Take Lord's. In 1979 Viv scored a century against England in the World Cup Final and in the same year another hundred for Somerset in the Gillette Cup Final. There followed a hundred against England in the 1980 Test, and in 1981 yet another in the Benson and Hedges Cup Final.

He made his first-class début in 1972 and was signed up by Len Creed for Somerset in 1974. There he acknowledges that he learned much of his batting skills on English wickets from Brian Close. It helped that basically he was always a front-foot player. Figures can be a bore, but I think his performance in 1976 is worth recording. In the eight months between January and August he made 1,710 runs in 11 Tests at an average of 90.00. His opponents included Australia, India and England. Enough said.

He was always athletic and in spite of his height (five feet eleven inches) and his strongly built frame he was a brilliant fielder anywhere, with a devastating throw. In later years he was most often at first slip, where he made the most difficult catch appear easy, and he 'pouched' 120 for the West Indies. He was also quite a useful off-break bowler and could bowl seam at medium pace. With so many fast bowlers playing for the West Indies he sometimes had to fill the spinner's place and ended with 32 Test wickets to his credit.

He took over the captaincy of the West Indies in 1985. He started by beating New Zealand and England, but then followed three drawn series against Pakistan, New Zealand and Pakistan again. There was talk of a West Indian decline and an end to their world dominance. Naturally the new captain was partly blamed, but he was learning the job and had the difficult task of following Clive Lloyd. Furthermore, the West Indies were gradually introducing new players into their team. By the time they came to England in 1988, however, they were right back on top with Viv very much in command.

Admittedly, they were a far better side than England, and

Richards's task with his battery of four fast bowlers may not have seemed too difficult, but in fact his captaincy was a revelation. On the field he was astute with his field placings and changes of bowling. He obviously knew the faults and weaknesses of the England batsmen. He also made sure that his side were one of the fittest I have ever seen. I watched one of their work-outs, which they did every day for forty minutes before each day's play. I was exhausted, just watching, but it meant that they completely outshone England in the field and I think were the best fielding side since Jack Cheetham's South Africans in 1955.

Off the field Viv was also a great success. In the past he had always appeared to be rather haughty and aloof, and there is no doubt that he was a very proud man. He was the first captain from the Leeward Isles – he was born in Antigua in 1952 – and he put them on the map so far as providing Test players is concerned. They even displaced Barbados as *the* cricketing island. Anyway, off the field in 1988 Viv did everything right. His relationship with the media was excellent, and he made a point of mixing and greeting us all with a smile.

Viv was knighted in 1990 – the same year as Richard Hadlee – and retired from cricket a year later, having captained the West Indies in fifty Tests. For nearly twenty years he delighted crowds around the world with his own unique style of batting. But don't try to copy him!

Mike Brearley

You would never have thought that he had captained England thirty-one times, and has been rated as one of the greatest of all Test captains. There he was on an autumn afternoon in the playground at Primrose Hill, pushing his young daughter on a swing. Curly grey hair, open-neck shirt, old jacket and jeans. A slow, welcoming smile of recognition – a quietly spoken voice: 'Hello, Johnners, how are you?'

Mike Brearley, possibly the most successful, certainly the most intellectual of England's captains. Under him they won six rubbers, halved three and lost one. As captain of Middlesex from 1971 to 1982 he led them to win four County Championships and two Gillette Cups.

He was a truly remarkable all-rounder. He took a first in

Classics and a good second in Moral Sciences at Cambridge. To cap this he came top in the Civil Service examination in 1964 – a gateway to a top job in almost any occupation. He played cricket for Cambridge for four years from 1961 to 1964, and in that time made a record 4,310 runs, captaining them in the last two years. Just to prove his versatility, he scored two hundreds in the Varsity matches at Lord's, and was also their wicket-keeper on two occasions.

I first got to know him well on Mike Smith's 1964–5 tour of South Africa. Coming straight from his triumphs at Cambridge, Brearlers – as I have always called him – had an inexplicably unsuccessful tour. He had scored 2,178 runs in the summer of 1964, yet on the tour he played in none of the Tests, and scored only 406 runs at an average of 25.37 in the other matches. He started well enough with a couple of sixties, but the second half of the tour was a complete disaster for him. It was a tremendous test of his character, but he took it remarkably well. I never once heard him complain, and throughout he played his part in supporting Mike Smith and the team in every possible way.

You get to know people well over a bridge table, and that's how I got to know and like him. Charles Fortune, the South African broadcaster, and David Brown made up our four and we had some hilarious games. Brearlers was by far the best player, though Charles Fortune probably thought *he* was! Big Dave and I were 'instinct' players and didn't worry too much about conventions. We were rather like the very poor player whose erratic bidding had got his partner into terrible trouble. At the end of the game, the poor chap left the room to go and spend a penny. After he had been away for about half a minute, his partner said brightly: 'Well, for the first time this evening, I know what he's got in his hand!' I'm bound to say that it didn't seem to matter what Brearlers had in *his* hand. He always seemed to win.

His standing as a batsman is difficult to assess. IIe had the benefit of the easy Fenner pitches during his four years at Cambridge, but even so he scored a lot of runs elsewhere. He had a correct, pleasant style with sound defence and all-round strokes, and liked to open the batting. In fact, I wonder how many people realised that he actually opened for England forty times. Twenty of these were as Boycott's partner, without a single run-out! So he had plenty of chances to prove himself as a Test batsman, but never quite did so. His batting always showed character, however, and time and time again he came up with a useful score just when it was needed.

In the field he gave up serious wicket-keeping after his first two years at Cambridge, giving way to Mike Griffith in the last two years when he was captain. But he later proved himself a first-class slip catcher (52 catches for England), and was perfectly adequate in any other position. I saw him make one of the best catches that I have ever seen in the Prudential Final at Lord's against the West Indies in 1978. He was fielding at wide mid-on when Andy Roberts took an enormous heave at Mike Hendrick, who was bowling from the Pavilion End. The ball soared high in the sky towards the boxes in the Tavern Stand. Brearlers turned and ran fast in that direction with the ball coming from *behind* him. He was going at full tilt, looked up at the right moment and took a brilliant catch as the ball came over his shoulder. He had to suffer the indignity of being kissed by most of his side! But it emphasised his own skill as a fielder, which was an important factor in his success as captain. By his own example he was able to make the England side into a magnificent fielding machine, possibly the best it ever was.

On balance, therefore, he did not earn his Test place as a batsman, but was well up to standard in the field. Certainly, since I have followed cricket England captains have generally earned their place by their playing merit. Exceptions to this might be the old amateurs like Arthur Gilligan, F. T. Mann, Percy Chapman and, latterly, F. G. Mann. But, as Yorkshire proved for so many years, no matter how strong a team may be, a good leader is essential.

The secret of Brearlers' success as a captain was that he loved the job. Both for Middlesex and England he revelled in the many challenges. Cricket is a complicated art, and gives so much scope for thoughtful captaincy. A deep knowledge of the history of the game and its laws, tactics, field placings, study of opponents' strengths and weaknesses are all essential ingredients for good captaincy, but a one hundred per cent pass in all these is still not enough. A cricket captain has not only to lead his team *on* the field but also *off* it. Cricketers spend so much time together during an England summer, or on winter tours. A great captain has also to be a father figure to keep them happy and help to solve their personal problems.

This was Brearler's great strength. With his psychological approach he got to know and understand every member of the team. He studied each one separately and decided on the best way to handle him. (Stuart Surridge did the same thing in his five successful championship years for Surrey. He found that to get the best out of them he had to be gentle with Jim Laker, for example, but tough with Tony Lock.)

Rodney Hogg was quoted in Australia as saying that 'Brearley has a degree in people' – a very perceptive remark for a fast bowler! But Brearlers was deceptive until you knew him well. On the surface he was a gentle person, with his slow friendly smile, but underneath he was tough and strong willed, and expected to get his own way. At the same time he supported his players and looked after their interests, especially where money was concerned. He wasn't exactly a barrack-room lawyer, but he always tried to see their side in any discussions or disputes.

I will end by showing how important to his success was his understanding of individuals. A perfect example occurred on the last day of the famous 1981 Test at Headingley, which England won so sensationally by 18 runs.

Brearlers had been recalled to the England captaincy for this third Test in the series. Under Ian Botham England had lost the first at Trent Bridge and drawn the second at Lord's where Botham scored a pair and then resigned the captaincy. Things didn't seem to be going much better for Brearley. England had to follow on 227 runs behind and then lost 7 wickets for only 135 runs, but thanks to a magnificent 149 not out by Botham and 56 and 29 from Dilley and Old, Australia were set 130 runs to win with most of the last day available to get them.

At the start of their innings, to our surprise Botham was put on to bowl downhill and downwind from the Kirkstall Lane End. Poor Bob Willis, aged thirty-two but still by far the fastest bowler in the side, had to bowl *up*hill and *up*wind from the Football Stand End. Botham took the early wicket of Wood, but came off after seven overs. Old replaced him for a few overs, and then at last Willis was switched round. He proceeded to bowl with tremendous speed and ferocity, generating high bounce from the pitch. He ran through the side – with a rest at the lunch interval. I have never seen him bowl better or with more fury, venom and bite in every delivery. He finished with 8 for 43 – by far his best Test analysis ever.

Coupled with Botham's great innings, Willis was undoubtedly the cause for one of the greatest turnarounds ever in Test cricket.

I asked him after the match why he had started uphill and upwind. He said the same thought had quickly occurred to him! So he went up to Brearley and said: 'Skipper, why am I bowling from the Football Stand End, into the wind and up the slope?' Brearley smiled his slow smile, 'To make you angry,' he said. How's that for captaincy?

22 Ian Botham, David Gower, Allan Border

Ian Botham

THERE HAVE BEEN MANY *great* Test players, but very few who merit the classification of being a colossus. I can think of only three: W. G. Grace, Sir Donald Bradman and I. T. Botham (Guy the Gorilla or Beefy to his friends). The dictionary defines a colossus as 'more than life-size, a gigantic person standing astride over dominions'. W. G. *was* cricket in Victorian times and dominated the game throughout the country. Don Bradman brought a new concept into the art of accumulating runs and was head and shoulders above his contemporaries. And lastly there is Ian Botham, who for sixteen amazing years hit the world's headlines, either with his remarkable performances on the field or his equally remarkable behaviour off it! Is there a common factor between the player and the man? One word comes immediately to mind – aggression. So let's take the player first.

His figures in themselves clearly show him to be one of the greatest ever all-round cricketers, perhaps sharing the rostrum with Gary Sobers alone. Between 1977 and 1992 he played in 102 Tests, made 5,200 runs, took 383 wickets at 28.40 each, caught 120 catches and took 5 wickets in an innings 27 times, second only to Richard Hadlee (36). In comparison Gary Sobers played in 93 Tests, made 8,032 runs, took 235 wickets and caught 109 catches.

Like so many modern Test cricketers, his figures for his country are far better than those for his county. There are several reasons for this. Test bowlers, especially fast ones, cannot be expected to give continuously of their best whilst taking part in three one-day internationals and six Test matches. With fewer Tests and no one-day internationals bowlers like Trueman and Bedser did manage to take 100 wickets regularly for their county, but in those days they had the spur of big crowds. No great players – like 'great' actors –

enjoy playing before an empty house. They are only fully inspired and give of their best in front of big crowds or audiences. It may be unfair on the counties but it is understandable.

Ian was quite simply the best hitter of a ball that I have ever seen. He was physically immensely strong, powerfully built in forearms, thighs, legs and bottom (important for a fast bowler). One of the main reasons for his success was that he hit the well-pitched-up ball *straight*, most of his sixes going in an arc from wide long-on to wide long-off. To anything short on or outside the off-stump he would strike a tremendous blow off the back foot through the covers. In addition to his enormous strength and wonderful eye he always used a heavy bat, well over 3 lb., which meant that he was never able to produce a genuine cut. This may have been his excuse for the occasional reverse sweep, which so shocked the older generation like myself!

Anything short of a length on the wicket or outside the leg-stump he hooked to square or long leg. He could never resist a challenge. If a bowler placed a man at deep square leg, then Ian would try to hit the ball over his head for six. It was his competitive spirit, combined with his aggression, that made him such enormous value to a side. He always tried to come out on top. I shall never forget him at Old Trafford in 1981. Dennis Lillee had just taken the new ball and bowled Ian three bouncers, which Ian promptly hooked off his eyebrows for sixes over long leg. This was perhaps the best exhibition of hitting I have ever seen in a Test, better even than his remarkable 149 not out in the Headingley Test a month earlier. He – as *Wisden* put it – 'plundered' 118 in 123 minutes with 6 sixes (a record in England and Australian Tests) and 13 fours. It is worth noting that he played himself in, his first 28 runs taking 70 minutes. He then went berserk and in only 53 minutes made the remaining 90 runs. This proved that he was not just a hitter. Not for nothing was he on the ground staff at Lord's, where young boys are taught all the right techniques. This meant that he had a correct and sound defence, although there was always the matter of his temperament. He could never allow a bowler to dictate to him for too long. He just had to prove himself top dog.

It should be easy to assess a Test bowler who in sixteen years took 383 wickets. When he started he was a lively fast-medium, bounding in off a longish straight run with a high knee action.

Once at the wicket he got sideways-on and, because of the
pivot of his body, was able to bowl devastating out-swingers. In
the early 1980s, however, his action gradually altered, owing
largely to the development of his figure – though looking back
it may also have been the beginning of his back trouble which
handicapped him. He ran in more slowly, without the previous
bound and energy, and bowled more square-on, but remarkably
he continued to take wickets, quite often with bad balls (though
a bad ball becomes a good ball if it takes a wicket!)

Even when he had lost some of his bounce, pace and swing,
however, he continued to bowl short with two deep legs, and
defy the batsman to hook him for six. Many fell for the trap
and perished – none more so than Hilditch and Wood on the
Australian tour here in 1985 – but to me it was rather sad, and
a fall from the high standards of his early Test career.

One of his troubles was that he was such a competitor that
he wanted to bowl all day, which he often seemed to do,
especially when David Gower was captain. David found it difficult to prise the ball away from him, when he obviously wanted
to take him off.

There was, however, one famous occasion when Ian actually
did *not* want to bowl. It was during his golden year of 1981 in
the fourth Test at Edgbaston, following England's amazing win
by 18 runs at Headingley. In their second innings Australia
needed 151 runs to win. It was the fourth day of the Test – a
glorious Sunday afternoon. It seemed plain sailing for Australia,
who were 105 for 4, needing only 46 more runs when Border
was out caught off his glove from a surprise lifter from
Emburey.

Brearley had been about to bring Willis back, but suddenly
changed his mind and in a moment of inspiration turned to
Ian. He had only taken one wicket in the first innings and
none so far in the second. He seemed tired and dispirited and
suggested several alternatives to Brearley – anyone but himself.
But the captain insisted and 'ordered' him to bowl. The result
was unbelievable. Ian proceeded to take 5 wickets for 1 run in
28 deliveries and Australia were beaten by 29 runs. So the great
all-rounder had performed yet another miracle.

To complete his all-rounder tag Ian was a magnificent and
unique fielder at second slip. He caught many brilliant catches,
standing about two yards in front of first slip. He saw the ball
so quickly that he made catches off balls which would not have

reached him had he been standing in the normal second-slip position alongside first slip. But I would not recommend mere mortals to copy him, nor to stand with both hands on the knees as he did, as the bowler ran up to bowl.

As if his all-round performances were not enough, Ian also captained England twelve times. He took over from Mike Brearley in 1980 for the first Test at Trent Bridge against the West Indies. The West Indies just won this match by two wickets and the other four were drawn. He then captained England in the drawn Centenary Test at Lord's, followed by four Tests on the controversial West Indies tour, when the second Test was cancelled because the Guyanan government refused Robin Jackman an entry permit. The West Indies won the first two, and the other two were drawn. On top of all this Ian suffered a severe blow when Ken Barrington so sadly died at Bridgetown. So it was an unhappy tour, and a somewhat chastened Botham returned to captain England against Australia, who won the first Test at Trent Bridge. England managed to draw the second Test at Lord's, where Ian suffered the embarrassment of making a pair. This was too much for him. The media had already been after his blood and he promptly resigned the captaincy just before, so it is said, Alec Bedser could tell him that he had been sacked.

So the story of his captaincy is not a happy one. Perhaps he was too young (twenty-four) and inexperienced. It was certainly asking a lot of such a vital all-rounder to have the extra strain and worry. He always protested that it did not affect his performance as a player, but it certainly did not help his batting. In twenty-one innings he only averaged 12.09, with 57 his top score, but he did take 34 wickets at 32.3 apiece, about four runs a wicket more expensive than his Test career figure. Finally, he had the bad luck to be captain against West Indies in nine of his twelve Tests. Funnily enough, however, I believe that if he had been asked to captain England again he would have leaped at the chance.

So much for the player. Now for the man – a complex character if ever there was one. Aggressive, courageous, loyal, compassionate and larger than life. Wherever he was, whether on the field, in the dressing room or at a party, his strong personality and mere physical presence outshone everyone else. He was able to influence some of his fellow players, not always for their good, and had a slightly warped sense of humour. You never stood near a swimming pool at an outdoor party if he was anywhere nearby. And you had to be prepared for leg-pulls and practical jokes, all done in a boisterous friendly way.

After a few drinks Ian could be a dangerous man to cross or argue with. His whole career was blighted with brawls and fights in bars, hotels, airports and even in aeroplanes. He was seldom contrite afterwards, and usually blamed the media for the publicity. The same applied to the many accusations of his drug-taking and sexual exploits. He finally admitted the former after suing various newspapers, but he would blandly stand in front of the television cameras and deny everything – always blaming the media.

And here one must be fair. I went on ten tours from 1958 to 1973 as a commentator and saw plenty of off-the-field activities by players which would have made news today, but my colleagues and I were there to report *cricket*, not personal conduct. Nowadays, however, the editors of the tabloids send special reporters to stalk and spy on the players in their off-duty hours. Hence the headlines. Whilst not excusing some of the excesses reported, I do deplore the gutter press paying large sums of money to anyone – especially beauty queens – prepared to reveal all.

It is something which Ian brought on himself, however, and he has had to learn to live with it. What he has needed all his life is strong but friendly leadership, and he has not often had it. Whenever he has, however, he is a different person. His friends have not always helped him and he has been tempted by large sums of money to do some extraordinary things, such as being groomed to become a Hollywood star.

There is of course another side to him – the family man who loves his wife Kathy and his three children, and likes nothing better than living in the country with them and his dog, and rough shooting. There's also the fishing, where he overcomes his natural impatience and enjoys a long fight against the salmon. He will try anything so long as it offers a challenge, hence his learning to fly and his notoriously fast driving. And of course there's the compassionate man who believes in action rather than words – as proved by his walk from John O'Groats to Land's End and his journey over the Alps. Though often in pain and great discomfort he never gave up, and through his courage and determination made millions of pounds to help fight leukaemia.

Finally there's his loyalty to his friends, as when he resigned from Somerset when he thought Joel Garner and his special friend Viv Richards had been unfairly treated. I am always a sucker for anyone who is nice to me, and Bothers has always been that, so I wish him well.

David Gower

Few Test players have had as many gifts showered on them by the gods as David Gower: good looks, fair curly hair, charisma, charm, good manners, a sense of humour, intelligence. In addition he was athletic, six feet tall and moved like a gazelle with speed and lightness of foot.

As a batsman he had a wonderful eye, and a sense of timing which stroked the ball to the boundary. There was no brute force nor bludgeoning of the ball – everything he did was graceful and elegant. Tom Graveney is the nearest living batsman to compare with him. Of course, being a left-hander helped him. To my mind there is nothing to beat a left-handed off-drive through extra cover.

It all sounds too good to be true, and of course there were a few minuses. He was – rightly, I think – criticised for being too casual, careless and irresponsible. He earned himself the soubriquet of 'laid-back' both on and off the field, and he certainly was. This had both advantages and disadvantages. It meant that, outwardly at least, he remained calm and didn't panic. He accepted umpires' decisions without question and could ignore the pressures to which modern cricketers claim they are subjected.

This also gave him the appearance of being a non-fighter, however, and not seeming to care when disasters happened. It was the main criticism of his captaincy: an apparent air of laissez-faire, with insufficient attention paid to discipline, dedication and practice. He seemed to rely on everyone giving of their best, without the necessary encouragement or criticism. On his West Indies tour he gave the impression of preferring a day off on the beach or sailing, rather than a hard session at the nets. His natural talent may not have needed much net practice (Denis Compton was the same – he hated it), but lesser mortals *do* need continuous practice, to keep the eye in and to iron out various faults in technique which crop up from time to time. In this respect cricketers could take a lesson from the star golfers and tennis players – who never seem to stop practising.

It must be said on his behalf that in his first spell of twenty-six Tests as England's captain he had the bad luck to play ten of them against the West Indies, and lost them all. But he did have a successful tour of India in 1985 when after losing the first Test, he managed the difficult feat on India's slow pitches of fighting back and winning the series 2–1. And in the same summer he beat Australia 2–1 in England.

Like Norman Yardley, he may have been too nice and not ruthless enough ever to be a great captain. His handling of Ian Botham is a case in point. He often seemed to have difficulty in taking Ian off, even when he was bowling badly and a change was clearly needed. I won't say that Ian refused to give the ball up, but it looked jolly like it!

David lost the England captaincy in unhappy circumstances after the Lord's Test against India in 1986. They won by five wickets and, following immediately on the five defeats in the West Indies in the winter, his fate was sealed. Unlike Ian Botham, who, after the Lord's Test against Australia in 1981, got in his resignation *before* he was sacked, David had the news of his sacking broken to him by Peter May after Mike Gatting had already been appointed in his stead. Sacking anyone is never easy but in the case of some past England captains, it does seem that some of them have been dismissed rather abruptly and unfairly. After seeing all the traumas and dramas of Mike Gatting's brief captaincy, David must have been relieved that he was sacked when he was. But he had enjoyed the captaincy, and when he was offered it again, he accepted and was England captain for a further six Tests.

He undoubtedly played far too much cricket during the eighteen years after he first played for Leicestershire in 1975, including 117 Tests and goodness knows how many one-day internationals. He rapidly became stale and played out and wisely took the 1987–8 winter off, thus missing the World Cup and the tours of Pakistan and New Zealand. In truth it didn't seem to do him much good, and in the summer of 1988 he had a run of poor scores for Leicestershire. Nor was his form against the West Indies up to his highest standards, and he was dropped for the fifth Test at the Oval. Even so, he did better than most of the others, with 211 runs at an average of 30.14. Only Gooch and Lamb did better. At least he had the satisfaction of reaching exactly 7,000 runs in 100 Tests, but he never really showed the determination, concentration and fighting qualities which were needed against the battering of West Indian fast bowlers.

From the moment, at the age of twenty-one, when he scored four runs to square leg against Pakistan at Edgbaston off his first ball in Test cricket, he was both a delight and a torture to watch. He was what I call a 'touch' player, relying on eye and footwork acting in perfect harmony. When they didn't he seemed strangely vulnerable. In his early days he was a sucker to the ball on his legs. Time and time again he tickled it to a leg slip or short fine leg especially placed there, and sometimes to the wicket-keeper. At one time he appeared to have mastered this, though he occasionally half-drove a ball into the hands of mid-wicket.

In later years his footwork let him down, and by not moving his feet he tended to give catching practice to second or third slip. He sometimes appeared unable to resist playing a ball wide of the off-stump which he should have left alone. It was as if his bat was attracted like a magnet to the ball. His supporters despaired, and so did he, because no matter how he looked, he *did* care. On the other hand, when everything was coordinated he was still as good a batsman to watch as any other in the world. His off-drive was perfection, and he wafted away anything short to the boundary. He also had the great asset of being a good judge of a run and very fast between the wickets.

Some of what I have said may seem to be too critical, because after all to have made 7,000 runs in 100 Tests means an average of 70 for every Test, and that can't be bad! His final total of 8,231 Test runs at an average of 44.25 puts him seventh in the list of the highest scoring Test batsmen, between Viv Richards and Geoff Boycott. So laid-back he may have been, but the figures show that it stood him and England in good stead. Furthermore, his eighteen Test hundreds contained several where he was prepared to get stuck in and battle on after passing his century – as scores of 215, 212, 173 not out, 166, 157 and 152 go to prove.

As a fielder his swiftness and ease of movement made him into a brilliant performer, especially in the covers. He used to have a fine arm, but then damaged his right shoulder so that he could not throw at all – a severe handicap. When he chased a ball to the boundary he often had to run back with it quickly or give it to someone else to throw.

Oh, yes. As a bowler he took one Test wicket against India at Kanpur in 1982 – and he wasn't even captain! His analysis read: 1–0–1–1. He treasures that, especially as his victim was that fine all-rounder Kapil Dev.

David retired in 1992 at the early age of 35 after being rejected by the England selectors and left out of three consecutive tours. But he will have been less affected than most other first-class cricketers. He has so many interests. He loves travelling and could be described as a *bon viveur*, with an expert knowledge of wines and a special penchant for port. He likes music, is a keen photographer and at least for short periods enjoys lying on a beach in the sun. He is a naturally active person, so enjoys sailing and water-skiing.

His other love is winter sports, and each year he likes to toboggan down the famous Cresta Run at St Moritz. He has also been a member of a bobsleigh team. Both sports must be terrifying – on the Cresta Run especially, when you travel headfirst within inches of the icy track at speeds of 60 mph or more. One year I asked him how he thought that I would fare with my long nose. He replied that I would plough a deep furrow in front of me as I sped down the run. And apropos of that conversation, he was one of the easiest people to interview of all the Test cricketers. He never dodged a question, but fended the awkward one off with disarming wit and a smile.

One final thought. He was born in Tunbridge Wells and educated at King's School, Canterbury. How Kent must have kicked themselves for allowing him to slip through their net and escape to Leicestershire. It was just like the man from Decca Records who turned down the Beatles!

Allan Border

You could spot him easily on the field. He looked smaller than his five feet nine inches and walked with tiny steps, bearded chin resting on his chest, eyes down, green cap pulled over his eyes. Even when captain he was an unobtrusive figure, and off the field quiet and modest. He could also be emotional, as proved by his reaction after England had beaten Australia at

Brisbane on Gatting's tour of 1986. He proved himself a good leader, however, and became not only the greatest accumulator of runs in cricket history, but also one of the most correct players with immense powers of concentration. A left-hander, batting usually at number four, sometimes at number five, time and again he rescued Australia from early disasters. He scored more Test fifties than any other batsman and his 27 hundreds put him third in the all-time list, behind only Bradman (29) and Gavaskar (34).

When Allan first came over here in 1980 for the Centenary Test, and then again in 1981, he was an unexciting player to watch – placing, nudging and cutting the ball rather than hitting it – but when he came as captain in 1985 he was completely transformed. He had a wonderful tour, scoring a hundred in each of his first four matches. He made more runs than any of his batsmen, both in the Tests where he averaged 66.33, and in all matches, with 1,355 runs at an average of 71.31.

But it was his change of style which was so noticeable. He had become a hitter of sixes and used his feet delightfully to drive the bowlers back over their heads. In his first hundred against Somerset there were 4 sixes, against Worcestershire 6 sixes, against MCC no sixes but 22 fours, and against Derbyshire 5 sixes. It was a complete transformation, and ever after he was a joy to watch. His defence was sound, and he was strong and sturdy and scored with drives, cuts and strokes off his legs.

Allan was a glutton for cricket, as proved by his spending his Australian winters over here playing for Essex. He was signed by them to replace Ken McEwan, and got off to a terrible start in his first season, not reaching 50 until the end of May. But then he had a purple patch, scoring 1,287 runs at an average of 51.48 before returning to Australia in the middle of August. He fitted splendidly into the Essex team – always a happy one. He didn't act like a star Test player but was very much one of the boys, and when asked was helpful with his advice. He seemed to play cricket non-stop, but returned again in 1988 as keen as ever to undertake the hard grind of county cricket and scored another 1,393 runs, average 58.04.

He was an excellent fielder in the covers, mid-wicket or round the bat and set a new Test record of 156 catches. He was also a more than useful slow left-arm bowler, who could pick up the odd wicket and break up a stand. He formed an efficient partnership with Bobby Simpson as his manager, and together they shared the triumph of unexpectedly winning the World Cup in Pakistan and India in 1987.

Allan retired in 1994 after a record-breaking 156 Tests and a remarkable 93 Tests as Australian captain. He is top of the list of Test batsmen with 11,174 runs and an average of 50.56, ahead of Sunny Gavaskar in second place with 10,122 at an average of 51.12. He was not the most glamorous of cricketers, nor the most spectacular personality, but his sturdy character and outstanding skill as a batsman made him one of the most successful Test cricketers ever.

23 The Tale End

CRICKET IS FUN, not only to play but also to read or talk about. More stories are told about it – many of them true – than any other game. And behind all these stories laughter is never far away. Few of them are new, but the old ones get reburnished as they are handed down from generation to generation, with the characters sometimes changing.

As laughter is such a part of cricket, I thought we should end with a few cricket stories. Some of them are from my own personal experiences and others are old favourites. If, when you finally put down the book, you have a smile on your face or laughter in your heart, then you will have caught or recaptured some of the true spirit of cricket.

In the 1950s I used to run an annual match against the village of Widford in Hertfordshire. I usually got some well-known players such as Richie Benaud and the former West Indies player Gerry Gomez to join me alongside my broadcasting friends like Jim Swanton and Rex Alston.

We had numerous 'incidents' such as when Jim Swanton was brilliantly caught and bowled low down by a young bowler from the village. Rex Alston the non-striker applauded and shouted 'well caught'. But Jim stood his ground and said: 'I'm not going for that one' and didn't!

Another year we thought that Jim had made enough runs, so we told Gerry Gomez to run him out. Alas Jim saw what was up, sent Gerry back and ran *him* out! John (Pom-pom) Fellows-Smith had also once been in too long, but no matter how hard we tried we could not run him out. In spite of each incoming batsman telling him to get out he soldiered on regardless. We were so annoyed that we thought we would rob him of his hundred so when he had reached ninety-six we all applauded and a small boy even put 100 up on the tiny scoreboard.

But 'Pom-pom' paid no attention and did not even touch his cap. He proceeded to make four more runs, *then* touched his cap, and got out deliberately next ball. He always counted his runs!

When he was up at Oxford, Pom-pom used to have his leg pulled unmercifully by Jumbo Jowitt. One day Pom-pom was sitting writing letters in the dressing room in the Parks. This is at the back of the pavilion and is underground so that it is impossible to watch the game from it. Jumbo rushed in and said: 'You are in, Pom-pom.' Pom-pom picked up his batting gloves and bat and walked out, and as usual with him, kept his eyes fixed on the ground with his bat trailing behind him. When he had got about halfway to the wicket he heard roars of laughter from the crowd. Looking up he saw that the game was going on in the middle and that no one was out.

In the next match against Middlesex he was again writing letters in the dressing room when a young chap being tried for the University went in to bat. Pom-pom was the next man in. After about two minutes Jumbo Jowitt again rushed in and said: 'Lawrence is out, you are in, Pom-pom' – but this time Pom-pom refused to believe him and went on writing letters. He wasn't going to be caught out twice! However, a few moments later Lawrence came into the dressing room and began taking off his pads, so Pom-pom realised that this time his leg had *not* been pulled.

He picked up his batting gloves and again rushed out to the wicket. But still determined not to be caught out a second time he looked up as he walked, and to his surprise he saw that there was no one on the field except the two Umpires. J. J. Warr, who was captaining the Middlesex team had been let into the joke and had taken all his team and hidden them behind the sightscreen!

During the third Test against the West Indies at Trent Bridge in 1950, Worrell and Weekes put on 283 for the fourth wicket and on the Friday evening were hitting the England bowling all over the field. In the television commentary box we were getting a bit tired of showing four after four, so to vary things I said: 'This is an enormous problem for Norman Yardley. I wonder what he's thinking as he stands there at mid-on.'

This was a hint to the camera to pan in on Norman. He filled the television screen, but unfortunately at that moment he was scratching himself in a very awkward place. I was speechless for a moment but managed to blurt out: 'It's obviously a very ticklish problem.' He told me later that he got a tremendous rocket from his wife Tony when he got home!

A southerner who was staying in Leeds decided to watch the annual Roses Match between Yorkshire and Lancashire. Before the game started he found a seat and went off to get a drink – placing his hat neatly on the seat where he had been sitting. On returning a few minutes later he found that his hat had been removed to the floor and a large Yorkshireman was sitting in his seat. Somewhat diffidently he said, 'Excuse me, Sir, I think you are sitting on my seat. I reserved it with my hat.'

The Yorkshireman replied, 'I'm sorry, lad. It's bums what keep seats up 'ere, not 'ats!'

At another Roses match in Sheffield, father arrived early and kept a spare seat for his son, who arrived half an hour after the start of play, breathless and pale with excitement.

'Dad,' he said, 'I've got some terrible news for thee – house is on fire.'

'Aye –'

'Mother's been taken to hospital with bad burns –'

'Aye –'

'And she says she forgot to send insurance money –'

'Aye and I've bad news for thee too – 'Utton's out!'

He was a *very* slow bowler and had been hit more or less out of sight when at last the batsman missed a ball which pitched straight – like the others it was devoid of spin – and struck him on the pad. The bowler turned round with a howl of triumph to the umpire and cried, 'How's that?'

'Not out,' said the umpire. The bowler was a very well-bred cricketer and it was not until the end of the over, when he had been hit for three more sixes, that he said to the umpire:

'That one pitched straight, didn't it?'

'Yes.'

'It didn't turn did it?'

'No.'

'He didn't touch it, did he?'

'No.'

'Then why wasn't he out?'

'It wasn't going fast enough to dislodge the bails!'

This story is about the customary annual match between Durban and Pietermaritzburg. The Mayor and skipper of Durban had represented his side for fifteen years and, during that period, had only captured two wickets and made 17 runs, and had never held a catch. The game was duly played in Durban and after a few wickets had fallen, in strode the Mayor of Pietermaritzburg to take strike. All of a sudden he took an almighty swing and the ball went soaring into the heavens straight to the Durban skipper. His apprehension was terrific and in the dying moments he closed his eyes and the ball landed safely in his left hand. His jubilation was fantastic – tossing the ball in the air and then lying down and rolling the ball on his forehead – his first catch ever in such class cricket. He then held the ball aloft to receive the congratulations of his team mates, but was confronted by a rather irate mid-on who said, 'For God's sake throw the ball back – it was a "no-ball" and the batsmen have run seven already!'

A Kent amateur wicket-keeper used to enjoy his pints of beer at the end of a day's play. One morning he had a dreadful hang-over and entered the dressing room apparently in a trance. Kent were fielding so his colleagues helped him on with his pads, box and wicket-keeping gloves and 'steered' him out to the middle. They set him down about fifteen yards behind the stumps as the opening over was to be bowled by a young fast bowler.

The first ball went 'whoosh' past the wicket-keeper's right ear. He never moved and the ball went for four byes. The second ball went past his left ear and still the wicket-keeper remained in a crouching position without moving. Another four byes were signalled. But the third ball was down the leg-side and the batsman, trying to glide it, just got an outside edge off his bat.

The wicket-keeper took off and diving full length to his left, held a miraculous catch inches off the ground. He got up, tossed the ball in the air and walking across to the slips said: 'Do you know, gentleman. That's the first time I've ever caught a batsman off the *first* ball of the day!'

In a village match a batsman came in wearing only one pad. When this was pointed out to him, the batsman replied, 'Yes, I know, but we only have five pads between us.'

'But,' he was told, 'you've got it on the wrong leg.'

'Oh no,' said the batsman, 'I thought I would be batting at the other end!'

Surrey were playing Middlesex at Lord's when Pat Pocock, always known as Percy, came in to bat. The Middlesex spin bowler Fred Titmus noticed that Pocock was wearing glasses. 'What are you wearing those for, Percy?' he asked.

Percy, knowing that Titmus was a bit deaf, replied: 'So that I can *hear* the ball better, of course.' Percy then took guard and was immediately clean bowled by Titmus.

As Percy passed him on his way back to the pavilion Titmus said to him: 'You didn't hear that one very well, did you Percy?'

J. J. Warr was invited to Bill Edrich's fourth wedding. When he turned up at the church J. J. was asked by the usher which side of the aisle to put him: 'Bride or bridegroom?'

J. J. promptly replied: 'Season ticket!'

Brian Close was captain of Derrick Robins's eleven in South Africa in 1974–5. On one occasion, to his disgust, they were soundly beaten after he had declared. He locked the dressing-room door and berated the team for all the inefficient things they had done wrong. After about half an hour of cataloguing the reasons for their defeat, he asked if anyone could think of any other reason why they had lost.

One member of the team was Lancashire wicket-keeper John Lyon. He was a shy and reserved person who had hardly spoken a word to anyone on the tour, but he plucked up courage, held up his hand and said: 'Yes, skipper. You declared too bloody early!'

During a different tour of South Africa Derrick Robins had to thank the Mayor of Durban for a reception which he had given for the Robins team. He started his speech with the unfortunate phrase: 'I'd like to ask you all to give the Mayor the clap he so richly deserves.'

It was followed by a deadly silence.

In a village cricket match a very fat batsman came in to bat, and as he was taking up his stance at the wicket the local umpire confided to the visiting bowler: 'We have a special rule for him. If you hit him in front it's lbw. If you hit him behind it's a wide!'

On the 1936–7 MCC tour of Australia, Gubby Allen was the England captain. England won the first two Tests and in the third Test at Melbourne Gubby decided to set a trap for Bradman. He placed Walter Robins just backward of square leg and, sure enough, Bradman hit a ball in the air straight at Robins. He was normally a brilliant fielder, but, possibly because he had a sore finger, he dropped the catch. He felt very downcast and at the end of the over went up to Gubby and apologised profusely. 'Don't worry, Robbie,' said Gubby, 'it doesn't matter at all. It's only lost us the series!'

He was right. Bradman went on to make 270, and Australia won that Test and the next two!

On another MCC tour of Australia, the team were travelling by train. A girl was nursing a baby in a carriage, the only other occupant of which was a man who kept staring at the baby. He couldn't take his eyes off it, and the girl became more and more embarrassed and annoyed. Finally she could stand it no longer and asked the man why he was staring so. He replied that he would rather not say. But when the girl persisted he said he was sorry but he was staring because the baby was the ugliest baby he had ever seen in his life. This naturally upset the girl who broke into floods of tears and, taking the baby, went and stood in the corridor.

She was still crying when the MCC team came along the corridor on their way to the restaurant car. They all passed her except one of the players, who being a decent chap, stopped to ask her why she was crying. She told him that she had just been insulted by a man in her carriage. So he said: 'Well, cheer up. I'll bring you back a cup of tea from the restaurant car. That should make you feel better.'

So off he went and returned in about five minutes. 'Here's your cup of tea,' he said to the girl, 'and what's more I've also brought a banana for the monkey!'

Before the start of the Melbourne Test at the end of December 1924, the headlines in the local papers featured the story of a well-known midwife called Nurse Blank, who was involved in an abortion case.

On 1 January 1925, Hobbs and Sutcliffe of England batted all day against Australia, putting on 283 for the opening partnership, in reply to what was then a record Test total of 600 runs by Australia. There were 75,000 people on the ground, and as the day wore on they began to barrack their team more and more. (It is worth remembering perhaps that the bowlers included Jack Gregory, Charlie Kelleway, Arthur Mailey and Arthur Richardson.) But the barrackers were merciless on them: 'You'll never get them out – you'll have to burn 'em out – send for the Fire Brigade, they'll get 'em out – put the roller on – put the clock on – and so on.'

But the culminating point of the whole day's play came between the tea interval and the close of play. There was a momentary silence, which was broken by a terrific raucous voice which yelled out: 'Send for Nurse Blank – she'll get the b–––s out!'

During an MCC tour of India, under the captaincy of Lionel Tennyson, half the team were down with dysentery. Alf Gover had to leave his sick-bed to make up the eleven for a match. Ian Peebles, in his own inimitable way, has described what happened then.

Alf's first few overs were uneventful, but during the third, only the most acute observer would have been alarmed at the tense expression on his face as he started on his long, hustling run. It was when he shot past the crouching umpire and thundered down the pitch with the undelivered ball in his hand that it became obvious something was amiss.

The batsman, fearing a personal assault, sprang smartly backward, but the flannelled giant sped past looking neither to right nor left. Past wicket-keeper, slips and fine leg in a flash, he hurtled up the pavilion steps in a cloud of dusty gravel and was gone. That he has never received full credit for this record is due to the lack of timing apparatus and the distance, from the start of his run to his uncomfortable destination, not being a recognised one.

As, in the tight-lipped precipitation of his flight, he had been unable to give any hint of his future movements, fine leg, after a moment's thought, followed up the steps and rescued the ball from the bowler's convulsive grasp!

There used to be a tradition in pre-season matches and charity matches of bowlers giving an incoming batsman one to get off the mark. But it didn't always work out. Colin Ingelby-Mackenzie told me of a charity match in which Hampshire played Lord Porchester's eleven at Highclere. 'Butch' White, the fast bowler, had restrained himself admirably, bowling well-pitched-up military medium at all the club batsmen. When Lord Porchester himself came in, Colin went up to Butch and said, 'Give him one, Butch,' then walked away without seeing what Butch was doing.

Butch's eyes had gleamed at the welcome instruction from his skipper, and he hurriedly paced out his usual thirty yards' run. Before Colin could stop him he came charging in at full speed and bowled a terrifying bouncer which nearly removed Porchy's head.

I *believe* the fixture was renewed the next year, but I'm not too sure!

From our commentary box at Lord's we can always hear the bell of St John's Church ringing for Evensong, just before close of play. I usually make a comment about it, as it's my parish church where all my five children have been christened and my daughter married. Some years ago our Rector was called Noël Perry-Gore and one day he told me of how he had won a bet with his children. They were listening to me commentating from Lord's one lunchtime, whether on television or radio I am not sure. He said to his children: 'I bet you I can make Brian Johnston mention St John's Church during his commentary.'

Of course they thought he was joking, so took him on. With that, he ran out of the rectory, went into the church, and rang the bell lustily. After about a minute's ringing, he went back to his children. They were in a state of great excitement: 'You've won, Daddy,' they said. 'Just now Brian Johnston said, "That's the bell of St John's Church, by the roundabout at the Nursery End. I wonder what on earth it's ringing for at this time of day. The Rector must have heard some good news from somewhere!" '

I have always tried to 'sell' cricket and put it across the air in the best possible light. I remember that in the 1950s, when I was the staff television cricket commentator, I felt it my duty to get the game as much coverage on television as possible. Paul Fox, later the managing director of BBC Television, was then running *Sportsview* and *Grandstand*. I had to work hard to persuade him to include a cricket item in either of the programmes. When I saw I was losing the argument I used to say to him lamely, 'Well anyway, it's a lovely game.'

Sometimes he laughed and let me have my way, but in fact he didn't know *too* much about cricket. He was directing *Grandstand* one Saturday afternoon, and we were televising the Roses match. We had been on the air for about twenty minutes when I heard him through my earphones say to our producer: 'OK, at the end of this over tell Johnners to cue over to the Athletics. We'll be coming back to you later. Let me know when it will be and we'll come over for the fall of the next wicket!'

Even if *he* didn't, *I* still think 'it's a lovely game'.

Index